John Henry Blunt

Dursley and Its Neighbourhood

Being historical memorials of Dursley, Beverston, Cam, and Uley

John Henry Blunt

Dursley and Its Neighbourhood
Being historical memorials of Dursley, Beverston, Cam, and Uley

ISBN/EAN: 9783337094409

Printed in Europe, USA, Canada, Australia, Japan

Cover: Foto ©ninafisch / pixelio.de

More available books at **www.hansebooks.com**

DURSLEY

AND

ITS NEIGHBOURHOOD;

BEING HISTORICAL MEMORIALS OF

DURSLEY, BEVERSTON, CAM, AND ULEY..

BY

JOHN HENRY BLUNT, M.A., F.S.A.,

Rector of Beverston,

AUTHOR OF "TEWKESBURY ABBEY AND ITS ASSOCIATIONS,"
&c., &c., &c.

LONDON: SIMPKIN, MARSHALL, & Co.
DURSLEY: WHITMORE.

1877.

PREFACE.

THERE are few parishes of which there is not something interesting to be recorded, and few of which the records are satisfactorily dealt with in County histories. Of the four parishes which are dealt with in this little volume, each however has a special interest of its own, one being the site of a burial place belonging to the earliest times of our national existence, and of a Roman Camp; a second containing the interesting remains of a Castle that was inhabited by a great branch of the Berkeley family for several centuries; and the two others possessing parish books which illustrate, in a remarkable manner, the parochial life of the district from the time of Queen Elizabeth downward.

The author felt it to be a duty, when he became Rector of Beverston, to gather what information he could about the history of his parish, and to place it upon record. A wish was expressed by his friends that the memorials so gathered should be put into print; and a suggestion was added by the publisher that it should be accompanied by notices of Dursley and some of the adjoining parishes. Thus the volume grew into its present form, and would have included several other parishes but that the author has been obliged to take up work which has occupied all his time, and has thus been prevented from carrying his local enquiries further. He has not been able, for the same reason, to lay before the reader quite such full accounts even of these four parishes as he had originally intended: but those who are interested in them may be glad to possess a more detailed account of each than has hitherto been in print, and antiquaries may find a fresh illustration here and there of English country life in former times.

The reader is indebted to Mr. Falconer Madan, Fellow of Brasenose College, Oxford, for the description and panoramic sketch of the view from Stinchcombe Hill. The author begs also to express his obligation to Mr. Vizard, of Ferney Hill,

Dursley, for the loan of valuable printed books and manuscripts; and to Mr. W. P. W. Phillimore, of Queen's College, Oxford, for many manuscript notes that have much facilitated his enquiries respecting Cam and Uley. The two views of Beverston Castle are Heliotype copies of Photographs by Mr. Keene, of Derby, the woodcut of the Uley Cairn is copied by permission from the Archæologia [vol. xlii. p. 213.] of the Royal Society of Antiquaries, and the plan of Uley Bury is from an earlier volume [xix. page 161.] of the same invaluable collection.

BEVERSTON, JANUARY, 1877.

CONTENTS.

ILLUSTRATIONS.

DURSLEY.

The picturesque little town of Dursley nestles down in a
Cotswold bottom which forms the end of a valley that opens
out northward on to the vale of Gloucester, fifteen miles
south of that City, just where the Severn begins to broaden
into an estuary, with the Forest of Dean on its further bank,
and beyond that the border hills across the Wye. All around
the town the hummocky Cotswolds have been tumbled up in
quaint mounds that look too large to be the work of pre-
historic Titans, and too small to be the work of geological
epochs; while the town itself seems to lie at the bottom of a
creek whose waters were drained off into the Severn a few
thousand years ago. On the southern shore of this creek the
slopes are clothed with lovely hanging woods of beech, while
northward they are chiefly pasture lands, dotted here and
there on their sides with cottages and "break-neck" farms,
bearing clumps of trees on their summits, and marked by the
enduring footsteps of the Roman Legions.

The town has a railway all to itself, one of the shortest
lines in England, yet effectually connecting it with the life and
vigour and bustle of the busy world; for it starts off, two
and a half miles away, from the Gloucester and Bristol branch
of the Midland line which runs through the Vale, and creeping along the bottom runs till it can run no further because
of the ten or twelve miles of high land that lie between its
terminus and the vale of Malmesbury. Some generations ago

B.

this branch railway would have turned Dursley into a busy manufacturing town after the modern pattern; for there was a time when it was famous for its cloth and blankets, and when other towns came to it for woolcards wherewith to turn tangled wool into fibres fit for the spinners and weavers.

But the manufacturing days of Dursley belonged to the ages when spinners and weavers worked at home, when steam engines had not been heard of, and when water power was the only force in use to supplement the power of strong arms and skilful hands: when manufactures did not bring desolation to lovely landscapes, and when the Cotswolds were a great pasture ground like the downs of Wiltshire. Now, Stroudwater turns the mill wheels of many a large factory, and scantly watered Dursley has subsided into a market for agricultural produce gathered off the arable land into which so many Cotswold pastures have been broken up, though hill and vale still send good mutton to market, as well as many a dairyful of "single" and "double Glos'ter." [1]

In the old English days of which it is the custom to speak as "Anglo-Saxon," Dursley was known as "Dersilege" or "Dureslega;" and though no injustice is done to it when the town is called scantly watered as regards manufacturing power, yet its name is explained as being derived from "Dwr" and "ley" or "lege," which are very old English for water and pasture. If such be really its derivation Dursley gives a happy illustration even in its name of the way in which the Ancient Briton and the Saxon mingled together to form

---

[1] There is an old proverb about the Cotswold grain of ancient days on which Fuller discourses in his usual quaint style, " 'It is long coming as Cotswold Barley.' It is applied to such things as are *slow* but *sure*. The Corn in this cold Country on the Woulds, exposed to the winds, bleak and shelterless, is very backwards at the first; but afterwards overtakes the forwardest in the country, if not in the Barn, in the Bushel, both for the quantity and goodness thereof." [*Fuller's Worthies Glouc.* 377]

the great nation of mixed blood: for " ley " is undoubtedly
" Anglo-Saxon," and it is equally certain that our brethren
across the border would claim " Dwr " for " Welsh ." That
the town should derive its name from water is also probable
from the circumstance that it seems to have originally
gathered around the cluster of springs called the Broadwell.[1]
These springs, which rise vertically over a space about 15 feet
square on the south side of the Church, maintain a constant
head of pure water of that size and two feet deep, a life-giving
supply for a rising town, and which might well supply a
name to it also among primitive settlers on the land around.
The overflow of the Broadwell forms a brook called the Ewelme
from very ancient times, and this brook runs on to join the
Cam river, the united waters flowing into the Gloucester
and Berkeley Canal near Slimbridge. The Broadwell itself
seems once to have gone by the name of Ewelme, and this
was also once corrupted into New Elme; both which names
are familiar as those of a village near Wallingford where a
similar cluster of springs may be seen as a distinctive feature
of the place bubbling out of the hill on which the Church
and Hospital stand.[2]

---

[1] There is a frequent charge of " xij^d " in the early Churchwardens accounts for " riding the Broadwell," that is *ridding* it of
rubbish. Later it runs "for cleansinge of ye broadwell."

[2] In ancient deeds of the Hospital the Berkshire Ewelme is called
Aquelme, which seems to connect the syllable " Ew " with the
Norman " Eau." The spring or brook which bounds King's College,
Cambridge, on the west, and runs into the Cam is described in the
Statutes as "aqua vulgariter l'ee nuncupata." So E-ton is the town
of water. Perhaps the second syllable may be explained by a
quotation from Chaucer,

" In world is none so clere of hewe
The water is ever fresh and new,
That *whelmeth* up with waves bright
The mountenance of two fingers height"

Ewell in Surrey is another village of springs.

[Quoted in *Lye's Junius' Etymologicon* 1743]

B 2

As the Roman Legions bivouacked on the hills near Dursley so some of them built villas in the valley, the remains of one such villa, at least, having been discovered a few years ago under Stinchcombe Hill.[1] But the earliest historical notice we have of the town is in connection with its ancient Lords, the Berkeleys of Dursley, who had their home on large estates here long before the Fitz Hardings had set their feet in England.   They were of the Royal blood of England, Roger de Berkeley, Lord of Dursley immediately before the Conquest, being a cousin (of what degree is not on record) of Edward the Confessor.   A large part of what is now the great Manor of Berkeley had become Crown property on the death of Earl Godwin and the exile of his son, Earl Sweyn:[2] but Roger de Berkeley possessed a manor at Dursley when Doomsday Book was compiled, and thus seems to have escaped spoliation from the hands of the Godwins as well as confiscation at the Conquest.   He also possessed lands at Cobberley, Siston, and Doddington, but the ancient residence of his family was Dursley, where they had built a Castle; which existed as such when Berkeley was a Nunnery, as it was until it came into the hands of the Godwins first and then of the Crown.

But the Conquest brought an accession of property to the Lord of Dursley, for Doomsday records that he not only had his old inheritance there, one hide (or 120 acres) of land, on which his Castle stood, and three hides (or 360 acres more) held on lease of the Crown, but that William I. granted to him the whole of the hundred of Berkeley and Berkeley Hernesse in fee farm at the yearly rent of £500. 17s. 2d. which was a mere bagatelle, though representing £8,000 or

---

[1] The site of it was on the Stancombe Estate, in the adjoining parish of North Nibley, and is now grown over with trees. The curiosities dug up were sold in London.

[2] See the account of Beverston, page 101.

£10,000 of our money, considering the large extent of country comprehended in the grant.

This Roger de Berkeley, the earliest 'of the family known, founded the Benedictine Priory of Stanley St. Leonard's, four miles from his Castle at Dursley, but on the property of his brother Ralph. Being wifeless and childless he retired to this monastery in his latter years, and died there some time after 1091. His brother Ralph had died before him, and the estates of both went to William son of Ralph, and nephew of the Lord of Dursley. William also became the founder of a Monastery, that of Kingswood near Wotton-under-Edge, which was one of the earliest of the Cistercian Order in England, being founded in 1139, eleven years after the importation of that Order. Bishop Hooper, whose monument stands near the Palace at Gloucester, was a Cistercian Monk, and may, from his associations, have belonged to this Monastery.

But although the English Lords of Dursley had got on well with the Norman Sovereigns from the Conqueror to Henry I., the death of the latter unsettled them, and eventually brought ruin on their estate. Henry's nephew, Stephen, obtained possession of the crown, but all his antecedents were foreign, his only association with England being that he was a grandson of the Conqueror. Henry's daughter, Matilda, the ancestress of all the Plantagenets, was an Englishwoman born, and when she fought with Stephen for her father's crown many Englishmen sided with her. But a woman on the throne would have been an intolerable novelty to others, and, notwithstanding their sympathies, the Berkeleys, that is William the founder of Kingswood and his son Roger, took the side of Stephen. The father was taken prisoner at a time when the forces of Matilda and her illegitimate brother, the great Earl of Gloucester, were triumphant, and he died in prison. The son,

Roger, escaped for a time, but at the accession, in 1154, of Matilda's son, Henry II. as the successor of Stephen, the Lord of Dursley lost all his great estates, and they were granted by the King to Robert Fitz Harding, the founder of the family which afterwards took the name of Berkeley from them.[1]

Thus for a short time Dursley Castle and Manor passed into the hands of the Fitz Hardings. But eventually inter-marriages were brought about between the sons and daughters of the gainer and the loser. Roger de Berkeley's daughter, Alice, was married to Robert Fitz Harding's son Maurice, and Robert de Berkeley, son of the former was married to Helena Fitz Harding, daughter of the latter. These friendly marriages are said to have been brought about by the young King himself, and he made it a condition that Dursley Castle should be restored to Roger de Berkeley and his successors, a new Castle being built at Berkeley for the Fitz Hardings.

By this compromise, therefore, Dursley reverted to the ancient English family which had so long held it, and it afterwards descended from father to son in regular suc-cession until the year 1382, when the last son of the line died without children. Upon his death the Castle and Manor passed to his sister Maud, who was married to Roger de Cantelupe. From her, by several generations of daughters it descended to a representative of the old Berkeleys who was married to Thomas Wyke, and then for about a century it passed by male heirs to Robert Wyke, who sold it in 1567.

The descendants of these old English Berkeleys of Dursley down to Maud de Cantelupe are shewn by the pedigree on the next page. The descent of the Wykes is also shewn, but the connecting link between them and Maud de Cantelupe is not certainly established.

---

[1] See account of Beverston, page 102.

Descent of the BERKELEYS of DURSLEY
and the WYKES.

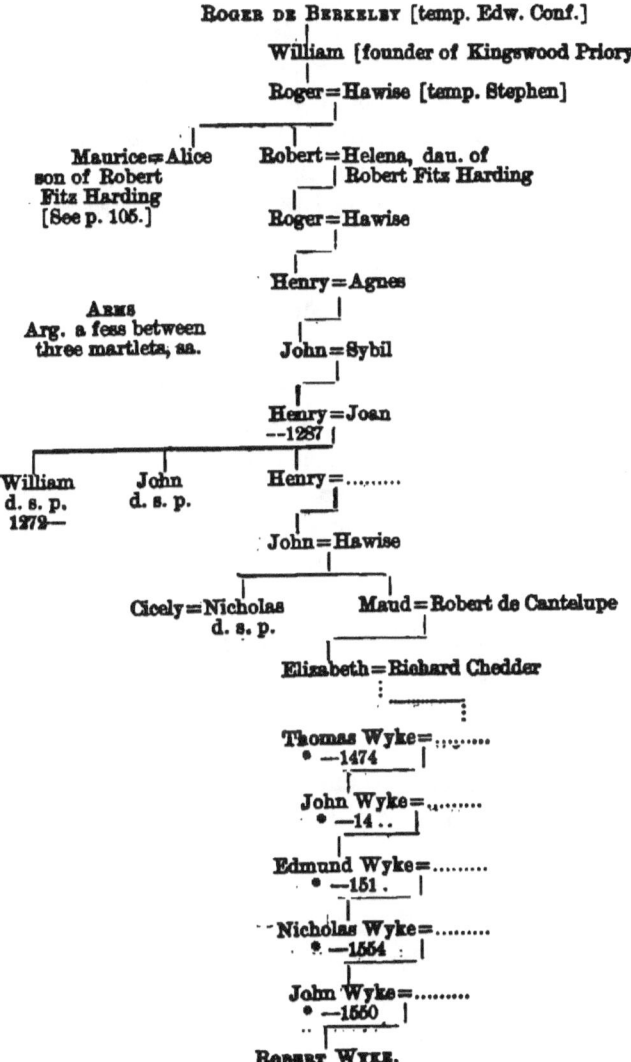

ROGER DE BERKELEY [temp. Edw. Conf.]

William [founder of Kingswood Priory]

Roger=Hawise [temp. Stephen]

Maurice=Alice
son of Robert
Fitz Harding
[See p. 105.]

Robert=Helena, dau. of
Robert Fitz Harding

Roger=Hawise

ARMS
Arg. a fess between
three martlets, sa.

Henry=Agnes

John=Sybil

Henry=Joan
--1287

William
d. s. p.
1272—

John
d. s. p.

Henry=.........

John=Hawise

Cicely=Nicholas
d. s. p.

Maud=Robert de Cantelupe

Elizabeth=Richard Chedder

Thomas Wyke=...........
• —1474

John Wyke=..........
• —14..

Edmund Wyke=.........
• —151.

Nicholas Wyke=.........
• —1554

John Wyke=.........
• —1550

ROBERT WYKE.

By the time that the Castle and Manor were thus alienated from their ancient possessors, the Wykes, their lineal representatives, seem to have fallen into poverty. " I have divers times, within twenty-six years past," writes Smyth the historian of the Berkeleys, about 1620, " beheld Mr. Wikes (the heire of this ancient lyne,) then not more old than poore, in Chancery Lane and in Fleet Streete, London, picking up the shreds of rags cast into the streets from the sweepings of taylers' and seamsters' shopps, to get thereby a farthing token for his sustenance : somewhat harsh to be written by me, when myself, and others then in my company, knowing his honourable descent, and seeing his present condition, have given him sixpence or twelvepence from amongst us, concealing ourselves and eke our knowledge of him : howbeit, conscious of his ancestors and discent (and of the mount from whence hee was tumbled down,) hee would never begg of any, for ought I could ever see or learne."[1]   Of the old castle of this ancient family nothing now remains.   Rudder says that in his time the ruins of the foundations were still visible in a garden which formed part of " Castle Fields" about a quarter of a mile north-west of the town, these fields being on the right hand of the road, immediately opposite the Rectory: and the inequalities of the ground shew that the foundation walls still, probably, remain there.   Leland says that it was built of " Towfe Stone," and that it had a moat around it, but that it had fallen into decay, and when he visited the town, about 1530, it was clean taken down.   It had, in fact, been taken down by Edmund Wyke for the sake of the materials, which he had removed to Dodington for the purpose of building the Manor House there.   Smyth wrote in the middle of the seventeenth century that the ruins which still remained were " fruitfull with Barley and Woode there growinge."

---

[1] Quoted from Smyth's MS. Lives of the Berkeleys p. 92, in Fosbrooke's Gloucest. i. 428.

It may be doubted whether Dursley was ever a town of its present size in mediæval times; and while it was thus the residence of the old Berkeleys its feudal connection with that family was probably the life of the place. But it is spoken of in the reign of Edward I. [A.D. 1281] as one of the five ancient boroughs of Gloucestershire, and was therefore a place of some dignity though not of much size. It was made a market town by a charter of Edward IV., granted in the year 1471 at the petition of the Marquess Berkeley, or at least no earlier charter is known.[1] About the same time the Church was being enlarged and the ecclesiastical position of the town made independent of the monastery of Gloucester, to which it had formerly belonged; and this conjunction of circumstances seems to indicate that Dursley was undergoing some change which was raising the number of its population and making it a place of more importance. Probably this was the time when Dursley began to take its share in the revived and almost newly-created Cloth manufacture for which England, especially in Gloucestershire and Yorkshire, was afterwards to become so famous. Fifty or sixty years later, when Leland collected materials for his Itinerary, he calls it "a pretty clothing town," and the change in its fortunes is indicated not long afterwards by the change in the name of its leading man, Wyke the representative of the old feudal interest giving way to Webb the representative of the new manufacturing interest which was then beginning to grow strong.

Mr. Webb's name appears in the Churchwarden's Register as early as 1566, about which time a Robert Webb received a patent from Queen Elizabeth privileging him to farm for

---

[1] This is the date given by Bigland from Archdeacon Parsons' MSS. But Leland says the town was "privileged at nine years since with a Market." This grant by Henry VIII. may have been a renewal of the old privilege. It was again renewed in 1612.

31 years the taxes on all woollen cloth that was sold in Gloucester and Bristol. But the Webbs were already an old clothing family, for according to Fuller the founder of their family was a Flemish cloth maker invited over to England by Edward III. and dubbed by the King with an English name appropriate to his calling. One of the family seems to have built a Mansion in Dursley so early as the reign of Henry VIII., an old house bearing outside the date 1520, and on a beam within the Cypher E. W. and date 1539. Descendants of these elder Webbs were still clothiers at Nailsworth so lately as the beginning of this century, the family being thus engaged in the trade for nearly 500 years.

But the mention of Fuller's name is a reminder that he put into his Church History of Britain a charmingly quaint account of the re-establishment of this staple industry in England which will amuse the reader and perhaps give some information not very generally possessed on the subject.

"The King and state" says Fuller "began now to grow sensible of the great gain the Netherlands got by our English wool; in memory whereof the duke of Burgundy, not long after, instituted the Order of the Golden Fleece; wherein, indeed, the *fleece* was ours, the *golden* theirs,—so vast their emolument by the trade of clothing. Our King therefore resolved, if possible, to reduce the trade to his own country, who as yet were ignorant of that art, as knowing no more what to do with their wool than the sheep that wear it, as to any artificial and curious drapery; their best clothes then being no better than friezes, such their coarseness for want of skill in their making. But soon after followed a great alteration, and we shall enlarge ourselves in the manner thereof.

The intercourse now being great betwixt the English and the Netherlands, (increased of late, since king Edward married the daughter of the earl of Hainault,) unsuspected emissaries were employed by our king into those countries, who wrought themselves into familiarity with such Dutchmen as were absolute masters of their trade, but not masters of themselves, as either journeymen or apprentices. These bemoaned the slavishness of these poor servants, whom their masters used rather like Heathens than Christians, yea, rather like horses than men! Early up and late in bed, and all day hard work and harder fare, (a few herrings and mouldy cheese,) and all to enrich the churls their masters without any profit unto themselves.

But O how happy should they be if they would but come over into England, bringing their mystery with them, which would provide their welcome in all places! Here they should feed on fat beef and mutton, till nothing but their fulness should stint their stomachs: yea, they should feed on the labours of their own hands, enjoying a proportionable profit of their pains to themselves; their beds should be good, and their bed-fellows better, seeing the richest yeomen in England would not disdain to marry their daughters unto them; and such the English beauties, that the most envious foreigners could not but commend them.

Liberty is a lesson quickly conned by heart; men having a principle within themselves to prompt them, in case they forget it. Persuaded with the premisses, many Dutch servants leave their masters and make over for England. Their departure thence (being picked here and there) made no sensible vacuity; but their meeting here all together amounted to a considerable fulness. With themselves, they brought over their trade and their tools; namely, such which could not as yet be so conveniently made in England.

Happy the yeoman's house into which one of these Dutchmen did enter, bringing industry and wealth along with them. Such who came in strangers within their doors, soon after went out bridegrooms, and returned son-in laws, having married the daughters of their landlords who first entertained them. Yea, those yeomen in whose houses they harboured soon proceeded gentlemen, gaining great estates to themselves, arms [1] and worship to their estates.

The king having gotten this treasury of foreigners, thought not fit to continue them all in one place, lest on discontent they might embrace a general resolution to return; but bestowed them through all the parts of the land, that clothing thereby might be the better dispersed. Here I say nothing of the colony of old Dutch, who frighted out of their own country with an inundation, about the reign of king Henry I. possibly before that nation had attained the cunning of cloth-making, were seated only in Pembrokeshire. This new generation of Dutch was now sprinkled everywhere, so that England

1 This assumption of arms by the old clothing families of Dursley, Cam, and Uley is very conspicuous on their monuments.

(in relation, I mean, to her own counties) may bespeak these inmates in the language of the Poet :—*Quæ regio in terris vestri non plena laboris ?* Though generally, where left to their own choice, they preferred a maritime habitation.

EAST.—1. Norfolk, Norwich Fustians; 2. Suffolk, Sudbury Baize; 3. Essex, Colchester Sayes and Serges; 4. Kent, Kentish Broad Cloths.

WEST.—.1. Devonshire, Kerseys ; 2. Gloucestershire, Cloth ; 3. Worcestershire, Cloth ; 4. Wales, Welsh Friezes.

NORTH.—1. Westmoreland, Kendal Cloth; 2. Lancashire, Manchester Cotton; 3. Yorkshire, Halifax Cloths.

SOUTH.—1. Somersetshire, Taunton Serges; 2. Hampshire, Cloth; 3. Berkshire, Cloth; 4. Sussex, Cloth.

I am informed that a prime Dutch cloth-maker in Gloucestershire had the surname of WEB given him by king Edward there; a family still famous for their manufacture. Observe we here, that Mid-England,—Northamptonshire, Lincolnshire, and Cambridge, having most of wool, have least of clothing therein.

Here the Dutchmen found fullers' earth, a precious treasure ; whereof England hath, if not more, better than all Christendom besides: a great commodity of the quorum to the making of good cloth, so that nature may seem to point out our land for the staple of drapery, if the idleness of her inhabitants be not the only hinderance thereof. This fullers' earth is clean contrary to our Jesuits, who are needless drugs, yet still staying here, though daily commanded to depart ; whilst fullers' earth, a precious ware, is daily scoured hence, though by law forbidden to be transported.

And now was the English wool improved to the highest profit, passing through so many hands, every one having a fleece of the fleece,—sorters, combers, carders, spinsters, weavers, fullers, dyers, pressers, packers: and these manufactures have been heightened to a higher perfection since the cruelty of the Duke de Alva drove over more Dutch into England. But enough of this subject : which let none condemn for a deviation from Church History: First. Because it would not grieve one to go a little out of the way, if the way be good, as this disgression is, for the credit and profit of our country. Secondly. It reductively belongeth to the Church History, seeing many poor people, both young and old, formerly charging the parishes, (as appeared by the account of the church-officers,) were hereby enabled to maintain themselves." [*Fuller's Church Hist.* vol. i. pp. 418-420. *ed.* 1837.]

The connection of Dursley with spinning and weaving is indicated not only by the name of Webb. In the Parish Register there are frequent entries in which the person is designated as Clothier, Shearman, Millman, Weaver, Broadweaver, Silkweaver, Matmaker, Drawer, Scribbler, and Card-maker.[1] Mr. Webb is also sometimes called "alias Woolworth," and the name of "Woolwright" occurs early in the register of the neighbouring parish of Cam.

But it is to be feared that there is also another trace of the old Dursley manufacture in a certain proverb of wide acceptance, "You are a man of Dursley." Fuller says, "It is taken for one that breaks his word and faileth in performance of his promises, parallel to 'Fides Græca,' or 'Fides Punica.'" De Foe, in his "Tour through Great Britain," says that Dursley is "a good clothing and market-town governed by a bailiff and four constables, and has been formerly noted for sharp, over-reaching people; from whence arose a proverbial saying of a tricking man, 'He is a man of Dursley.'" There must have been something damaging to reputations in the cloth trade, for has not the world been accustomed to use the same sort of language of a "Yorkshireman?" But then there really were complaints to Parliament in early days [A.D. 1399.] that Gloucestershire—not to say Dursley-men—

---

[1] "Scribbling" is the process by which the dressed wool is tortured by scrubbing brushes of brass into the form of a continuous sheet or "lap." The process of "carding" is of a similar kind, but it converts the "lap" into small rolls about half an inch in diameter, which are afterwards twisted by the "slubbing-billy" and the "spinning-mule" into yarn fit for spinning.

The "cards" which were formerly and are still made in Dursley are now turned out in a state of great perfection by machinery. They may be described as scrubbing brushes in which the bristles are represented by wire and the wooden backs by thick leather. After having served their time with the spinners they are very useful to Church restorers for scrubbing off churchwardens' whitewash.

"tacked and folded together" their lengths of cloth in such a manner, that though they looked sound enough on the outside of the roll they were bad in colour and narrow in width, and wrought of diverse wool (was it 'shoddy'?) in the part within. And when this was cured by one Act of Parliament another was required enacting that cloths were not to be overstrained to give them a false appearance of length and breadth,[1] not to have starch or chalk put in to increase whiteness or weight, nor to be mixed with inferior wools such as flocks and pell wool.

Could it have been Dursley that the Bishop of the Diocese—that very plain-spoken preacher old Latimer—had in his mind when he preached as follows about certain loud "professors of the Gospel?" "I hear say" he preached "there is a certain cunning come up in the mixing of wares. How say you: 'were it not a wonder to hear that the cloth-workers should become 'poticaries?' Yea and I hear say in such a place, whereas they have professed the Gospel and the word of God most earnestly of a long time, 'See how busy the devil is to slander the word of God.' Thus the poor Gospel goeth to wrack. . . . If his cloth be seventeen yards long he will set him on the rack and stretch him out with ropes, and rack him till the sinews shrink again while he hath brought him to eighteen yards. When they hath brought him to that perfection they have a pretty feat to thick him again. He makes me a powder for it, and plays the 'poticary: they call it flock powder—they were wont to make beds of flocks, and it was a good bed too, now they have turned the flocks to powder, and play the false thieves with it. Oh! wicked

---

[1] In the old days when Shrewsbury still had a market hall for Welsh flannels there was an old buyer who won for himself the name of "Tam o' th' broad thumb," for the dexterity with which he added the width of his thumb, liberally taken, to every yard of cloth as he measured it before paying the Welshmen.

devil, what can he not invent to blaspheme God's word! Woe worth that these flocks should slander the word of God! As he said to the Jews, 'thy wine is mingled with water,' so might he have said to us of this land, 'thy cloth is mingled with flock powder.'"

But those were old times. Bishop Latimer preached against racking cloth and filling it up with "devil's dust," just fifteen years before Mr. Thomas Thackham began to keep the Churchwarden's book which has told us so much of the history of Dursley in the following pages. In the next century an equally plain spoken old Churchman who has been previously quoted so largely seemed to think better of Dursley spinners. " Dursley is a market and clothing town in this county," says Fuller, " the inhabitants whereof will endeavour to confute and disprove this proverb; to make it false now, whatever it was at the first original thereof. Besides, the worst places, in the midst of epidemical viciousness, have afforded some exception from the wicked rule therein. " The Cretians are always lyars," was the observation of a Poet, and application of the Apostle; yet we find some Cretians whom the Holy Spirit alloweth for 'devout men.' Thus sure I am, there was a *man of Duresley*, who was a *man of men*, Edward Fox by name, a right godly and gracious Prelate, of whom hereafter. However the men of Duresley have no cause to be offended with my inserting this proverb; which if *false*, let them be angry with the *Author*, the first man that made it; if *true*, let them be angry with the *Subject*, even themselves who deserve it." And let us hope that the men of Dursley took the old Church Historian's advice a long while ago, and that the proverb " You are a man of Dursley " lost its sting many generations gone by.

But Proverbial Philosophy has dealt rather harshly with the town of Dursley. A century or so ago it was known to its enemies as " Drunken Dursley," a name which there is

no reason to think that it ever deserved, and which it
evidently owes to the terribly tempting trick of alliteration.
Another hard reflection on the character of Dursley folk took
the form of rhyme :—

> " Dursley baboons
> Who 'yet their pap a'thout any spoons."

Now " pap " was the " hasty-pudding " or " parritch "
which formed the evening meal of Gloucestershire labourers,
and doubtless of Gloucestershire artizans also, before the
invention of tea and potatoes.   They concocted it of wheat
flour, though in hard times of barley-meal and butter-milk;
and well-to-do-people used to add a little treacle to make it
more tastey.   In Lancashire the forefathers of the manufacturers who now " eat off silver plate " were accustomed to
eat a similar porridge of oatmeal, and they ate it out of great
wooden trenchers.   The master and his apprentices sat together around a table, in the centre of which was placed the
bowl of " pap," and each with his wooden spoon took his dip
of the savoury supper till the porringer was empty.   No
doubt Dursley manufacturers once did the same: but the
statement that they fed like monkeys, and that they dispensed
with the use of spoons, need hardly be taken as historical.
Perhaps such allegations were malicious slanders of some
envious rivals the name of whose town history has charitably
left unrecorded.

That such was the case is a conjecture confirmed by the
imputations cast upon the cookery of Dursley, and especially
of its porridge, by a Yorkshireman named John Jackson,
who wrote " A Diary of a Journey to Glastonbury Thorn,"
from Woodkirk in his own county, a journey made in the
Autumn of the year 1755.   In this Diary, which has been
recently printed in the " Reliquary," he relates that on his
return home he spent the night of January 4th, 1756, in
Dursley, and thus spitefully he records his experiences of the
town :—

Dudley in 1873

"At morn I left Philip Jones [at Berkeley] and went and took leave of my very good friend Mr. William Jenkins, and both found and left him sewing Sail Cloth, and I tarry'd a good while and we discoursed very freely, and I was very civilly entertained and had some copper coin given at my coming away. And so I set off for Dursley, and lodged at Robert Goodwins, ye Sign of the White-Hart in Dursley, and in Dursley is a neat beautiful Market House, and in this town I saw 2 swine lay killed and burnt as black as a toad, and one lay on a table and ye other ith' mucky miry way, ye ugliest object I thought yt ever my eyes beheld, and that and more of their cookery is more proper for dogs and swine than men. Their toad-back bacon [1] and Cabbage-kettle stinking porrage like Traynoyl or like the stink of ye Hog Sty." Mr. Jackson then quotes, with other verses, these:—

"God sends good meat, the Deel sends Cooks
    To spile and marr the same;
With sulky, saucy, simpering looks,
    Maid, Mrs., and Mad Dame."

Woodkirk is now better known as Ardsley West, and being near Wakefield in the West Riding has a good deal to do with coal and woollen cloth. But it may be safely asserted that no Dursley clothier ever wrote of it, or of its Maids and Madams, in such uncomplimentary terms as John Jackson did of his Gloucestershire entertainers.

---

[1] "Toad-back-bacon" is a term known in Gloucestershire for bacon that has been smoked in the chimney until it is black on the outside, and hard within. North country people seldom smoke their hams or bacon, and the Yorkshireman's palate was evidently not yet trained to the more luxurious bacon-curing habits of the West of England. The "Cabbage-kettle indicates a time when Cabbages were the staple vegetable of a poor man's household, the "potatoe-pot" being a novelty introduced about the end of the last century.

When this visit was paid to the town its clothing trade was in full vigour. Rudder writes of it, in the middle of the last century, as having enriched many of its inhabitants, and as being still, with card-making, their chief support. Rudge, writing about 1803, says that it was at that time carried on by means of the best machinery by John and Edward Wallington, William Phelps, and Mr. Tippets. In the present day not a yard of cloth, and not much card, owes its origin to Dursley manufacture: but some of the old Dursley clothing families have become large landowners and county people, and have doubtless become so through persevering adherence in prosperous times to a proverb said to be indigenous to the neighbourhood, "Saving must equal Having."

The Corporation and Court Leet.

Dursley has never been incorporated by Royal Charter, but it is a Borough by prescription; and it was called one of the five "ancient," or prescriptive, boroughs of Gloucestershire so long as 600 years ago. Its municipal head has the title of Bailiff, and those who have served the office of Bailiff receive the honourable title of Aldermen. The officers under the Bailiff are

Two Constables.

Two Carnals, or Meat Inspectors, now called Cardinals.

Two Ale Conners or Tasters.

One Hayward.

One Crier.

One Leather sealer, not appointed lately.

The Bailiff represents the ancient English "Reve" or governor elected to preside over themselves by the inhabitants of a Borough, and hence called the Borough-reve, or in port towns and cities, as in London, the Port-reve. A similar officer was elected by the freeholders of a county and was called the Shire-reve: and as " Sheriff" is the shortened form of Shire-reve so possibly " Bailiff" (though usually said to be of Norman origin) is a corrupted form of Bailiwick-reve, the tendency of popular pronunciation being always in the direction of making hard words easy. But whether the present title of this head municipal officer is Norman or " Anglo-Saxon " it is certain that his office existed under the title of Borough-reve, either by Royal grant or by custom, long before the Norman Conquest, and that the un-chartered Corporation of Dursley represents the most ancient form of English municipal institutions.

Until the time of the Norman Conquest both towns and counties had the privilege of electing all their officers except the County " eorlderman " or Earl, and as he was, officially, much what the modern Lord Lieutenant is, so among the ranks of the nobility he represented the Continental " Count " or " Consul;" the same Latin word " comes " being used for both. But when the out-at-elbows Normans got possession of England, through the too easy hospitality which we always show to foreigners, the principal object of the new comers was to enrich themselves at the expense of the English, and hence William the Conqueror's government was almost entirely one in which the Chancellor of the Exchequer was Prime Minister: a government for the collection of taxes. Moved by these Whig principles the Conqueror substituted Crown officers in every direction for the old officers who had been elected by the people themselves: so that instead of the old Shire-reves there came Viscounts [*Vice-comites*], and instead of the old Borough-reves there came Provosts [*Præpositi*], both kinds of officers being neither more nor less than publicans and sinners whose duty was to extort the utmost possible amount of revenue from the conquered people.

c 2

Thus instead of its ancient domestic system of local government by a Borough-reve or home elected Bailiff, Dursley had thrust upon it a stranger appointed by the Crown, a Crown Bailiff, whose only orders in respect of government were to get all the money he could out of the oppressed inhabitants of the town.

But although the Normans got the better of the old English people for a generation or two, time worked its revenges, the conquerors were absorbed into the ancient nationality, and the cry for a restoration of " the laws of Edward the Confessor," which was so often heard at the court of our Norman Kings, was only an indication of the persistent determination with which Dursley (and the rest of England) " harked back " upon old national institutions. At length, in the thirteenth century, when Kings of England began to speak English again, and even the titled nobility were getting less Frenchified, the obnoxious Crown Bailiffs were turned out of the house, and the old system of municipal Government was, to a great extent, restored. The larger towns were permitted to revive their Borough-reves, under the new title of Mayors, and subject to such regulations as were laid down in the Royal Charters by which the privilege was conceded to them. In the smaller towns, or those to which Charters were not granted, such as Dursley, Westminster, and Southwark, the ancient system was revived without any other change than the alteration of the head officers' title from " Borough-reve " to " Bailiff; " if, indeed, even that was a change. In later times, in the reign of Queen Elizabeth, the borough of Westminster, not long before made a city by the appointment of a Bishop, had its ancient government modified and then stereotyped by Act of Parliament. Dursley and Southwark were left untouched, but the latter being less fortunate than the former possessed an overwhelming neighbour, and the City of London has so absorbed the Borough of Southwark that scarcely more than the title of Bailiff is left to indicate its ancient independence; the Alderman of the "Bridge Ward Without," and the Magistrates of the County of Surrey, usurping nearly the whole of his jurisdiction.

The original mode of electing the Bailiff of Dursley would be by the vote of all the people of the town at an open-air court or "hustings," the last representative of which was the hustings court for the nomination (and election if there was no opposition requiring a poll) of Members of Parliament. But election at the hustings court of the *borough at large* has long been superseded by election at the Court Leet, which is the *borough by representation* in the form of a jury presided over by the Steward of the Manor of Dursley. Perhaps it was found that the introduction of cloth manufacturing roughened the edge of Dursley manners; and that the courteous system of "give-and-take" with which elections used anciently to be carried on in the borough, was supplanted by strong party-spirit and disorderly tumults. So the lovers of order fled to the ancient institution of the Court Leet and its Jury, and looking on the latter as a fair representation of the Inhabitants, established the system of submitting to it the names of three persons, any one of whom is accepted by the town as its Bailiff when so chosen by a majority of the Jury.[1]

---

[1] The following is the oath taken by the Bailiff:—

"You shall well and truly serve our Sovereign Lord the King and the Lord of this Leet in the Office of Bailiff within the Burrough Town of Dursley until you shall be thereof Discharged according to due course of Law: During which time you shall carefully see to the preservation of the King's Peace and to the good Government of this Burrough; to the suppressing of Riots and unlawful assemblies and the punishment of offenders. You shall also see to the Weights and Measures that the same be according to the Standard and orders of this Kingdom; You are likewise to look to Forestallers, Ingrossers, and Regrators of the Market and all other things appertaining to your office and which have accustomarily been used to be done for

This election of the Bailiff of Dursley takes place at the sitting of the Court Leet on some day during the month of October: but the person elected does not enter upon his duties practically until New Year's Day, when his year of office is inaugurated by ecclesiastical solemnities and municipal festivities.

After entertaining all the Aldermen at breakfast the Bailiff walks in procession with them to the Parish Church, accompanied by the Steward of the Manor, and attended by the officers of the Corporation: the Bailiff being clad in an official robe of scarlet bound with fur, and the Aldermen in gowns of a tawney colour.[1] Thus another good old

---

the good Government of this Burrough you shall well and truly do and execute to the utmost of your knowledge and understanding,

So help you God."

[1] In the reign of Edward the Sixth when the Privy Council gravely decided that the use of black in mourning was a relic of idolatry, the official robes of Mayors and Aldermen began to be disused. Some towns made a stand against the innovation, and a little later the town books of Leicester contain an order that "from hensforthe all and every person that shall be elect and chosen to execute the office of the mayoraltye within the said town of Leycester, at every principal feast and other times accustomed shall wear for the honour of the King and Queen's Majesty and their successors, and for the worship of the said town, scarlet, as of ancient time it hath been accustomed; upon pain of every person so chosen to the said office of mayoralty refusing the wearing of the said scarlet during his said time of mayoralty to forfeit and pay to the chamber of the town of Leycester five pounds."

An improvement on this order graces the municipal records of Canterbury: for there, about the same time "Mr. Mayor is ordered to provide his wife the Mayoress with a scarlet gown and a bonnet of velvet upon the pain of forfeiting £10." [N & Q. III. iij. 514., II. v. 263.] Mistress Mayoress must have had a large following in the Town Council when this order was made: but silver cradles are still habitually provided for the ladies of municipal heads on certain interesting occasions.

tradition is kept up, that of asking a blessing upon the exercise of civil authority by associating its assumption with a celebration of Divine Service. May the State in all its degrees long continue to value the blessings which it derives from association with the Church, and may the Church always have reason to value its official recognition by the State.[1]

Nor must it be left unrecorded by the .pen of history that the good old traditions of "civic hospitality" have been retained in Dursley as well as elsewhere. The very Church-wardens' Register bears traces of these traditions, for it records the expenditure of thirteen shillings in the year 1688 on "six bottles of wine and a pound of Biskey that ye Bayley sent for to treat the Lord Bearkley:"' and in 1704 a similar entry declares that £3. 10s. 0d. was spent "For treating the Deacon," who was probably Archdeacon Parsons. These were exceptional cases of hospitality, and appearing where they do, may perhaps be ranked by the reader with the famous record that

"Mr. Jones, of his great bounty,
Built this bridge at the expense of the County."

But the day on which the Bailiff enters on his office is always celebrated by really hospitable entertainments, provided not out of the Church Rate or at the expense of the County, but from his own liberality. These entertainments are not exactly turtle-feasts or Mansion House balls, but they are such respectable equivalents for these as a small country town appreciates; and although there is no salary attached to the office of Bailiff of Dursley, while the Lord Mayor of London

---

[1] In the Churchwardens' accounts for 1569 there is an entry "It. gathered on New Yeare's Eve vj^s. iiid. spent of ye same xvjd." This seems to have some association with the Bailiff's admission to office on the following morning. But New Year's Day in England was at that time March 25th, and remained so until September, 1752, when the New Style was adopted. [See "Hoggling Money."]

gets his £10,000 for his year of office, it is not on record that the one any more than the other ever flinches from the courteous hospitalities customary on his inauguration. Nor are such hospitable customs without a certain real constitutional value. The course of legislation ignores the office of Bailiff and shunts him aside when he could well perform many of the duties assigned to newly-invented officials : and it is well to keep up these honourable traditions, for they may prove to be a foot-hold by which he may some day regain a firmly established place among our borough institutions.

The Aldermen of Dursley are also the representatives of a most ancient municipal tradition. It seems as if the little town hidden among the shadows of the Cotswolds had been overlooked by the ruthless eye of "Reform" both in the old days when municipal reform meant the renewal of privileges, with or without reconstruction, by means of Charters bought at a great price from the Crown; and in more recent times, also, when it mostly meant the destruction of everything that the reformers did not like or did not understand.[1] For a Corporation of Aldermen, as the term is received in towns which have Charters, was unknown until the thirteenth or fourteenth centuries; the borough eorlder-men of more ancient days being those who had been distinguished by having had some position of trust or honour assigned to them by their fellow-townsmen, and being thus ranked, ever afterwards, as honourable "elders" of the town. But the Borough-reve or chief magistrate was alone responsible for the government of the town, and whatever the aldermen did, they did either as his assessors and councillors, or as deputies

---

[1] Birmingham was the first borough to sell its ancient regalia after the passing of the Reform Bill. It was also one of the first to repudiate Vandalism as a part of Reform by having a new set manufactured, after a Mediæval design, a few years ago.

acting under his authority. Little is known from records respecting the position and office before it was defined by Charters, but traditions in these matters are kept up with great exactness, and thus a later generation fairly represents one of a much earlier date solely from the custom of each generation doing as its predecessor had done. It may be, therefore, that the ancient office of Alderman was chiefly honorary as it seems always to have been within memory in Dursley.

The COURT LEET is the most ancient criminal court known to our constitution, although now superseded as regards the greater part of its jurisdiction, by the wide-spread net-work of the County magistracy. It consists of a jury presided over by the Steward of the Manor, as deputy to the Lord of the Manor; the Lord himself being, in the first instance, the representative of the jurisdiction of the Crown within the boundaries of his Manor.

It is an institution which originated in the constitutional principle that every man should have at his door an authority for the redress of wrongs, the preservation of the sovereign's peace, and the enforcement of justice: thus answering, in a borough, to the Sheriff's "tourn" or periodical tour through his county. The Court Leet was empowered to take cognizance of all such criminal matters as are now carried to the Quarter-Sessions, or the Assizes, with the exception of those crimes that are punished with death. Knavish bakers and brewers it sent to the pillory, drunkards it set in the stocks, common scolds it placed on the ducking-stool or temporarily silenced with the gossips' bridle: and it inflicted fines where a pecuniary composition was considered a sufficient satisfaction of justice. And not one of its least merits is thus stated by a panegyrist: "The proceedings in the leet are without expense, the suitor pays no fees, and advocates or attorneys of course never enter it." [*Ritson's Court Leet. 2nd ed.* 1809.]

This list is taken from the Bailiff's Book; the earlier part, from 1566 to 1758, having been carefully extracted for that book from the Churchwardens' Register, and preserving the original spelling of the names :—

A.D.		A.D.	
1566	John Smallwodd	1598	
1567	James Smallwodd	1599	
1568	Roger Pytt	1600	
1569	Christoph. Webbe	1601	
1570	William Berry	1602	
1571	Richard Berry	1603	John Plomer
1572	William Webbe	1604	
1573		1605	
1574		1606	
1575		1607	
1576		1608	
1577		1609	
1578		1610	
1579	Richard Marton	1611	Maurice Tyler
1580	William Tratman	1612	Arthur Vizar
1581		1613	Richard Tippetts
1582	Alexander Biztoy	1614	John Martin
1583	Thomas Tratman	1615	
1584	Thomas Carvar	1616	William Hardinge
1585	John Tiler	1617	Isaac Smyth
1586	Richard Maxtone	1618	
1587	William Purnell	1619	
1588	Thomas Tratman	1620	
1589	John Plomer	1621	Richard Tippetts
1590	Thomas Austen	1622	Henry Trotman
1591	Richard Marten	1623	
1592	Richard Brownynge	1624	William Harding
1593		1625	Thomas Hyett
1594		1626	Thomas Smyth
1595		1627	Richard Merick
1596		1628	Philip Biggs
1597		1629	Richard Browninge

A.D.		A.D.	
1630	Issac Smith	1670	William Lytton
1631	Richard Oliver	1671	John Purnell
1632	John Tyler	1672	Arthur Crew
1633	William Purnell	1673	William Purnell
1634	Nicholas Dangerfield	1674	John Watkins
1635	George Grace	1675	John Oliver
1636	Isaac Smythe	1676	William Merrick
1637	John Browninge	1677	William Partridge
1638	Samuel Harding	1678	Daniel Knight
1639	William Hill	1679	Thomas King
1640	Henry Smith	1680	Thomas King
1641	John Tucker	1681	William Tippetts
1642	Nicholas Dangerfield	1682	Samuel King
1643	Nicholas Dangerfield	1683	Richard Tippetts
1644	William Pitt	1684	Walter Maye
1645	John Hodges	1685	Jacob Wallington
1646		1686	John Williams
1647	John Philips	1687	Isaac Smyth
1648	Augustin Phillipps	1688	William Lytton
1649	George Martaine	1689	Thomas Purnell
1650	William Tippetts	1690	John Partridge
1651	Henry Adye	1691	John Purnell
1652	John Arundel	1692	Benjamin Symonds
1653	Isaac Smith	1693	Samuel Clarke
1654	John Purnell	1694	John Webb
1655	Obadiah Webb	1695	Robert Whatcley
1656	William Purnell	1696	Richard Merrick
1657	John Watkins	1697	Thomas King
1658	Josias Arundell	1698	Joseph Pulley
1659	John Oliver	1699	Maurice Philips
1660	John Till-Adams	1700	Samuel King
1661	William Partridge	1701	Richard Tippetts
1662	Edmond Perrett	1702	James Bayley
1663	John Tucker	1703	William Purnell
1664	William Tippetts	1704	Jacob Wallington
1665	Thomas Everett	1705	Isaac Smyth
1666	Henry Smith	1706	Isaac Smyth
1667	Samuel Symonds	1707	John Philips, jun.
1668	John Arundell	1708	Maurice Smith
1669	William Smith	1709	

A.D.		A.D.	
1710		1751	Maurice Smith
1711		1752	John Plomer
1712	Roger Whateley	1753	Lewis Hoskins
1713	William Symonds	1754	William Long
1714	Josiah Arundell	1755	Joseph Faithorne
1715		1756	William Heaven
1716		1757	John King
1717		1758	William Plomer
1718		1759	William Blake
1719		1760	Samuel Lewton
1720		1761	Thomas Cam
1721		1762	Josiah Tippetts
1722		1763	Samuel Phillimore
1723		1764	Morgan Pully
1724		1765	Hugh Everett, senior
1725		1766	Thomas Morse, junior
1726		1767	Thomas Tippetts
1727		1768	Benjamin Smith
1728		1769	Samuel Wallington
1729		1770	Benjamin Millard
1730	James Selwyn	1771	Richard Williams
1731	Giles Hodges	1772	Isaac Danford
1732	John Purnell	1773	Isaac Jones
1733	Richard Oliver	1774	John Ball
1734	James Nicholas	1775	William Roach
1735	Samuel Wallington	1776	William Drew
1736	Thomas Morse	1777	Samuel Griffin
1737	Timothy Wallington	1778	William King
1738	Samuel Clarke	1779	Thomas Lewton
1739	Richard Cooper	1780	Benjamin Millard, junior
1740	Jacob Stiff	1781	Daniel Dimory
1741	Thomas Purnell	1782	William Jackson
1742	Josias Clarke	1783	John Wallington
1743	Thomas Wallington	1784	James Wheeler
1744	William Browning	1785	Nathaniel Blackwell
1745	John Moody	1786	Richard Williams, jun.
1746	John Gethern	1787	Jonathan Hitchins
1747	George Faithorne	1788	Thomas Moore
1748	Nathaniel Lawson	1789	John Long
1749	Joseph Till-Adam	1790	
1750	Richard Tippetts	1791	

A.D.

A.D.		A.D.	
1792		1833	George Vizard
1793		1834	James Harding
1794		1835	Joseph Player
1795		1836	Robert Rowles White
1796	William Troughton	1837	Edward Bloxsome
1797	Edward Wallington	1838	James Hammet Howard
1798	William Smith	1839	Thomas Williams Richards
1799	James Player	1840	John Tilton
1800	John Harding	1841	John Vizard
1801	Thomas Richards	1842	Henry Bishop
1802	James Danford	1843	William Richards
1803	John Millard	1844	John Hurndall
1804	Samuel Trotman	1845	Charles King
1805	John Wood	1846	Joseph Shellard
1806	William Harris	1847	William Champion
1807	George Harris	1848	Edward Goodwin
1808	Samuel Champion	1849	Charles Hamilton
1809	Harry Dimery	1850	George Leonard
1810	Richard Roe	1851	Edward Augustus Freeman
1811	John Cartwright	1852	Edward Gazard
1812	Thomas Clarke	1853	Thomas Woods
1813	Thomas Williams	1854	John Hurndall, junior
1814	Thomas Williams	1855	Richard Godwin
1815	John Trotman	1856	John Davis
1816	Thomas Morse	1857	William Philip Want
1817	Edward Bloxsome	1858	William Philip Want
1818	Henry Vizard	1859	George Wintle
1819	Henry Vizard	1860	Frederick Vizard
1820	Henry Vizard	1861	Henry Moore
1821	Charles Vizard	1862	Henry Moore
1822	Edward Wallington	1863	Daniel Crump
1823	William Fry	1864	Charles Workman
1824	James Young	1865	Henry Owen
1825	Charles Frederick Richards	1866	George Ayliffe
1826	William Cox Buchanan	1867	Richard Garn
1827	Baptist William Hicks	1868	George Wenden
1828	John Williams	1869	John Morse
1829	Robert John Purnell	1870	Thomas Trewren Vizard
1830	Edward West	1871	James Lang
1831	John Wallington	1872	James Whitmore
1832	John Wallington	1873	William Henry Hancock
		1874	John Benjamin Champion

ECCLESIASTICAL DURSLEY.

The earliest authentic history of England is its Church History, and so it eventually proves in the case of every town or parish. But the ancient history of a place is often written by the light of modern discovery, and much local observation and research is required before the necessary materials for such history, if they exist, can be pieced together. Such research and observation in respect to Dursley has been unfortunately neglected, and if the details of its early history are ever recorded it will be by some other writer.

THE ANCIENT CHURCH.

But when they are brought to light it will probably be found that Anglo British Dursley became a Christian town as soon as most places in Gloucestershire. Perhaps earlier than some, for the last homes of British heathenism appear to have been on the breezy plains and downs, while Dursley lies in a quiet valley such as early Christian missionaries, whose energies were not of a combative kind, loved to visit and settle down in. Moreover, the Roman armies were one means by which the world was Christianized, many a centurion and many a soldier having learned the faith from the lips and life of Apostolic men; and Pudens, the .Gloucestershire friend of St. Paul, being very probably at some time of his military life, quartered in the Roman Aldershott on Uley Bury. It may be reasonably concluded, therefore, that the proverb "God is in Gloucestershire" was true of those early days when the Lichfield martyrs, and St. Alban, and the first Christian Emperor, Constantine, bore witness by their lives and deaths to the Christianity of our then land of the far-west; and that long before the fifth century the Christianity which had become almost universal among the Romans had become so among their British subjects, the camp at Uley Bury bringing the standard of the Cross as well as the Imperial eagles to the knowledge of Dursley people.

When, however, the heathen Germans seized upon the county which the Romans had first disarmed and then left unprotected, they came upon the Christian Britons as the Philistines came upon the Israelites in the days of Deborah and Barak: " was there a sword or a spear found in all the coasts of Israel?" While they were making their swords and their spears they were driven step by step out of the southern counties until all who were left free had taken refuge among their Christian brethren in the Welsh valleys. It was some time before peaceful relations between the conquerors and the conquered were sufficiently established to permit of any Christian Britons coming eastward to evangelize the Saxons of the new kingdom of Mercia, of which Gloucestershire formed part, but Theocus the hermit [1] from whom Tewkesbury took its name was doubtless one among many who eventually did so: and in the seventh century the district around Dursley was comprehended within a great Christian trilateral of which the Abbeys of Gloucester [A.D. 680], Bath [A.D. 676], and Malmesbury [A.D. 673], formed the protecting fortresses.

Thus we may well suppose the Church of Dursley to date from the days of early British Christianity, and if it was driven out of the quiet valley among the western Cotswolds by the Saxon invasion, its restoration would certainly take

---

[1] There was a hermitage on the high lands to the south-west of the town of Dursley, but whether it was an early one or only mediæval there is nothing to shew. All we know is, that the last hermit was falsely accused of having stolen a horse in the year 1517.

place when the Saxons themselves became English and Christian, and when the Monks of Gloucester as they explored the Vale passed up the streams of the Cam and the Ewelme until they found the end of the valley and the town that nestled there.

It is almost a proverb in Gloucestershire that the Berkeleys have always been great supporters of the Church, and there can be no doubt that the Church of Dursley prospered when it was under the protection of Dursley Castle. There seems, indeed, to have been an extensive range of Ecclesiastical buildings in the town near to the Church itself, a fine pointed arch near the Broadwell having evidently belonged to some important structure, perhaps to the "Priory." Yet the only documentary evidence bearing on the subject is that which records that a grant of land was made in Woodmancote to the Nuns of Clerkenwell by Maurice de Gaunt of Beverston [*Dugdale's Mon.* j. 432. *old ed.*]; and that in which is a reference to the "Prioress of Dursley," which is contained in the Inquisition taken after the death of Thomas Lord Berkeley in the year 1417.

But about the same time that the place began to rise in importance by becoming a clothing town, some considerable additions were made to the fabric of the Church, and the parish began to occupy a distinguished position as the Benefice and Cure of Souls of the Archdeacons of Gloucester.

In Mediæval times Dursley was one of the livings belonging to the Abbey of Gloucester, that Monastic corporation being Rector, and serving the Cure either by a permanent Vicar or by a clerical monk acting as Curate in sole charge, and liable to be at any time recalled and replaced by one of his brethren of the Abbey. This latter was the more common plan adopted by the Monasteries, and it occasionally happened, as at Tewkesbury, that there was a standing contention on the subject between the Monastery and the

Bishop, the latter wishing to appoint a Vicar so that there might be a particular person always responsible for the care of the parish, and the other arrangement being more convenient to the monks. But the Bishops had little or no authority in Monasteries, and many abuses arose in their dioceses from this interference with their jurisdiction. An opportunity arrived, however, which enabled the Bishop of Worcester—the county of Gloucester being then part of his diocese—to place Dursley on a better ecclesiastical footing.

The Archdeacons of Gloucester had, in Mediæval days, a very large jurisdiction, extending over all the district which now forms the two dioceses of Gloucester and Bristol. They lived in Gloucester in an official residence, and it is extremely probable that there was a standing rivalry between the semi-Episcopal Archdeacons and their near neighbours the semi-Episcopal Abbots. For this, or for some other reason, it was agreed between Alcock, Bishop of Worcester, and the Abbey of Gloucester, in the year 1475, that the Archdeacon should give up his residence in Gloucester, and that the house in which he had resided should become the property of the Abbey. As compensation for this advantage the Abbey made over to the Bishop all its rights in the parish of Dursley: and these the Bishop annexed to the Archdeaconry. As the appointment to the Archdeaconry rested with the Bishop he thus became Patron of the Benefice of Dursley; the Archdeacons becoming *ex-officio* Rectors of Dursley. This arrangement lasted for all but 400 years, namely, from 1475 until 1865. But it does not seem to have worked any better for the Parish than the old one, for the Archdeacons of Gloucester rarely resided in Dursley, and they mostly held other preferments. The list of them printed further on will shew that during the first sixty-five years after the change was made as many as five out of the eight Rectors of Dursley became Bishops. Since the Reformation only one has risen to the Episcopal Bench, namely

Bishop Hurd, who became Bishop of Lichfield nearly 300 years after 1475: but the Rectors still continued to be pluralists, seldom lived on the spot, and often appointed as their Curates men of inferior position and abilities who were not competent to take the lead in so important a Parish.

The ancient Church of the town was not originally so large as it is at present. It consisted only of the Nave, with a much lower roof, a Chancel which was probably much smaller than the present one, and a western tower surmounted by a spire, both of which were destroyed in 1699. There may also have been small aisles on either side of the Nave, but if so they were replaced by the larger ones now existing at a period not very long before the Reformation.[1]

These two larger aisles were built in connection with Chantry Chapels which occupied their eastern ends, the one in the North Aisle—hence called St. Mary's Aisle—being dedicated in the name of the Blessed Virgin, and that in the South Aisle in the name of the Holy Trinity. Nothing is known respecting the foundation of St. Mary's Chantry, but that of the Holy Trinity is traditionally known as the foundation of Thomas Tanner, a merchant who lived in the middle of the fifteenth century, and whose effigy in the form of a stone *cadaver* has always stood at the east end of it. That portion of the aisle is also called the "Tanner Chapel" in the Churchwarden's accounts of the following century, and has always been known by that name in recent times.

Chantries were built, during the fourteenth and fifteenth centuries, for the purpose of containing Altars at which the Holy Communion might be specially celebrated for the departed souls of the persons who built them and of their relatives. Lady Chapels—such as St. Mary's Aisle seems to have been—were of earlier date and were used for the daily celebration of the Holy Communion as the daily service of

---

[1] A description of the Church will be found in the section on "Dursley as it is."

the Church, independently of the special celebrations for departed persons which also took place there, and from which they too acquired the name of Chantries in later times. The Chantries were thus specially endowed by their founders, and Clergymen were presented to them by the Patrons who were not otherwise associated with the Church in which they were situated, and who were called " Chantry Priests." The special office of these extra-parochial clergy was abolished by Act of Parliament [1 Edw. VI. ch. 14.] in the reign of Edward VI., and their endowments were confiscated by the Crown.

In the year 1546 Henry VIII. issued a commission of enquiry respecting all Colleges of Priests and Chantries throughout the country, as also did Edward VI., a second time, in the year 1548, and the returns made by these Commissions being preserved in the form of " Certificates" among the Records of the Court of Augmentations, some particulars are still to be found respecting their original endowment and their final dissolution. The Certificate Rolls for the County and City of Gloucester and the City of Bristol contain the report of the Commissioners respecting the Dursley Chantries.[1]

From these reports it appears that " Our Lady's Service " was founded by persons whose names were not then known, and that it was endowed with lands and tenements by divers persons and the same put in feoffment with the rents and profits. Out of these endowments part had been used for the maintenance of a Priest to sing service at our Lady's Altar for the souls of the Founders and for all Christian souls ; and part had been distributed yearly among the poor. The lands were of the yearly value of £7. 19s. 8d. : the priest's salary being fixed at £6. 13s. 4d., the Poor receiving yearly 13s. 4d., and rent amounting to 14s. having been " with-

---

[1] Abstracts were made by Benjamin W. Greenfield, Esq., in 1866, and have been used for this work by the kindness of John Vizard, Esq., of Ferney Hill, Dursley.

drawn by Nicholas Wykes these 14 years past."[1] The value of the Ornaments of the Chapel was reckoned at 23s. 4d. in 1546 and at 6s. 8d. in 1548 : but at the latter date there is reported, in addition, Plate and Jewels, weighing 23 ounces and worth £5. 7s. 4d. The Incumbent of the Lady Chapel in 1548 was Richard Berye, aged 58 years, and he had also a stipend of £2. 8s. 0d. a year as Chantry Priest of Tokynton Chapel in the parish of Olweston.

The " Trinity Service " was founded by divers persons not then known, and the lands put on feoffment for the maintainance of a Priest to sing at the Altar of the Holy Trinity in the said Parish Church, praying for the Souls of the Founders and Benefactors thereof and all Christian souls. The profits of the land and tenements belonging to this Chantry amounted to the yearly value of £7. 4s. 2d.; the Ornaments were valued at £2. 13s. 4d. in 1546, and 13s. 4d. only in 1548, but in the latter year there are also entered Plate and Jewels weighing 17 ounces and worth £3. 10s. 10d. The yearly stipend of the Chantry Priest was £6. 13s. 4d., and the Incumbent in 1548 was Sir John Coderynton, who was eighty years of age and had no other living.[2]

It appears also from the report of 1546 that there was a third Chantry in the Church of Dursley, which is called the " Service of Jesus " by the Commissioners. This was endowed with lands of the annual value of £5. 9s. 4d. " of whiche landes dyverse of them ar evicted and takyn away. That is to sey one parcell of grounde callid Whitchester worth by yere xvj s by one of Sir Willm Kyngstons servaunts aboute xij yeres last past; and ij other parcells takyn away by one Nicholas Wykes Esquyer about ij yeres last past, by yere liij s. iiij d. And so ther remanyth nowe in the said ffeoffes hands xl s wch they occupy to ther owne use."

Where there were many Chantry Priests in a parish, or

<hr>

[1] To bring these sums to modern money multiply by twelve.

[2] The title "Sir" was formerly given to the Clergy as that of "Reverend" is now given.

perhaps in the neighbourhood of a central parish, they were accustomed to live together in a " College," such a College still standing at Higham Ferrers in Northamptonshire. Where the number was few, as at Dursley, their house of residence was called the " Chantry," and the house on the Church side of Long Street now known by that name is doubtless the one occupied by the Chantry Priests. From a taxation roll in the Worcester Register for 1513 it appears that there were then four Chantry Priests residing in Dursley, namely William Rogers, Richard Berye, Thomas a Powell, and Richard Salmon ; all four being called " chaplains."

When the Crown had taken possession of the endowments and valuables belonging to the Chantries it interfered with them no further. The buildings themselves were sometimes retained by the representatives of the Founders as burial places and pews ; and in other cases, as at Dursley, they were incorporated with the Church of which they had formed a part ; the screens which alone divided them from the Church being mostly removed.

These slight records respecting the dissolution of the two Chantries are unfortunately all that can be given with reference to the early progress of the Reformation in Dursley, the eighteen stirring years between 1548 and 1566 being quite a blank. From the documents above quoted, however, one interesting particular is obtained, namely that in the end of Henry the Eighth's reign the parish numbered 500 " houselling people" or communicants.

THE MODERN CHURCH.

For the parochial history of Dursley after the Reformation there is more material than for that of the preceding ages, for it was the good custom of the Churchwardens to keep their accounts and other memoranda in a thick folio volume which possesses a bulky dignity that has conduced to its preservation. This volume is called a Register, the name being taken from the books which were used for recording the Annals of Monasteries, and those which are still used as the official Journals of Bishops. It begins in 1566, and ends in 1758.

§ *The Churchwardens' Register.*

' The title of this valuable volume was thus written on its first page by Thomas Thacham the senior Churchwarden in 1566 :—

☞ A Book or Rigester prouyded to be a Ligear in the Storehouse to the vse of the p'ishe of Dursleye as well ffor the yearlie Accompts to be made by the Churchwardens as for the safe keaping in memorie of all those things that of right belongeth to the said p'ishe : wherein also anye mann yt will may haue his Testament or last will regesterid. &c. Dated the ffyrst day of April : in the yeare of the Lorde. 1566°. And in the Eight yeare of the Reigne of our Soueraigne Ladye Elizabeth by the grace of god Queene of England of frannce and Ireland Defender of the ffaithe. &c.

Ecclesiastic. 42. Be not thou affraid if thou gyve any thing by nomber and weight to put all in wryting bothe that whiche is gyven owt and that which is receauyd againe.

Si deus nobiscum quis contra nos : sed si Dominus contra nos quis nobiscum. Igitur in domino confido et non erubescam.

Per me Thomam Thacham

☞ Anno Dni 1566. ☜

On the back of the title page Mr. Thacham has also written the following inscription : [1]

This Book cotayneth xj Quires of paper.

Wryte true and spare not. If thou blott yet spare not.

Let wryting remayn : from cutting refrayne.

---

[1] A Thomas Thacham is mentioned by Foxe and Strype the Church Historians, who was a Grammar schoolmaster in Reading in 1556, who received an appointment as a schoolmaster in Gloucestershire, and who was a clergyman at Northampton in 1572. The Dursley Thacham knew more Latin than one would expect from an ordinary Churchwarden : was he this Schoolmaster ? See page 153.

> Too keepe your consience
> poure and there so may
> you be churchman another yere [1]

In the accounts for the year is the enty "*It.* to Samuel Byrton for this register book iiijs. " The volume was rebound a hundred and twenty years afterwards, in handsome stamped leather with brass clasps, on the one cover being also stamped in gold letters " W.L. 1686 CHVRCH " and on the other " I.G. 1686 WARDENS," these initials standing for William Litton and John Grace. The initials " I S." are also stamped irregularly upon the front cover, standing for Isaac Smyth who was Bailiff in that year.

A search through this volume not only gives the reader some insight into the Ecclesiastical affairs of the parish of Dursley for two centuries, but also furnishes some curious illustrations of parochial matters that are now obsolete and forgotten. These latter may be noticed first. ·

BRIEFS.

These were a relic of "rank Popery," being licenses to collect money in Churches, which were originally issued by the Pope, but when the Pope's authority in England was abrogated were issued by the Crown. In later times they were called " King's Letters " or " Queen's Letters," being in the form of " Letters Patent " but sealed with the Privy Seal instead of the Great Seal.

---

[1] This wise counsel may be supplemented by some parochial poetry which appears in one of the Overseer's account books of Dursley, about two centuries later, in the year 1775 :—

"Epitaph on the late Overseer J. H." [*i.e.* John Hurlstone.]
" Here lies one J . . n H . . l . . . ne that pinching Old Dog
Why should he lie here, and so much like an Hog ?
When on Earth not a Soul of him could speak well,
The Cries of the Poor now reach him in Hell.
He got up in the world by practicing Evil ·
Then fulfilled the proverb and rode to the Devil."

Briefs were granted at the pleasure of the Crown to those who petitioned for them in due form, and were addressed to all Archbishops, Bishops, Clergy, and Churchwardens, enjoining them to assist the petitioners in collecting money within their respective jurisdictions for the purposes specified in them. They were then read out in Church after the Nicene Creed, according to the rubric still extant in the Prayer Book, and the collection made in Church. The purposes for which briefs were granted were very various, as may be seen by the following receipts given by the official collector to the Churchwardens, and either written on a page of the Register or on small printed forms which the Churchwardens have occasionally preserved by pinning them in. Some of earlier date are noticed under " Poor Relief " further on,

"March ye 15th 1660.[1]

" Recd of ye Churchwardens of Dursley ye summe of foure shillings and seaven pence gathered there by a briefe for John Davis of Hereford, by me James Draper."

" Recd of ye Churchwardens ye sume of five shillings and nine pence gathered at Dursley by a briefe for ye inhabitants of Esthagborne in barkshcere

by me Moris Lewis "

" Collected for the Inhabitants of flimster the sume of ten shillings ten pence halfe pency "

" Recd eight shillings and eight pence wh was gathered ye 26th of May 1661 for ye repairing of a Key or peare in Watchet in ye County of Somersett, and also five shillings and scauen pence halfepeny wh was gathered ye 2 day of

---

[1] Briefs appear by the following entry to have been issued by Cromwell during the time of the Commonwealth, " Anno Dom : 1653, August 1. Collected in the pish of Durslye in commt Glouster towards the releife of the Inhabitants of Marleborough the summe of ffourteene pound eight shillings and seauenpence. wee say 14l. 8s. 07d. When they had greate losse by fyar.

Richard Nash } Churchwarden
John Hiatt }   Obadiah Webb."

June 1661 towards repairing of yᵉ Church of Condover in yᵉ County of Salope

Pr me Maurice Lewis for Jos Eglington High Constable."

Other receipts entered in a similar manner are as follows :

1661	Great Drayton, Salop, for loss by fire	6s	3d
1661 Jan. 16.	Elianor Davis, for house burned	4s	0d
1661 March 12.	For Bridgnorth, Salop	4s	9d
1661 March 13.	Elmsley Castle, Worcester, for a fire	11s	10d
1661 August 7.	Henry Harrison, Mariner ..	7s	1d
1661 August 20	For A fire in London . ..	6s	5d
1661 October 26	For the City of Oxford	5s	6d
1661-2 February 19	For Several persons burned out at Quatt, Salop	3s	7d
1661-2 March 12	For building Church of Blingbrooke, Lincolnsh.	4s	3d
1661-2 March 12	For " the prodisture Churches in the Dukedom of Lithuania "	27s	3d
1664 August 16	For " Grantom " Lincolnsh. ..	6s	1d
1664 July 30	For repairing Church of Lydney, Gloc...	3s	8d
1664 December 5	For Henry Lyster, of Gisborough, Yorks	6s	8d
1664 December 12	For repair of Basing Church, Southhamptonsh.	3s	1d
1665 May 12	For fire at Broughyn, Herts	3s	9d
1665 May 12	For repair of Witheham Church, Suff.	3s	0d
1667 Feb 23	For redeeming " Captives out of Algerie and Salley and other parts of the turks dominions "	12s	4d

1669 Feb 20	For fire at Tiberton, Salop ..	6s	4d
1670 April 24	For fire at Cotton end in the parish of Hardington, Northauts	8s	1d
1671-2 March 11	For fire at Oxford..	18s	1½d
1672 May 19	For fire at "ligrane in the County of Bedford.".. ..	8s	2¾d
1676 September 10	For repairing Oswestry Church	4s	7½
1676 October 15	For fire at Eton	7s	0d
	For fire in Southwark	62s	4d
	For fire at Cottenham, Cambs.	11s	8d
1677 Feb. 23	For fire at Wem, Salop.. ..	26s	8d
	For-fire at Combe in the parish of Wotton	7s	1d
1978 May 17	For fire at Towcester, North-ants	6s	3d
1678 May 17	For fire at Blandford, Dorset	4s	11½d
1682 May 19	For building Church at Kid-welly Carmarthen	6s	4d
1683 July 6.	" For Westminster Brief " ..	8s	10½d.
1683 Oct. 1.	For fire at Wapping .. £5.	2s	8d
1683 Oct. 25	For fire at Newmarket £1	19s	2½d
1683 Oct. 25	For fire at Bradwinth, Devon	6.	9¾d
1686 May 29	" Collected in ye p'ish of Dursley by a Briefe fro House to House towards ye reliefe of ye French Protestants " ..	2 11	0
1686 Oct. 1	" Collected in ye p'ish of Dursley by a briefe fro House to House for White Chappell "		17 11
1687 Dec. 5.	" Collected in ye p'ish of Dursley briefe from House to House for Stanly St Leonards "	4 5	0
1687 December 15	" Stanley's Briefe "	85s	0d
1692 June 22	" for ye reliefe of Mr. Clopton	10s	6d

1692 June 22	For fire at Hedon, Yorks.	..	4s	6d
	do do		3s	6d
1692 November 17	For fire at Chagford	.. ..	31s	0d
	For fire at " Drutige "	.. ..	7s	0d
	For fire at Elseworth	.. ..	4s	8d
	For fire at Havant	.. ..	6s	8d
1694 January 8	For fire at York	.. .. ..	18s	2d
1694 January 22	For Nether Haven	.. ..	11s	10d
1694 April 2	For fire in Warwick	.. ..	81s	7d
1694 July	For fires at Gillingham, Wrock-			
	wardine, Towyn, and Gran-			
	chester	.. ..	23s	1½d
1694 Septr 1	Wooller brief	.. .. ..	5s	10d
1694 Septr 1	Yalding brief	.. .. ..	4s	3d

" Sep. j 1684 Receiv'd of the Minister and Church-wardens of the Parish of Dursley in the County of Gloucester the sum of one pound seventeen shillings sevenpence farthing being collected on their Majesties Letters Patent, for the Relief of the *Poor French Protestants*, bearing Date the 31st of March, 1694. I say Receiv'd by me Tho : Burgis."

After this date there are no notices of Briefs until we come to one which was granted for Dursley itself, of which particulars are given further on. Had Dursley ceased to contribute towards repairing the misfortunes of its neighbours ? And is it in retaliation for such want of charity that the parish books of Ormsby St. Margaret, near Yarmouth, have the following entry in the year 1707 ?

" November 16. Collected to yᵉ rebuilding of Dursley Church and steeple fallen downe in yᵉ County of Gloucester, one peny." [1]

But the system of collecting by Briefs was full of abuse;

---

[1] See a list of about one hundred Briefs that were collected during thirty-three years in Ormsby Parish, printed in *Notes & Queries* 2nd Series, ij, 222.

sometimes the briefs were farmed, at the least about half of
what was collected throughout the country was paid to officials,
and the remainder was also subject to robbery. In 1704,
therefore, an Act of Parliament was passed [4 Anne ch. 14],
which stated that " many inconveniences arose and frauds were
committed in the common method of collecting charity money
upon briefs," and regulated their use with the purpose of
preventing them from becoming financial speculations, and of
making them honestly efficient for the purpose intended. Still
the abuses grew up again, and at last, in 1834, the Act of
Queen Anne was repealed by a new Act [9 Geo. IV. ch. 28],
which reserved to the Crown the power of granting Briefs
for Incorporated Church Societies alone. When Lord Palmer-
ston was Prime Minister he declined to advise the Crown to
issue any Briefs or Queen's letters even to these Societies,
and thus they have now fallen into disuse.

POOR RELIEF.

Very frequent entries occur in the Church accounts of
Dursley during the seventeenth century, of money being
given by the Churchwardens out of the Church Rate for the
relief of poor travellers, wounded soldiers and sailors, and
especially of many Irish people.

The earliest of such payments of any amount is in 1588
when there is " Item. pd to the poore for xiiij weekes
xvj ˢ iiijd." In general separate entries are made for such
payments, as in 1592, a poor man 2s. 6d. ; in 1603, A Captain
maimed in Ireland 2s. 6d. ; in 1615, To a man of Uppom
which came with license, 6d. ; in 1617, to a poor man with
Letters Patent—that is a Brief—2s. 6d. ; in 1621, to a man
and his wife travelling out of Ireland unto York, 6d. ; in
1622, unto one that came with the broad seal, 6d. ; in 1624,
to a traveller that came with a brief, 1s. ; to a poor woman
that her husband was taken prisoner by the Turk, 6d. ; to 3
poor people that came with a pass, 6d. In 1630, there are

as many as fifteen such entries, five being of Soldiers, two
of "a Minister"—a not unfrequent subject of this charitable
relief,—and several of Irish men and women.   In following
years many similar ones appear, but only one "Scottish man"
is on record as receiving charity: he, however, receiving two
shillings, which was considerably more than the usual sum,
a fact that will be interpreted by the reader's ideas as to
the canny people of the North.   In 1673 "Maimed soldiers
and seamen in their distress" received as much as £7. 6s. 10d.,
and in 1678, £2. 18s. 10d.   These were probably wounded
men who had served under the Duke of Monmouth in the
battles fought between the armies of Louis XIV. and the
Prince of Orange ; and Chelsea Hospital was not ready for
soldiers until 1690, nor Greenwich Hospital for sailors until
1704.

But the County authorities found it necessary to bring down
the hand of the law with weighty severity upon "travellers"
of this kind in the year 1678, and four closely-written pages
of the folio Register are occupied with the copy of an order
made on the subject in a General Quarter Session.   This
begins by reciting how "the Grand Inquest hath informed
this Court the dayly concourse and great increase off Rouges,
Vagabonds, and Sturdy Beggars, is a greate Grievance and
annoyance to the inhabitants of this County, and through the
negligence or ignorance of those officers who have been in-
trusted in this Concerne they are now grown soe insolent and
presumptious that they have oft by threates and menaces
extorted money and victualls from those who live in houses
ffar remote ffrom neighbours . . . . And have putt the people
in A general Consternation or ffeare that they will ffier their
house or steale theyr goodes, ... Whereffore this Courte·
. . . . doe order and commande all Chiefe Constables, petty
Constables, Headboroughs, Tythenmen, and all other officers
herein concerned that they doe fforthwith cause all the lawes

and Statutes heretofore mad against Rouges, Vagabonds, and
Sturdy Beggars, wandering and idle persons, to be putt in
execution, and to that end itt is here ordered." Then follow
a series of orders compiled from Acts passed in the reigns of
Elizabeth, James, and Charles I. The Officers were to search
every suspected place for beggars during the night once a
week or oftener; and also to apprehend "all such Rouges
&c. who trauell with fforged and counterfeited passes in the
day time : " and when they have duly apprehended them by
night or day " the Constable, Headborough, or Thythenman,
being assisted with the minister [!!] and some other of the
p'ish shall cause them to be stripped naked ffrom their middle
upward, and to be openly whipped untill theyr Bodyes be
Bloody." Then the minister, or high constable, was to add to
this work of charity a certificate that the man had been duly
whipped, and direct him to pass by the nearest road to his
native parish within ten days. The other orders provide for
carrying out this principal one, and for the fine or other
punishment of those who obstruct the officers in their duty.
But there are some humane provisions for the assistance of
soldiers and mariners lawfully passing on their way home
which offer a happy contrast to the severity of those made
for the benefit of " sturdy beggars."

It may be naturally supposed that this stringent execution
of the laws in force diminished the number of those who
came to the Churchwardens of Dursley for relief, and certainly there are very few entries of relief in following years
compared with those of preceding ones. They occasionally
make their appearance, however, until at last the Parish took
the matter into its own hands as is shewn by the following
entry. " Sept. 24. 1738. It is agreed at a publick Vestry
that no Churchwarden or Overseer shall be allowed to give
anything to Travellers on ye Parish Account. Saml. Clarke,
Thomas Gethen, Churchwardens; Jno Phelps, Jno Purnell,
Sam. Wallington."

Probably this order did not interfere with such domestic charity as is indicated by the items " Paid Dr. Berks for setting Edward Curtaise's child's bone, 1s 0d" and " Pd Mary May for Powltissinge of Gilles Davis his legg." Nor did this Parochial sternness prevent the Churchwardens who paid the ringers eleven shillings for celebrating the proclamation of peace in 1749 from adding afterwards " pd for drink the same day £2. 10. 0."

VERMIN.

In the neighbouring parish of Cam vigorous efforts were made by the Churchwardens to exterminate their fellow parishioners the sparrows. Those of Dursley waged war chiefly against foxes, pole cats, and hedge hogs : and their Register contains the following curious record of old legislation on the subject, which appears to have been written about the end of the sixteenth century :—

" According to a statute made the 8 yeare of Quene Elizabeth chap 15 and continued 13 of Elizabeth chapter the 25 : and after 14 Elizabeth chap 11 there ought to be chosen yearely on ester monday or tuesday by the Churchwardens and six other persons to be Required by the Churchwardens of the same parish to tax and assesse every farmer propriator and euery person and every other person haiueing the possession of any land or tythes to pay such soms of money as they shall thinke meete acording to the proportion of their lands or tythes and upon denyall or in default of payment shall forfeit 5s to be leuied by distress and sale of the offendors goods and the sums of money soo taxed and leuied to be delliuered to . . . . honest substantiall men of every parish which shall be elected and apoynted by the Churchwardens to hand the yearely distribution thereof and these persons soo nominated and apoynted shall be called the distributors of the provision for the destruction of noysom foule and vermine and the said distributors shall giue and pay

the same money soe to them delliuered to each person or
persons that shall bring to them the heads of such . . . . .
. . . . . . shall give account to the Churchwardens."

In handwriting of the same date there is also a tariff of
the prices to be paid for the "noysom foule and vermine"
which should be destroyed under the provisions of this
statute ; and the presence of wild cats, pole cats, and cormo-
rants, shews that the neighbouring woods were not very
different in Queen Elizabeth's reign from what they were in
that of Henry III., when that king licensed "William
Berkeley of Dursley for term of life to hunt the fox, wolf,
hare, wild-cat, and badger," there.

"The heads of ould crowes choughs pyes or Rokes taken
within the limits of the parish. for the heads of every three
of them one penny.

and for the heads of six of them young. or for six of their
eggs unbroken taken as aforesaid one peny

for 12 stares[1] heads one peny

for the head of a hawke. merton.[2] buzard. king tayle. mold
kite : scag. cormorant. two pence.

for every two eggs of them a peney

for the head of every Joy rauen kyte wood owle 1.^{d}

for a bull finch or kings fisher one peney

for a fox or Gray[3] one shilling

for a falchen : polecatt weasell slow faire badger [?] or wild
catt a peney for a otter or hedghog 2.^{d} •

for 3 : Ratts or 12 : mice 1.^{d} for euery. want[4] one halfpeny."

In the accounts for 1579 entry is made of a payment "to
ffrenshe for a foxe's heade xij^{d}," but there is no further
mention of such payments until 1622. After that date there
are frequent entries such as "p$^{d.}$ for hedghoggs 3s. 2d,"
"hedgocks 2s. 6d.," "Joyes, viijd" "jaye's heads, 2s. 6d,"
"pd for birds and other varments 0. 4. 7.," 48 dozen of

---

[1] Starlings.   [2] Marten.   [3] Badger.   [4] Mole.

Sparrows at a penny a dozen, "Paid" in 1690 "for foxes, grays, aud other varmant berds, 1. 4. 9½" "pᵈ for birdes and vermintes, 1. 6. 10.," "Pᵈ for varments of all sorts to severall people, 2. 11. 3." In 1702 sixteen foxes "by order" cost the parish as many shillings; in 1704 there is a charge of eight pence for two pole cats, and of twenty-four shillings for as many foxes. In 1705 the sum of 5s 4d was paid for 72 jays, 2s for woodpeckers, and 3s 4d for 230 tom tits. But the highest charge of all was in 1708, when as much as £5. 1. 3. appears under this head, including thirty shillings for thirty foxes brought in under "justice's warrant." A regular "sparrow-catcher" was appointed in 1658 to whom was paid yearly the not extravagant stipend of four shillings; yet promiscuous warfare was still carried on against hedgehogs, joyes, titmice, and foxes, especially the last. But the revival of fox-hunting probably brought the war to a close, the following entry being nearly the last on the subject. "March 4th 1722 at a Publick Meeting of yᵉ Parish it's this day ordered that no Church warden for the time to come shall be allowed to pay for Foxes or any other Vermin without a Lawfull order from a Justice of the Peace," The "Signatories" to this treaty of justice and peace with the unsportsman-like-persecuted foxes are Thos. Purnell, Isaac Smyth, Tho. Phelps, John Partridge, Henry Adey, John Tippetts, Jacob Stiff, Joseph Phelps, Nich. Neale, and Maurice Phillips.

Some miscellaneous entries.

HOGGLING MONEY.—The Churchwardens regularly received a small sum yearly towards the expenses of the Church under the name of "Hoggling Money." The entry occurs in 18 years out of the 47 years following and including 1579, the smallest sum being 5s. 11d., the largest £1. 6. 0. In 1621 the entry is "when wee went a hoggling," £1. 3 7.:

E

in 1622 "in going a hoglen" 16. 3.: and in 1626 "for hogling" 19. 5.[1] In several years there are entries of sums "receaved upon newe yeares day" or on "New year's eve," the sums being of similar amounts to the hoggling money and the latter being never entered in the same year. "Hogling" is a well known term for a lamb, as "Hog" is for a young sheep: and as New Year's Day was the twenty-fifth of March in the sixteenth and seventeenth century it is not altogether unlikely that Hoggling money was a tax upon the early lambs, those which had made their appearance before the Bailiff inauguration into his office, which was on New Year's Day. On the other hand the ancient New Year's Eve custom of "mumming," which is still known in the north by the name of "Hogmany," may once have been an official business gravely supervised by the Churchwardens. There were also two "Hoke-days," on the first of which the men placed ropes across the street and taxed all the passers by, the women doing the same on the second day. At Hock-tide, as at Christmas, plays were performed: and the two days seem to have been the Monday and Tuesday after Low Sunday.

This is the sort of thing they used to sing as their "Hagmena Song" in Yorkshire:—

"To-night it is the New Year's night, to-morrow is the day,
And we are come for our right and for our ray,
As we used to do in old King Henry's Day:
    Sing fellows, sing hag-man, ha !

---

[1] But the same entry is found in the Churchwardens' accounts of Cheddar in Somersetshire; and the amount received there in 1631 was £10. 3. 4. [*N. & Q.* III, iij. 423.] Another name for it appears to have been "Hoghall Money." Thus in *N. & Q.* VI. ij. 275, the following is printed as having been found "on the margin of an old folio;" "Mrs. Wright indebted to Richard Basset for keeping a mare four weeks for work, 5s 6d., by the Hoghall money, 1s 6d. 1784."

If you go to the bacon-flick cut me a good bit
Cut, cut it low, beware of your maw.
Cut, cut it round, beware of your thumb,
That me and my merry men may have some.
  Sing fellows, sing hag-man, ha!

If you go to the black ark, bring me ten marks,
Ten marks ten pound, throw it down upon the ground,
That me and my merry men may have some.
  Sing fellows, sing hag-man, ha!"[1]

Whether the Churchwardens of Dursley went about the
town singing such songs as part of their Ecclesiastical duties
when they "went a hoggling" is not on record.

FINES FOR SWEARING, AND TIPPLING ON SUNDAYS are not
unfrequently noticed in the Churchwardens' accounts. Thus
in 1702 the Churchwardens add to their accounts, "Recev'd
more P the Justices' Order for Swearing, and selling Beere
on the Sabath Day, and Drunkennes of those under—

	s	d
John Morgan for Swearing ..	06 =	00
Tho Clift for Selling Beare ..	10 =	00
Edw⁴ Jobbins for Ditto	10 =	00
Dan¹¹ Wyman being Drunk ..	05 =	00
Tho Archard for Sweareing ..	01 =	00
Edw⁴ Jobbins for Ditto	01 =	00
Jonathan Dallimore Ditto	01 =	00
Tho Heath Ditto..	01 =	00
Jn⁰ Vizard Ditto	01 =	00
Robert Hancok Ditto	01 =	00

$$£02 : 06 : 00$$

---

[1] Brand's Popular Antiquities, j. 461. *Bohn's ed.*

This money was distributed among 27 persons, and in the list appear "Tho Clift's Child .. 05 = 00," "Edw Jobbins's Apprentice .. 05 = 00," "Tho Heath .. 01 = 00," "Dan¹! Wiman's Children .. 04 = 00:" from which it is evident that the fines were not allowed to bear very heavily upon the culprits. But the most conspicuous year was 1757, and the most conspicuous offender Thomas Roe. Three times in that year a Justice of the Peace paid over the cost which Roe had to pay for his profane luxury of swearing. On June 10th he was fined twelve shillings, on June 18th two pounds, and on August 8th thirty shillings. There are long lists of the names of the poor people among whom these fines were divided, the 82 shillings being distributed among 120 people. The integrity of the last distribution is here also rather blown upon by the entry of Thomas Roe himself as the receiver from the Churchwardens of fifteen shillings out of the thirty which he had been obliged to pay to the magistrate !

Boys.—The Dursley boys of the seventeenth century were not so perfect in their behaviour at Divine Service that they could be judiciously left to themselves. So in 1657 the Churchwardens paid to "John Stockwell Master Corrector of the boyes" six shillings: in 1658 "To Walter Jenkins for keeping the boyes" two shillings and sixpence: and in 1694 "To John Mills for beateinge yᵉ boyes" three shillings. Let us hope that what an old woman once called this "catechizing" may have been serviceable to the boys in after years.

Elizabethan Churchmanship in Dursley.

The Churchwardens' Register begins, unfortunately, just thirty years too late to give us any information respecting the progress of the Reformation in the Church during the reigns of Henry VIII., Edward VI., and Queen Mary, its earliest entries being made in 1566, when Queen Elizabeth had been

seated on the throne for about eight years. But it is probable
that the purchase and use of the Register indicate the beginning of a new order of things, it having taken some years
entirely to displace that which had been brought about by
the re-action of Queen Mary's reign, and to introduce that
which was established by law not earlier than the third year
of Queen Elizabeth's reign.

Of this we find indications in the first pages of the Churchwardens' accounts, where there are payments entered for
work done in the Church which must have been of an important and extensive character.

It is curious to see that the very first entry of a payment is " To a man of Sadburie for xiij Sacks of Lyme
to whyt lyme the Church iiijs viijd." In the same year
12 more ·sacks were procured from " the Lyme brener of
Sadburie " " at xiijd a sack." The cheapness of lime accounts
perhaps for the profuseness with which it was used on the
interior of our Churches in those times : but it must also be
remembered that the walls thus whitewashed had almost
invariably been covered with colour decoration and paintings,
and that the whitewash was laid on thickly to obliterate
these. In the same way the entries for " glassing " and the
" plomer " and lead, are often of so large an amount that
they can only be explained on the ground that the painted
glass windows had been smashed to pieces and white glass ones
substituted. Taste for art, and especially for Christian art,
was at the lowest possible ebb during the Reformation period.
In books and pictures of the time we may see coarse nude
figures of heathen deities, satyrs, &c., which were supposed
to be characteristic of the revival of pagan learning, and to
be far more beautiful than the finely painted Scripture
subjects, or the gorgeously robed angels and saints, with
which books had formerly been adorned. This decline of
taste was also accompanied by an outcry of the Puritans

against paintings on the walls and in the windows of Churches as superstitious: and although the outcry was often much more superstitious than the condemned paintings, it set on the uneducated classes to destroy those works of art which the educated classes despised too much to take the trouble of preserving.

Hence, no doubt, the twenty-five sacks of lime which the Churchwardens of Dursley used in 1566 were for covering up the painting of the Last Judgement over the Chancel Arch, of our Lord in Divine Majesty over the East Window, of St. Christopher, the type of Christ-bearers, on the North-wall of the Nave, and of many a Scripture subject elsewhere throughout the Church. But perhaps this was a kind of work which was more acceptable to the Churchwardens than to the parishioners at large. For when Thomas Thacham comes to make up the accounts he makes the following note :—

"Summa totalis xijli xs jd ob.

Of this we receavid xjli

so that we haue laid out more of oure own charge xxxs jd ob whereof do acquytt the p'ishe by these p'sents.

Give god the glorye."

But this is still more conspicuous in the case of alterations which Thacham made in the Chancel. For there are two pages of accounts " ffor the Sieges about the Comm'on Table." These were seats or pews around the east, north, and south walls of the Chancel, such as are still to be seen in the Chancel of Deerhurst Church near Tewkesbury. On these workmen were employed by Thacham for nine weeks during November, December, and January, in 1566 and 1567, and from the accounts of their wages it appears that they were sawyers, joiners, and carvers, engaged on "frames," "panels," "wains-cotting," and "ledges;" a small amount of wages being set down also for masons who repaired the "wall by the

Chappell" and the pavement.[1] The cost of these works was £9. 6s. 11½d. an amount which represented, perhaps, £100 of our own money. To defray this a subscription was collected from the parishioners, but their sparing contributions amounted only to £2. 11s. 0½d., only one-fourth of the sum expended. Hence the zealous Churchwarden makes another entry in which he says,

" So that I have laid owt of my own charge more than I rec. as by iust Accompts it doth appear vj^{li} xv^{s} xj^{d}. ob. only for the Sieges besyde the Church Accompts in the former Summe."

The next piece of historical evidence furnished by the Churchwardens is their Inventory of the Church goods, the first of many that appear during the next hundred years. It is as follows :—

" The Inventorie of all the Church goods; and other thynges belonging to the p'ishe. [A.D. 1566.]
In pmis A Cupp for the Communion, doble gylt with A Case for the same.[2] *Itm.* j Table clothe of lynnen for the Communion Table of holland in length iij yards and di wth an A & F at one end and T & C. at the other end marked wth blewe thrydd.[3] *It.* ij bybles : *It.* the paraphrase of Erasmus upon the Epistles. *It.* A Book of Commune prayer of the ordere

---

[1] It is interesting to see the wages and prices paid in this year.

Joiners ..	10d a day	Laths ..	4d a bundle
Sawyers ..	9½ ——	850 Nails	2s. 6d.
Carvers ..	10d ——	Lead ..	14s 4d a cwt.
Tilers ..	10d ——	Candles..	3d a pound.

There is a frequent payment also for " mosse" at a penny a sack. This may have been dried ferns for strewing on the floor instead of rushes. Ferns abound near Dursley, but rushes are scarce.

[2] A Cover was provided for "the Communion Cupp " in 1583 at a cost of 22s.

[3] The length of these and of the Linen Cloths in the " Store House," shews that the Altar was at least 6 feet long by 3 feet high.

of the church of England. *It.* A nother book contayning the
same ordere of commune p'yer: and the psalmes as they are
appointed to be read:[1] with the psalmes in metre appointed
to be song ; and the first book of homelies appointed to be
read in the church: and all these iiij contayned in one volume
It. A psalter book. *It.* the Iniunctions sett foorthe by the
Queenes maiestie Elizabeth our Sovreign Lady the first year
of her grace's reign. Aº 1559.
It. A Regester book of ij quiers of paper: for the order of
baptismes, marieing, and burieing.[2]
It A book of prayer against the the Invasion of the Turk.
It. A book of the form of Prayer to be sayd twise A week,
wth an homilie of gods Justice annexed thereto.
It. A paper book of a Quier ffor the Accompte of the proctors
for the poore.[3]
It. the Paraphrase of Erasmus vpon the 4 Gospels. xˢ.
It. A book of ij Tomes of homelies wth the commun p'yer in
one. viijˢ.
It. there is belonging to the Church an Acre of Arable land
It. A faire house callid the Church house. *It.* A Almes
house, wth
It. the Churchyard.

It. in the Church A Cofer for the books : *It.* A Cheast with
iij Locks and iij Keayes.
It. in the Storehouse[4] A Cofer for the pewter. *It.* another
cheast bound wth yron : having iij locks and iij Keayes.

---

[1] In early Prayer Books the Psalter was printed with a separate
Title page, and from these two entries it appears that it was not
always bound up in the same volume with the Prayer Book.

[2] This Register Book is not now among the Church goods.

[3] *Overseers* for the poor were first appointed thirty-five years later,
under the first Poor Law, 43 Eliz. ch. 2. A.D. 1601.

[4] It seems as if this was the Vestry.

It. ij Table cloathes. j of iiij and iij qvarters and the other of iiij yards and A qvarter. *It.* ij shortt cloathes of ij yards and a qter a peece.

Itm. in the Church house : A Crock of brasse weying

It. A sqvare kettle of Coper weying

It. j paire of potthooks weying

It. ij hangings weying [" to hange pottes in " 1591]

It. ij brothes [?] weying

It. j payre of Beaths [?] weying

It. an yron barre in the halle chimney

It. A bucket wth ij yron hoopes. *It.* A lade payle and A stoupe.

It. iiij vates contayning :

It. xiij stondes contayning :

It. xix Trendles contayning :

It. xj platters. vj potingers. iiij saltt cellers and vj spoons."

One item in the preceding Inventory is worth further notice, namely, the " book of the Form of prayer to be said twice a week " &c. This was " A Form to be used in Common Prayer twice a week, and also an order of public fast to be used every Wednesday in the week during the time of mortality and other afflictions wherewith the Realm at the present is visited. Set forth by the Queen's Majesty's special commandment, expressed in her letters hereafter following in the next page. xxx July 1563." Archbishop Parker, writing to Cecil, describes the country as " molested universallie by warre, and particularlie at London by pestilence, and partlie here at Canterburie by famyn." There was in fact a terrible outbreak of the plague in 1563, which destroyed 20,000 people, about a fifth of the number who died in that of 1665.

The Form of Prayer has a Preface directing the " Curates and Pastors to exhort their Parishioners to endeavour themselves to come unto the Church .... not only on Sundays and holy days but also on Wednesdays and Fridays. It then appoints that Morning Prayer shall be said, with Special Lessons. After that a pause of a quarter of an hour and more is to be made, during which the people are exhorted to give themselves to their private prayers and meditations. Then the Litany is to be read in the midst of the People, with the addition of a penitental psalm made up from various parts of Holy Scripture and a very long Confession of sins. On Wednesdays the Holy Communion was to be celebrated. Then, both on Wednesdays and Fridays, followed a long " Homily concerning the Justice of God " which had been written for the occasion by Nowell, Dean of St. Paul's.

Such a Form of Prayer indicates that in Queen Elizabeth's reign people went to Church very generally on week days, at least when such special occasions for Prayer arose; that the celebration of the Holy Communion was the central part of such special national supplications; that habits of silent meditation and prayer in Church were encouraged and enjoined; and that very long services were the custom of the times   It may also be added that on these days the Puritans fasted until two or three o'clock in the afternoon, the ordinary dinner hour being eleven or twelve.

Another point that may be noticed in this Inventory is that it contains no notice of Church vestments of any kind, although subsequent ones always, till the time of the Commonwealth, include the Surplice. But in 1574 there are entries that the Churchwardens " pd for a surplus cloathe ixs vjd, " and also that they " pd for ye makinge of ye same ijs iiijd. "   In 1578 it is entered in the Inventory in company with the " porringers and saltcellars " of the Church House, from which it would appear to have been disused in the Church.

The Puritans in Dursley Church.

Puritan influences were evidently now gaining ground in Dursley. The Church seems to have been first pewed about

1579, when payments for seats began to be received by the Churchwardens. The first entry of this kind is " *It.* of Alexander Byrton for a seate place wth Edmond Wettmothe in ye seate belonginge to ye low^r Inn xij^d " About twenty more such entries immediately follow, most of them adding to the person's name " for a place for his wiffe ; " and in later times there are a great number of them. In 1591 " A carpet for the comm^n table," " a holland cloth for the same," " three books of Comon Prayar," and " one of Epistles and Gospels " seem to point out that there had been some strange neglect connected with the necessary furniture of the Church, although indeed there are entries of " *It*, for a byble of ye Largeste volume. xxx^s " in 1579 (the old one being sold for five shillings), and of " p^d for A communion booke iiij^s " in 1583. When we find Samuel Hallowes as Minister, with William Trotman and Richard Merick as Churchwardens witnessing that on September 26th, 1618, there was " An new table borde geuen to the church by Margerie Morse Widowe, alias called Mrs. Fullie," it seems almost certain that a novel " table borde " of Puritan fashion was substituted for the old Altar table for which the long linen cloths of fifty years earlier date had been provided.

It was the Puritan custom to place their " table bordes,"—which were often literally " boards " placed on trestles,—in the body of the Church that the Communicants might sit around them as round a " borde " of Christian hospitality and fellowship, instead of placing them at the East end and kneeling in front of them as before the Table of the Lord. To break up this custom Archbishop Laud and his " High Church " coadjutors enjoined that the table should be uniformly placed at the East end of the Chancel, and rails set up in front of it which would prevent its removal into the body of the Church and would offer a support for kneeling Communicants. This was done in Dursley Church in the year 1636, and the Churchwardens enter in their accounts "*It.* paid for 2 posts and settinge up the Rayle at the Communion Table," £3. 6. 0. and *It.* for a payre of Jemells" [hinges] "for the Raile Doore that goethe before the Communion Table" £1. 0. 8.

At the same time "the way into the pulpitte" was turned at a cost of ten shillings, a pulpett door was provided for two shillings and sixpence, and an iron to hold the hour glass for four shillings. These entries may shew that while there was a party in the parish which supported the principles of the Reformation in the High Church sense which looked towards the altar as the centre of Divine worship, there was also a Puritan party which set great store by preaching, and loved those preachers best who after an hour's discourse would say "let us have another glass" and turn the full side of their time keeper upwards to run out its sands again as they themselves ran out their yard long periods.

The full flow of the tide of Puritanism is indicated in the Churchwardens' Register by the disappearance from the Inventories in 1643 and the following years of the Surplice, the Book of Common Prayer, and the double gilt Communion Cup, with its cover and case. Instead of the Prayer Book there then appears the Scottish Presbyterian " Directory for Public Worship ; " instead of the silver gilt chalice appear two pewter platters, one pewter salver, and two pewter " Comunion boules," which cost 3s. 4d., the " scouring of the pewter " becoming also a regular item in the accounts.[1] Two

---

[1] The double gilt silver chalice was stolen by the "pure" supplanters of the Church and its customs. The pewter substitute was used till 1687, when it was sold for seven shillings and Plate bought for £2. 18. 0. A hundred years after the Pewter Age there appears the following entry in the Churchwardens' Register. "1748. January the 10. Given by Mr. N. Neale a Silver Patin for Bread and a Silver Cupp for Sacrament Wine for the Use of the Church of Dursley in the County of Gloucester.

Churchwardens { George Faithorn
{ Richard Tippetts "

and sixpence was also paid in 1648 "to James Attwood for settinge upp a thinge to houlde a bassone," and one shilling on "a screw for the fonte," which looks as if the latter was screwed up to prevent it from being used for baptisms and the former substituted. As much as £11. 5. 8. was paid for "glassing the Church windows," to replace with plain the stained glass which had survived: the Communion rails lately set up were now destroyed, and the altar again turned into a "table board" in the nave.

What treatment the Clergy received may be judged of by the treatment of the learned, and not High Church, Archdeacon Robinson the then Rector of Dursley, who was "seized at his living of Dursley, set on horseback with his face to the horse's tail, and thence hurried away to Gloucester prison."[1]

So Dursley took its part in the great Puritan revolution which seemed for a time as if it had exterminated the ancient Church of the land. In this retired valley among the Cotswolds as well as elsewhere the use of the Prayer Book was prohibited from 1645 until 1660 under pain of £5 fine for the first offence, £10 for the second, and for the third a year's imprisonment; the Clergy were turned out of the Churches, driven from house and home and deprived of their incomes. Some were sent to prison like the Rector of Dursley, some transported to the West Indies, and most of them left in great poverty, as it is not easy for an elderly clergyman to earn his bread in any other profession than that which he has been brought up to and engaged in all his life. Thus the face of all things parochial was altered for fifteen years. Instead of their old Rectors and Curates the Dursley people had to receive as a pseudo pastor, some ignorant layman (for educated laymen were above such work) who dubbed himself a minister and got into the old clerical nest

---

[1] Walker's Suff. of Clergy. ij. 33.

by the help of the few leading Puritans of the neighbourhood : and who dealt out to them in Church one long winded
homily as a prayer and another as a sermon, each being
chiefly conspicuous for bad taste, red hot politics, and male-
dictory theology,

Then the tide again turned. English people had hardly
tasted the true flavour of unadulterated Puritanism before
they found out that it was not at all to their liking ; and
although they could not get rid of it while Cromwell ruled
the land with his Ironsides, the Church bells rang out merrily
for its expulsion almost as soon as he was gone, and parochial
life flowed back again into its old channels. In 1661 the
Churchwardens record that they paid £6. 0. 0. "for the
Kings Armes,"[1] a shilling "for sending a letter to yᵉ Archdeacon, five shillings "to yᵉ Ringers at yᵉ Coronation day ;"
and early in the following year fourteen pence "to the paritor
for bringing of a booke set foorth by the King and his
Counsell to be read on the 30 Day of Janu : by the minister."
Then "a new Common Prayer Book" appears in the Inventory, for which the parish paid seven and sixpence, and
"the booke of yᵉ Directory" in a previous Inventory is
crossed through with an indignant dash of the Churchwarden's pen, he having evidently had enough of it.[2] A little
later there is an entry of payment for "9 ells holand at 5s.
to make the Surples, £2. 5. 0." and for making it ten
shillings more. Then a cover for the font is provided shewing
that it was again brought into use. A few years afterwards,
in 1684, rails were again set up before the Lord's Table at a

---

[1] Such was the penitent loyalty of the parish that in 1665 £4. 10. 0.
was again paid "for painten the Church Dyall and florishing the
Kings Armes" and in 1733 £5. 10. 0, again for the Kings Arms.

[2] Those who wrote or spoke against the Directory during the time
of the Commonwealth were liable to a fine of from £5 to £50, at the
discretion of the magistrates.

cost of £4. 13. 4., and in 1687, there was an expenditure
of £2. 18. 0. upon "pleat for the communion," seven
shillings being "Recd for the ould peuter for 'the communion" which had been bought in the place of the "double
gilt communion Cupp" of Queen's Elizabeth's time.

Nor was it with a grudging mind that Dursley people
received Episcopacy back again, for in 1663 when the Bishop
came on his Visitation the parishioners "Paid for Sack for my
Lord that we presented to him" Six shillings and two pence :
which being the price of four quarts at that time, it is to be
hoped that his Lordship passed round the hospitable tankard
to his Chancellor and Archdeacon.

The changes which were brought about by our next Revolution—happily our last—in 1688 are slightly but significantly
recorded in these financial annals of Ecclesiastical Dursley.
In that year the Churchwardens "pd to Paritor for two books
of thanksgiving for the Prince of Wales," one shilling and
sixpence. Shortly afterwards a shilling is paid to the same
person for King James the Second's " Declaration for Liberty
of Conscience," which so many of the Clergy refused to read
out in their Churches because it was considered as nothing
but a declaration for the Liberty of Popery. Then a shilling
was paid for "a proclamation to pray for the Prince of
Wales"—afterwards known as the Old Pretender. This is
followed by the payment of sixpence for " a proclamation to
pray for the Prince of Orange " and a shilling for " a Common
prayer book to pray for the prince," but which prince is not
stated. The ebbing and flowing of the tide is, however,
clearly shewn in the next entries, of which the first is a
shilling " for a prayer booke against invasion," the second
another shilling "for a Booke for thankes Given for the
prince of orang " the invader, and the third of a third shilling
" for a booke to Alter the prayers for King William." The
times were full of change, opinions were strong on both sides,

and doubtless in Dursley as elsewhere you might hear the bells ring out one day " God bless King James the Second," and the next day " God bless King William the Third." Happy that long generation which has been able to ring out a constant and happy peal of " God bless good Queen Victoria," without one serious thought of revolution either in Church or State.

The Fall and Rebuilding of the Steeple.

When Defoe wrote his Tour through Great Britain in the latter half of the seventeenth century he recorded that the Church of Dursley had " two ailes and an handsome spire." In the second edition of Sir Robert Atkyns' History of Gloucestershire, published about 1712, it is also stated that Dursley " had an handsome Spire at the West End, but now fallen down." A century earlier the Churchwardens' accounts contain charges, in 1570, " *It.* for lyme to ye use of ye toure and steple vijs vjd.," and " *It.* for pointing the steple vli. " The latter item is repeated in 1656, and is indeed one that frequently occurs.

In the year 1688 there seems to have been some apprehension that the tower was unsafe, for there is an item in the accounts, " Pd Edward Wicks for his Advise about ye tower 2s 6d.," and the result of the advice seems to have been some trumpery contrivance for propping up the tower inside as is shewn pretty clearly by the entry immediately following, " Pd to Jonathan Danford for A peece of timber, and drawing it up into the tower loft £1. 10 0." This temporizing with danger gave a sense of security and in 1694 the old entry comes again " Paid Richard Lathern for pointing the Tower and Steeple £10. 10. 0."

In 1699 some extensive repairs were being carried on upon the roof. Old lead weighing 46 cwt. 2 q. 24 lbs. was sold at a penny a pound, bringing in £21. 16. 0., and new lead was

bought of James Brown the plumber, weighing 52 cwt., and costing £37. 17. 0.; nine loads of tiles at £4. 10. 0. being also bought.   If it was a wooden spire the lead was probably used for re-covering it, and wooden spires were very common in those times: but the "pointing" of the "steple" and the mention of "y⁰ toure and steple" seem to shew that it was of stone.   However that may have been, it was in the same year in which these repairs of the roof were effected that the tower and spire were destroyed, the day of their fall being January 7th, 1698-9.

Bigland, writing in 1791, says that the Spire fell while the bells were ringing, and that several persons lost their lives by the accident.   As January 7th was not a Sunday in that year, and is not a ringing day ordinarily, it is probable that the bells were being rung to celebrate the completion of the repairs.   Whether it was so or not, the entries respecting the repairs are just followed by one recording the purchase of a new Prayer Book when there succeeds the melancholy record "Pd for pulling down the Ruins of the tower to the Church, £3. 1. 0."

Such calamities take place so suddenly that it is no wonder the details of them escape observation and record.   A magnificent spire, probably twice as large and high as that of Dursley, fell down at St. Chad's, Shrewsbury, on July 9th, 1788, and only one person, walking in the meadows at some distance, saw the dreadful occurrence.   They who crowded to the Churchyard beheld only a confused heap of ruins, the tall spire having fallen on the roof of the nave, and mingled in one hopeless wreck the stones, the timbers, the bells, the organ, and the monuments, of what had a few minutes before been one of our most glorious Collegiate Churches. The wreck at Dursley was not so bad, for the spire seems to have fallen outwards and not towards the nave; and thus although the tower tore down a portion of the west end of

F

the Church in its fall the ruin was kept within bounds and left the mediæval fabric of the nave substantially uninjured.

The cost of rebuilding the tower and spire seems to have been at once considered as far beyond the means of the town, although at this time it must have been a prosperous manufacturing place, with several wealthy cloth-making families as well as the landholders. The loss was estimated at £2,000,—though only about £500 was expended in repairing it,—but in recent times the sum of nearly £6,000 has been collected, much of it from the inhabitants of Dursley, for the restoration of the same Church to which this calamity had happened. But in 1699 it was at once determined to obtain a Brief, so that the expense of rebuilding the fallen tower and spire might fall on strangers and not on the parishioners.

The consultations that were held over this matter cost the parishioners, however, a good deal of money. It was evidently dry work, as if the dust of the ruins had got into the throats of the Vestrymen, and the Church Rate was saddled with the items " P^d at the Session when m^r Georg: Smijth and m^r Elliott and the Churchwardens delivered at the Sessions the Loos by the fall of the tower and Steple £6. 12. 2.   P^d the workmen that went to the Sessions that vallued the Loos £1. 4. 0.   P^d at Nibley for beere when the p'ish went to m^r George Smith for Advise.   P^d to John Mills for beere when the p'ish there mett severall times and for beere for the Laborers £6. 17. 8.   P^d at the Bell Inn in Dursley when m^r George Smijth went to Sessions 7s. 0d. John Mills for Drinke at the p'ish meeting and to workmen £2. 0. 11." This liberal expenditure of £17. 1. 9. on beer resulted in the presentation of a Petition to the Crown for a Brief, and in the determination to effect only such repairs as were absolutely necessary to make the Church useable, while that was being collected.

The following is a copy of the Petition, the original of which was formerly in the possession of Mr. Linton of Dursley :—

"Dursley in Com. Glouc^r 29o Martii 1699

To the King's most excellent Majestie The humble petition of the Inhabitants of yor Towne of Dursley in ye County of Glouc^r.

Shewing unto your Matie That on Satterday the Seaventh day of January last past the Tower and Spire Steeple of the parish Church of Dursley aforesaid with the Ring of Bells therein by casualty and great Mischance fell downe, and also broke part of the West end of the said Church, The Damage whereof and Charge of Rebuilding the said Tower and repairing the said Church is estimated by workmen to amount unto One Thousand Nyne Hundred Ninety ffive pounds at the least, And yor petition^s shew unto yor Matie that the said Towne and parish is very small the whole yearly Value of all the lands of the said Parish not exceedinge Six Hundred pounds by Estimation, and that greatly burthened with numbers of poore which takes up a ffourth at least of the yearly vallue of the said Parish, whereby yor petition^{rs} are unable to beare the Charge aforesaid of rebuilding the said Tower and repairinge the Church without some Charitable assistance.

Maurice Phillips, Baylif
John Arundel
John Tippetts
Thomas King
Isaac Smyth
John Parbeedge
Abrah Stiff
Will. Danford
Ob Baker

Wherefore yor petition^{rs} humbly beseech yor Matie to grant to y^r petit^{rs} your Gracious letters patents to aske gather and receive the Charitable benevolence of yor Maties Loving Subjects towards the great Charge and pious worke afores^d

And y^r petitio^{rs} as in duty

John Wood   bound shall ever pray.
Saml Kingg   Thomas Purnell
John Webb   Nicholas Neale
Jno Arundell Jur   James Harding
Samll Clarke   Richard Tippetts
Jooseph Dallemore   John Purnell "
Morris Phillips Sen.
Tho Fryer
William Litton
Joseph Pulley
Thomas Phelps

This petition was not granted probably for some years. An extract previously given from the accounts of Ormsby St. Margaret shews that it was being collected at the end of 1707, when that not too liberal Parish contributed one penny towards "the great Charge and pious worke." In the Dursley accounts for the same year there are also the two entries " 1707

Itt. at the first meeting for ye Brief 10s 0d.

Itt. wn you met to put yr hands to the Brief 9s 0d "

Perhaps the petition of 1699 had not been granted at all, and another was sent up in 1707 which met with better success.

Meanwhile the repairs decided upon were set in hand soon after the accident had occurred. The sum of £24. 5. 5. was paid " for building the piller in the Church and the Butreses against the Church walls," £1. 9. 4. " for quaryen and halling for the Church Bartlements." £12. 2. 11. for " carpenter's work about the Church." £8. 9. 5. for " laborers for Removing the Stone of the tower and steple and the Rubish in the Churchyard," and other work. £2. 6. 0. to " the free Mason for 23 dayes work about Carving and Seting up the New bartlements on the Church."

At the same time new roofs were put to " the three Iles "

the new timber for which cost £22. 16. 6. the tiles and lead £16. 4. 6: the tiles being 18,650 in number at 11s. a thousand, including carriage from the tile pits; and the tilers' labour £7. 16. 0., being 24 "pearch at 6s 6d Pr pearch."

In the Inventory for November 2d 1699, there is an entry of "five bells which did belong to the tower and the Clock," and "the stem of the weather cock" is added on Oct. 4, 1700, the clock being entered as "a ould Iron Clock." There were also received 3s. 6d. for "3 Cannons broke at the fall of the Bells, 7 lbs. at 6d," and for 106 pounds of "ould Iron" and "ould Cramps" 14s. 1d. These bells, or some of them, still remained useable, however, and a temporary wooden tower was erected to hold them, probably at the Church House. The labour for this cost £18 7. 9.; Timber cost £11. 12. 6.; Iron work and nails cost £2. 18. 11½.; and 329 "foote of Board for the wooden Tower, with 9 days work at it" cost £3. 15. 6. In 1701 there is still "Pd to John Mills for beere for workmen £1. 17. 6." and £6. 4. 7. for boards and lime. In 1702 there is a charge of three shillings paid to Henry Collier "for making a scaffold for him, and mending the tower and bell frame," which looks like work connected with the temporary re-hanging of the bells: but there is no other entry that throws light upon the matter, and no money was as yet entered for payments to ringers. In 1703, however, "a Rope"—a very familiar charge—again appears in the accounts at the usual price of six shillings: and payment of 4s. 6d. "att Gunpowder treason," and five shillings "at Thanksgiving day" in that year, together with four shillings "to the Ringers at Visitation," shew that the bells had now again come into use, though only in their temporary wooden tower.

As soon as the Brief had been collected the work of rebuilding commenced. This was in 1708, when the Churchwardens begin their account of much beer at the Bell and the

Lamb with the entry of 5s 3d spent "Att ỹᵉ Bell wⁿ yᵉ tower builders came first." There are very few details recorded respecting the work, and it appears to have been done by contract. The Brief had yielded only one fourth of the sum asked for and so all thought of rebuilding the Spire was abandoned. The first entry about actual work is "For cleaning yᵉ rubish from yᵉ old Tower, £1. 05. 00," in 1708; and the work appears to have occupied about two years, for the date of 1709 is inscribed on the tower under the clock, while in 1710 the Churchwardens paid £3. 1. 9. "for timber for the Ringing loft;" and then, for a wind up of the whole, £3. 0. 0. "ffor 2 Diners for the men yᵗ bild yᵉ tower."

The Petition for the Brief shews that the sum asked for was only £5 short of £2,000, the small diminution probably bringing it within a smaller scale of duty: but the final accounts shew how much short of this sum was contributed, or—what is more probable—how much stuck to the fingers of lawyers, officials, and other necessary evils, on the way.

"An Account of the p'duce of Dursley Breife [A.D. 1711].

	£		
1st Receipt	400		
2d Receipt	80		
3d Receipt	48.	6.	2
4th Receipt	21.	9.	11
5th Receipt	19.	17.	8
totall p'duce	£569.	13.	9

Disbursement of the Breife Money.

	£	s	d
paid Bawler and Samsion for Building the Tower	500.	0.	0
pd Rudhall for a Treble Bell	36.	10.	0

	£	s	d
pd Tho. Steight of painshaw for Clock and Chymes and Carridge from Berkeley	32.	18.	0

	569.	8.	0
pd John Phillipps and Nathaniel Webb p'sent Churchwardens the Ballance being		5.	9

	569.	13.	9 "

It is curious to observe that the parishioners of Dursley of that day did not think it necessary to contribute a penny—as even Ormsby St. Margaret's parish near Yarmouth did—towards the rebuilding of their Church Tower, and that when all was told they were richer by just five shillings and ninepence than they would have been if the disaster had not happened. Times are changed, and changed for the better. But whether they obtained the money from home or abroad it is certain that they who rebuilt the Tower did it in a manner deserving of very high commendation; and among the very few Church Towers of its date that of Dursley may claim to be one of the best, from being so closely in accordance with the ecclesiastical architecture of earlier date. Probably the builders were prudent enough to take the older Tower for their pattern as far as it could be remembered, and they may have used the old materials as far as was possible, though they do not seem to have been used to any great extent.[1] Not long ago it was nearly covered with ivy, but this was considered to be so injurious to the walls that it has been removed.

---

[1] In the year 1874 some alterations were made at the old Rectory house, now superseded by a new one, which brought to light some fragments of old ecclesiastical building of early fifteenth century date, which had been inserted into a wall, on the plaster of which was scratched the date 1709. These fragments are probably portions of the old Church Tower, and consist of portions of a large arch which may have been a doorway, together with some window mullions,

About thirty years after the rebuilding of the Tower, probably in 1738, the ancient Chancel of the Church was taken down and replaced by a smaller one at the cost of the then Rector, Archdeacon Geekie, but no record of this remains in the parish, and the rebuilt Chancel has itself disappeared before its present noble successor.

The recent Restoration.

The Church of Dursley had fallen into such a state of decay, however, in the middle of the present century that it was found necessary to carry out some very important repairs, and the opportunity was used for making several improvements.

In the year 1866, an Architect, who had been directed to examine the fabric, reported that it was in a most unsatisfactory condition. Owing to the failure of the foundations nearly all the north and south walls had fallen out of the perpendicular, and the pillars and arches of the Nave had followed suite, the north wall leaned over to the extent of fourteen inches, and the corresponding arcade as much as nine and a half inches. The western part of the South Arcade had been so twisted that one half leaned northward, and the other half southward: while the adjoining fine Porch with the parvise above it was crumbling to the dust as the tower had done. The modern low-pitched roofs were also of very inferior quality and character, galleries blocked up the

portions of pillars, and what looks like a piscina but may have been a holy water stoup. They are in the outer wall of the house, facing the road.

In the interior of the same house is a very fine stone fire place, which had been entirely concealed. This is about ten feet broad and five and a half feet high, with mouldings of a bold character, and some curious corner niches. In an upper room a smaller stone fire place was found, but this was of simpler character, and probably of later date. The larger one may belong to the fourteenth century.

Dursley Church

windows, and high pews held possession of the floor. If ever there was a fair case for the real restoration of a Church that of Dursley was one.

During the next two years this restoration of the fabric was effectually carried out, the Church being at the same time enlarged. The walls and arcades having been partly rebuilt a Clerestory was added to the Nave which has given a noble heighth to the interior and supplied it with abundance of light. The Chancel was rebuilt on a larger scale, being extended twenty-five feet eastward, and a considerable space was thus added to the Nave. A new Vestry and Organ Chamber were built on the South Side of the Chancel, and the division between the latter and the Nave has been marked by a fine arch with elaborately carved mouldings.

In effecting these repairs and alterations very great care was properly taken to make the work one of *restoration* as far as could possibly be done, and to avoid the destruction of anything which could possibly be preserved. To prevent the Church from falling into ruins it was necessary to take down tottering walls and pillars, but stones were carefully numbered as they were removed, and replaced in the same situation which they had previously occupied : and when each column was set up again on its new foundation of concrete two yards deep, it was, in fact, the column which the builders of the fifteenth century had erected restored rather than renovated, and made good for centuries as they would have wished to see done had they risen to look on their half-ruined work.

Church restorations are not effected without much expenditure of money, and the expenditure on that at Dursley amounted to £5,624. 13s. 0d., of which one fifth was provided by the Rector, and the remainder by freely-given contributions of the parishioners and their friends.

The Church is now a goodly structure of size proportioned to the requirement of its position, and with a Chancel suitable for the dignified performance of Divine Service according to those good old principles of the Book of Common Prayer, which are now so much better understood than they were in the last century.

It consists of a Nave with North and South Aisles which take in the small eastern chapels that were formerly screened off from their eastern end, of a Chancel with a Vestry and Organ Chamber on the South Side, a Western tower, and a fine South porch. The dimensions of the building are as follows :—

	Interior.		Exterior.	
	Ft.	In.	Ft.	In.
Length of Nave	101	8	106	0
„ North Aisle	83	8	89	4
„ South Aisle	70	4	76	0
„ Tanner Chapel	25	0		
„ Chancel	33	0		
Breadth of Nave and Aisles	60	0	65	8
„ Tanner Chapel	12	8		
„ Chancel	19	4		
Total length of Church	134	8	140	0

The oldest portion of the Church dates from the fourteenth century, but this consists only of a single window and a small part of the wall; and it may be called a late fifteenth century Church with an eighteenth century tower, and a Clerestory and Chancel of recent date. The outer walls are built of the peculiar "puff" or "tuff" stone which is found in Dursley, and which was also used for filling in the groined roof of Gloucester Cathedral and for building the Castle at Berkeley.[1]

---

[1] This peculiar stone is very similar in appearance to the volcanic "tufa" of the Catacombs near Rome, but is in reality a crystalline lime stone of aqueous origin similar to stalactite. It is said to exist only in two other places, one in Devonshire and the other in Germany·

There are no relics of the more ancient Church, with the exception of a slab of stone lying at the foot of the newell staircase which leads up to the room over the porch. This is a portion of a coffin cover on which is incised the head of a cross, similar to those which are built into the north wall of the nave at Beverston [page 113] : and it may have formed part of the floor of the Church in the thirteenth century.

The principal objects of antiquarian interest in the Church are the three fine sedilia in the north wall of St. Mary's Aisle, the roof of the Tanner chapel, and the memorial figure of the founder of that chapel. The monument of Tanner originally consisted of a table tomb, surmounted by a canopy of four arches under which lay one of those ghastly stone corpses which were so commonly used as memorials in the fifteenth and the earlier half of the sixteenth century. Similar ones may be seen at Tewkesbury Abbey, Bristol Cathedral, Winchester, Exeter, and many other churches. That of Tanner is now headless, the canopy has gone, and what remains has been built into the sill of the window. But a leaden plate is let into the stone above the place where the head has lain, and the inscription upon it shews that the remains of the generous Founder whom it commemorates have been treated with more respect than his monument.

| James Webster Arch^deac. of Glo'ster Rector 1789 | This Vault (in which the remains of TANNER founder of this Chapple were deposited) was opened & his bones collected & preserved in this place by W. F. Shrapnell Surgeon ANNO 1789. |

Notwithstanding the cavities in its substance the Tuff stone is exceedingly strong and durable ; for though it is softer when taken from the quarry than ordinary stone, it becomes extremely hard by exposure to the air.

THE BELLS.

Such history of the bells as there is, and it is very little, belongs to this period. It begins with the payment of £3. 19. 6. in the year 1639 " for the Sante Bell," and of 1s. 6d. for " bringing the Sante bell." The original purpose of the Sancte, Sanctus, or Sainte, bell, was that of warning persons outside the Church that the most solemn part of the Communion Service was commencing. that which is called " the Canon," or the portion associated with the Consecration.[1] This part of the Service was introduced by the Preface and the Ter Sanctus, and thus the Latin word for our " Holy, Holy, Holy," which is *Sanctus*, became the Christian name of this member of the Bell family : the English form of it being " Saints Bell," meaning not any personal Saints but the Three Saints or Sancts of the Seraphic Hymn. But when the Sante Bell was put up in its turret or " cote " at the east end of the South Aisle of Dursley Church in 1639, it was probably intended to be used for ringing in the " two or three " who " gathered together " to the daily services. This purpose is illustrated by the familiar passage in Barnabas Oley's Life of George Herbert, who died in 1633, six years before, that " he brought most of his parishioners and many gentlemen in the Neighbourhood constantly to make a part of his congregation twice a day : and some of the meaner sort of his Parish did so love and reverence Mr. Herbert that they would let their plough rest when Mr. Herbert's Saint's bell rang out to prayers, that they might also offer their devotions to God with him ; and would then return back to their

---

[1] The " Sacring Bell " was a small hand bell kept on one of the Altar steps and rung at the time of the actual consecration, the words of " sacring," or consecration, being said in so low a voice that without this warning the congregation would not have known when it took place. At Brokenborough in Wiltshire, not more than 12 miles from Dursley, there was a little peal of eighteen bells rung by one wheel for this purpose.

plough." It was also used as a "Sermon bell" in the afternoon when Sermons were not common at that time of the day, or for the young people to come to the Catechizing: a large bell being first rung or tolled for some time and then the "ting-tang" for five or ten minutes.[1] This use of such a bell is curiously mentioned in the Life of John Bold, who was Vicar of Stoney Stanton in Leicestershire, for the first half of the eighteenth century. "I have often" said an old man to his biographer " at the ringing of the bell on Saturday afternoon, left my plough for half an hour for instruction, and afterwards returned to it again." And another said, " Ah, Sir, that was a fine team I drove when I was young: but, Sir, whenever the Church bell rang at three o'clock on Saturday afternoon I always left my team when at plough to come to Mr. Bold to be catechized, and then went back again to plough."

It was probably the use of the bell for daily service by Archdeacon Robinson which led to its removal from the bell-cote when Puritan influence gained the ascendancy in Dursley; for in 1646 it is found in the Parish Chest and entered as "on saynts bell" in the Inventories until 1694. It was pawned for £1. 5. 9. in 1647 under the following order of the Vestry. " It is orderede by the p'ish that Jo. Tilladame and Edmond Perett to keepe the Saints bell till they be payd on pound and five shillings and 9d : wch they

---

[1] So a contemporary writer describes the use of a Sermon bell at Durham before the Reformation. " Every Sonnday in the yere there was a sermon preched in the Galleley [of the Cathedral] at afternonne, from one on the clocke till iij ; and at xij of the clock the great bell of the Galleley was toulled, every Sonndaie iij quarters of an houre, and roung the forth quarter till one of the clock, that all the people of the towne might have warnyng to come and here the worde of God preched." [*Rites of Durham*, Surtees Soc. *ed.* p. 33.]

The "ting-tang" between the Nave and Chancel is always rung for the last five minutes before Service begins at Over near Cambridge.

have layd oute in theire office of Churchwardens betwix this and $\mathcal{S}\mathit{t}^{1}$ Mychell the Archangell." In 1694 we come to the end of its history in the entry " Recevid for yͤ Saints Bell " £2. 2. 6.

In the same year in which the Sancte Bell was put up, 1639, a new ring of bells was cast out of the old ones and new metal: and curiously enough the casting seems to have taken place on the spot and not at a bell-foundry.

The first notice of this is the entry of a sum of 7s. 1d. " Paid for mͬ Purdie's expenses when he was sent for about the bells." The bell doctor seems at first to have tried an inexpensive cure for a cracked bell, for this is a subsequent entry, " *It.* pd to Pardy for cutting the peece out of the bell, 0. 0. 6 : " but a sixpenny remedy was not one likely to prove satisfactory, and so on the next page begins the record of " a Rate of Thirty four months pay for and towards the settinge up of the bells and other necessary repa*r*ations of the Church." This " rate " was a noble parochial assessment towards the new ring of bells, for out of £129 collected, about £120 was used (with other money) for that purpose alone. The highest amount given by one person was £7. 18. 8., the sum which stands against the name of " Ann Purnell widd.: " the lowest amount was five shillings. In addition to the legal assessment thus agreed upon, and for which 76 names are down, there is also another account of " More received of those yͭ paid of ffree gifte towards yͤ settinge upp of oͬ bells." This additional subscription amounted to £15. 7. 10, being made by 45 persons, among whom are " my lord Bishop" and " Docͬ Robinson " the Archdeacon and Rector.

The greater part of the sum thus collected was placed at once in the hands of the bell founder, the first entry in respect

---

¹ The Puritans objected to calling any one " Saints" but themselves. For themselves they used the name constantly.

to money "Disbursed and laide out towards the settinge up
of yᵉ bells and other things thereunto belonginge," [1] being
" Paid unto Roger Purdy' and unto Mr. Knowles for the use
of Purdy for mettell and for castinge and for frames
136li 0s 0d

The next entry shews that the belfry was used as the local
and temporary bell foundry, the Churchwardens having
" Paid unto Edward Harrell for the p'tition betwixt yᵉ Church
and bellfree 0. 16. 0." Then this financial " Song of the
Bell" has a few stanzas which indicate the progress made
though unfortunately without any indication of dates beyond
that of the year, and Gunpowder Treason day, when doubtless the bellfounders held high festival.

	li	s	d
gave to yᵉ bellfounders at the running of yᵉ bells	0	3	6
paid for carryinge the mettell unto yᵉ pitt	0	3	0
paid at yᵉ bringinge downe of yᵉ bells	0	2	0
Spent when the bells were weighed	0	5	0
Spent uppon the 5th of November	0	10	8
paid for massons worke	0	6	6
paid for bell ropes	0	8	9
paid for a Corde	0	0	3
paid to Morris Leauis for makings Cleane the Bellfree when the bells were to be rung ..	0	1	0
laid out for breade and beare and horsemeate uppon mʳ Knowles when he recd his last money ..	0	1	4
gave to the bellfounders at yᵉ making yᵉ moulds	0	0	6
Paide to James Prince for yᵉ lock and Jemells for yᵉ p'tition doore between yᵉ Church and bellfree and for nayles	0	0	6
Paide for Nayles for yᵉ Clockhowse	0	0	6
Paide to Richard Oliver for mendinge the Clocke and other Iron worke about yᵉ bells	4	0	0

---

[1] But these "disbursements" include the customary expenses
entered in the annual accounts.

	li	s	d
Paide to Edwarde Harrell for yᵉ Alterringe of yᵉ Clockhowse	0	5	0
Item paid for five bell ropes and for cariage of them from Dorchester	0	10	8

Strange to say, although before this re-casting of the bells there are regular entries of payments for ringing them, no such payments appear from that time until the Restoration. Here and there are charges for a bell rope and for repairing the wheel of the great bell, but it seems as if the trade of the ringers was gone and the bells were silenced for nearly twenty years, during the reign of Puritanism. Then comes an entry in 1661 of an event that set the heart of England beating with joy like the heart of a man who finds that he has come to his right mind after twenty years' madness, " pd to the Ringers at yᵉ Coronation day. .0. 5. 0."

A few more entries may be noticed as referring to events of national interest. In 1689 the Churchwardens paid one shilling and sixpence on beer for the ringers when the Seven Bishops were liberated from the Tower of London: three shillings on Thanksgiving day for the Prince of Orange: and seven shillings when he was proclaimed King in the place of James II. In 1707 there is an entry of five shillings paid for ringing at the Duke of Marlborough's victory of Ramillies, and in 1708 a similar payment was made at the Thanksgiving for the victory of Oudenarde ; and another " for the victory in Flanders."

The last entries of special interest which are connected with the bells are those which record that in 1716 the parish " Pd to the ringers for routing the rebells " four shillings, " when the Pretender fled from Scotland " six shillings, and half-a-crown for "some good news" which the Churchwardens do not seem to have been able more accurately to define.

The bells now in the tower are eight in number. They are all inscribed " T. Mears of London fecit 1824." and on the tenor is the further inscription " Edward Wallington and James Young Churchwardens."

THE RECTORS OF DURSLEY.

Robert Morton 1482—6. A nephew of Cardinal Morton.
Prebendary of Lincoln. Archdeacon of Winchester and York as well as of Gloucester.
Became Bishop of Worcester in 1487, died in
1497, and was buried in St. Paul's Cathedral.

John Dunmow 1487—8.

Simon Clement 1488—9. Was also Archdeacon of Worcester.

John de Gyglis 1489—97. An Italian who, with his brother
and successor at Worcester, received the profits
of English preferments and lived at Rome.
He was also Archdeacon of London. Became
Bishop of Worcester in 1497, and died at Rome
in 1498.

Geoffrey Blythe 1497—1503. Was also Dean of York.
Provost of King's College, Cambridge, Pre-
bendary of St. Paul's, and Archdeacon of
Salisbury. He became Bishop of Lichfield in
1503, and dying in 1530 was buried in his
Cathedral.

Thomas Ruthal 1503—1509. Was also Dean of Salisbury,
and became Bishop of Durham in 1509. He
was buried at Westminster with the title
" Secretary to Henry VII." on his tomb.
Ruthal was a Cirencester man, and the grand
Parish Church there was built at his expense.
But there is no record that he ever did anything for Dursley, though he was a great
builder, and though he was worth the enormous
sum of £100,000—to be multiplied by at least
twelve for our money—shortly before his death.

Peter Carmelian 1511—18. He was a man of considerable
importance; being Latin Secretary to Henry

the Seventh, and having matters of state entrusted to his management. He was also Poet
Laureate, and some of his poems are among
the very earliest works printed in England by
Rood, Caxton, and Pynson. He was unlike
most other authors in being very rich ; having
been able in 1522 to contribute £333. 6. 8.
towards the expenses of the King in France,
a sum not far off £4,000 of modern money.

John Bell 1518—39. He succeeded Latimer in the Bishopric
of Worcester in 1539, and dying in 1543 was
buried in Clerkenwell Church.

Nicholas Wotton 1540—44. Was also Dean of Canterbury
and York, being the only person who ever held
these two Metropolitical Deaneries together.
He was constantly employed in affairs of state
by Henry VIII., Edward VI., Queen Mary,
and Queen Elizabeth : and was said to have
refused the Archbishopric of Canterbury.

Guy Eaton 1544—54. Left England on accession of Queen
Mary.

John Williams 1554—58. Was also Chancellor and Prebendary of Gloucester.

Guy Eaton 1559—75. Returned on accession of Queen
Elizabeth.

George Savage 1575—1602. Was also a member of the High
Court of Commission, and in 1580 was ap-
pointed Commissary for his Metropolitical
Visitation by Archbishop Whitgift.

Robert Hill 1602—1607. Was also Rector of Tedington.

Samuel Burton 1607—34. Was also Rector of Dry Marston
for 36 years : and lies there in the Chancel with
an inscription which states that he was Archdeacon to five Bishops of Gloucester.

Hugh Robinson 1634—45. Was turned out by the Puritans and made to ride from Dursley to Gloucester with his face to the horse's tail. He was buried in St. Giles in the Fields.

Vacant 1645—60. Jos: Woodward appears as Minister for part of the time. Henry Stubbs was his assistant, and succeeded him. Stubbs was permitted to hold the benefice of Horsley, though not in holy orders, until 1678, and dying in London in that year was buried in Bunhill Fields. His funeral sermon was preached by his friend and "unworthy fellow-servant, Richard Baxter," and is in print.

John Middleton 1660—62. Was also Rector of Hamnell where he was buried.

Edward Pope 1662—71. Was also Rector of Walton on the Hill, Surrey, where he lies buried.

John Gregory 1671—78. Was also Rector of Hempsted, where he lies buried.

Thomas Hyde 1679—1703. Was also Professor of Hebrew at Oxford, and was buried at Handborough.

Robert Parsons 1703—1714. Was also Rector of Oddington, where he lies buried.

Nathaniel Lye 1714—37. Was also Prebendary of Gloucester and of Bristol, and Rector of Kemerton. Was buried in St. Michael's, Gloucester, in the 90th year of his age.

William Geekie 1738—67. Was also Prebendary of Canterbury and of St. Paul's.

Richard Hurd 1767—74. Became Bishop of Lichfield and afterwards of Worcester.

James Webster 1774—1804. He was also Vicar of Much Cowarne in Herefordshire, and Perpetual Curate of Stroud. His wife was a niece of Bishop Warburton; and Warburton's much loved sister, Frances, lived at the Rectory after her brother's insanity had become hopeless until her death in 1780   There seems to have been much affectionate intercourse between the Bishop and the Archdeacon, although Warburton held one of his fiercest of all fierce controversies with the Archdeacon's father. Archdeacon Webster, with his wife, two daughters, and Miss Warburton, was buried in the Chancel of the Church, and their monument is now on the South wall of the Nave.

Timothy Stonehouse Viger 1804—1814.

Thomas Rudge 1814—25.

John Timbrill 1825—65   Was also Vicar of Beckford. He was the last Archdeacon of Gloucester who was Rector of Dursley.

George Madan 1865—

CURATES IN ACTUAL PASTORAL CHARGE OF DURSLEY.

1618	Samuel Hallowes.
1653	Jos. Underwood [Puritan minister].
1662	Henry Stubbs [Puritan minister].
1662—70	James Whiting.
1670—84	Edward Towgood [— Edwards, — ffortune
1686—1703	John Elliott. — Hanley, Lecturers
1703—1705	William Evans with Mr. Towgood].
1705—1709	Richard Millechamp [Rector of Rudford].
1709—1710	John Jackson.
1710—1715	Edward Turner, Vicar of Cam, called on his Cam monument " sometime Vicar of Dursley."
1715—1737	Daniel Capel, buried in Dursley Church.
1737—1764	Charles Wallington, also Vicar of Frampton, buried in Dursley Church.
1764—1775	Thomas Gregory.

CHURCHWARDENS OF THE PARISH CHURCH FROM THE
YEAR 1841.

William Cox Buchanan	1841—2
Charles King	1841—2
John Vizard	1842—7
William Champion	1842—3
John Tilton	1843—4
William Harris	1844—5
Robert Blandford	1845—6
Joseph Cooper Player	1846—7
Edward Bloxsome, jun.	1847—8
Charles Hamilton	1847—8
George Vizard	1848—9
Joseph Shellard	1848—51
Robert John Purnell	1849—51
Henry Bishop	1851—4
William Tyrrell	1851—3
John Owen	1853—4
Edward Parker Shute	1854—6
Isaac Gardner	1854—6
William John Phelps	1856—7
Thomas Blackney	1856—9
William Philip Want	1857—9
Thomas Morse	1859—61
Frederick Vizard	1859—61
Fitzherbert White	1861—2
Richard Garn	1861—3
Isaac Gardner	1862—3
Henry Owen	1863—6
Daniel Crump	1863—6
John Vizard	1866—70
James Whitmore	1866—68
William Richards	1868—71
George Leonard	1870—2
George Ayliffe	1871—3
Thomas Trewren Vizard	1872—6
George Wenden	1873—6

DURSLEY CHARITIES.

The following Notes on the Charity Endowments of
Dursley are abstracted from the Tables in the Church, from
the Charity Commissioners' Report of 1827, and from the
Churchwardens' Register.

A.D. 1450. MR. SPILLMAN of Spillman's Court, Gloucestershire, and others, about the year 1450, gave an estate
called Oxlease, in Standish, then valued at £50 a year,
for the benefit of the poor. This was reduced to £4 a
year, after a suit in Chancery, the decree of the Court
being in issue in 1624. [See *Ch. Com. Rep.* 328.]
Traces of this charity are to be found in the Churchwardens' Register under the name of "the Oxlidge
money."

A.D. 1495. RICHARD YATE and THOMAS WHITHYFORD gave
the "Church House" and the "Torch Acre" to the
parishioners of Dursley, and in 1654 the proceeds were
applied to the repair of the Church ; a chief rent being
paid to the Lord of the Manor. In the Report of the
Charity Commissioners this benefaction is described as
"a burgage or tenement, now known by the name of the
Church House, with the gardens and grounds thereto
adjoining, within the borough town of Dursley next the
highway there, leading towards Woodmancote, on the
south side, and to the churchyard of Dursley on the
north side."—It is "now used as the parish poor-house."
The Report further states that it was the gift of RICHARD
FYNNIMORE and THOMAS HEVEN for the repairs of the
Church. The original Deed of this benefaction was lost
in the seventeenth century, but a new Deed of Charles
the Second's reign is among the papers in the Parish
Chest.

A.D. 1603. "Mr. Atwel's

Letts   Jesus

The towne of Dursley

"I geive to dursley thirtie three shillings and iiij^d for ever to keepe the poore at worke the gaine the poores to be disposed by the master and officers of the town and p'ishe or els such as they shall thinke fitt, for the true disposition thereof. Yo^r friende and wellwisher Hughe Atwell p'son of St Kewe in cornwell In times past p'son of Camberlye in Devonshere.

I pray returne yor letts wth sume of yor names and scale of the truthe for the true receivinge therof."
[From the *Churchwardens' Register.*]

A.D. 1617. The "Almshouses" are said to have been given to the Parish at this date. But entries of a chief rent paid for them to Mr. Webb are extant as early as 1566 in the Churchwardens' Register.

A.D. 1637. Hugh Smith of Dursley, mason, gave three tenements, part of the Broadwell House, to the poor, and 40s. as stock, the use of it for the Church.

"The Coppy of the Contents of the Last Will and Testament of Hugh Smith of Dursley deceased bearinge date the first daye of January 1637. Concerninge his gift by his said will to the use of the Church and poor of the p'ish of Dursley.

Item. I give and bequeath to the use of the poore Inhabitants of the towne and p'ish of Dursley for ever a parte of the Broadwell house that is the three Tenements that John Roac Thomas Adeane and Agnes Gilles nowe dwell in payeinge yearelye four pounds rente to Richard Smith and his heires and the rents and proffitts of these three Tennements from tyme to tyme to be att the disposeinge of the Churchwardens and Overseers and to be bestowed on such poore people as they in theire discretion shall see most fitt to have it.

It. I give fforty shillings to bee keepte by the Church-wardens from tyme to tyme as a stocke the use of it to bee bestowed on the Church and alsoe I give Twenty Shillings to the poore to be bestowed presentlye." [From the *Churchwardens' Register.*]

A.D. 1642. The rent of certain houses in Tetbury was given by SIR THOMAS ESTCOURT, 40s. for a lecture to be delivered four times a year at Tetbury, and the rest for the poor of Tetbury and Dursley equally. The amount for Dursley was fixed by a Chancery decree at £10 a year. In 1857 the Lord of the Manor offered to give up all his Manorial rights in the town of Dursley to the inhabitants if they would obtain a Charter of Incorporation. They wished first to be released from this Rent Charge, and this not being done the proposal fell through.

A.D. 1663. THROGMORTON TROTMAN of London, gave to the Haberdashers' Company £2000 to produce £100 a year, £15 of which was for giving a lecture "on the market days or some other day" at Dursley, and if that be not allowed, to the poor there.

A.D. 1678. HENRY STUBBS gave ten shillings yearly, chargeable on land in Horsley, for the purchase of Bibles and Primers. This Benefaction is entered in the Church-wardens' Register for many years, but is now lost.

A.D. 1703. JOHN ARUNDELL, Clothier, gave an acre "lying upon Breakneck" in Cam, the rent to be applied to buying books to teach poor children of Dursley to read English.

A.D. 1769. JACOB STIFF, Cardmaker, gave £30, the interest to be laid out at Christmas in bread, for widows and other poor people in Dursley.

A.D. 1781. In accordance with a previous will of MRS. ANN PURNELL, a piece of pasture land called "New Invention" in Cam, was charged, after a deduction of £3. 4. 6. yearly, with the annual sums of 10s. to the minister for a sermon on New Year's Day, 30s. to forty widows, 10s. to the minister for a sermon on Good Friday afternoon, and the rest to the same purposes as Stubbs' Charity.

A.D. 1781. In accordance with the previous will of NATHL. LAWSON, clothier, a piece of pasture land in Cam, called "Martha Nelmes's leaze," about two acres, was given to provide bread at Christmas for the poor of Dursley.

A.D. 1791. SAMUEL ADEY gave £100 to the Gloucester Infirmary, on condition that it should receive two in-patients from Dursley annually, and £100, the interest to be distributed in bread four times a year to the poor of Dursley who regularly attend Divine Service.

A.D. 1798. SAMUEL PHILLIMORE gave £150 to be invested in real property, one-third of the rent of which was to be given in bread at Easter to the poor.

A.D. 1811. RICHARD JONES of Dursley gave—

1. £250 consols to the Gloucester Infirmary, on condition that it receive one in-patient and two out-patients annually from Dursley.
2. A similar sum to the Bath Hospital, on the same conditions.
3. £450 consols to repew the Church, which was done in 1825.
4. £300 stock for the Boys' Sunday School.
5. £300 stock for the Girls' ditto.
6. Other sums (amounting to £700 stock, *Char. Comm. Report,*) for four friendly societies of Dursley.

A.D. 1836. JOHN HARVEY OLLNEY of Cheltenham, Lieut.-Col., gave £300 to be invested, for coals and blankets for the poor of Dursley at Christmas.

A.D. 1837. THOMAS GREGORY, apothecary of Dursley, gave
£50 to be invested, for bread on St. Stephen's day.

A.D. 1863. The REV. R. JERMYN COOPER, Rector of West
Chiltington, Sussex, gave £100 consols, for soup to be
given away in January and February.

A.D. 1854. GEORGE VIZARD of Dursley, banker, gave £200,
the interest to be expended in bedding and clothing for
the poor of Dursley.

A.D. 1834. HENRY VIZARD gave the National School house
and ground, and the Master's residence.

2 In 1843, he gave four cottages and a building in
Bower's Court for establishing and supporting an
Infant School, and endowed it with £1000.

. 3. In 1853, he gave six cottages and gardens for almshouses for three men and three women, and £2000
as an endowment, to be spent in repairs, payment
of taxes, and allowance to the inmates.

4. In 1855, he gave £200 to the Gloucester Infirmary,
on condition that it should admit one in-patient
and one out-patient annually from Dursley.

5. In 1856, he gave £500, for blankets and clothing
for the poor on St. Stephen's day.

———

WOODMANCOTE.

The town of Dursley extends itself eastward in a long suburb which is supposed to have been originally called Wodcmancote from being the residence of the officer who had charge of the vast woods which formerly grew in this district.

This Manor has always been separate from that of Dursley, and was for some time part of the great possessions of the Berkeleys of Beverston. It does not appear in Domesday Book, nor among the estates of the Berkeleys of Berkeley, and its history before the thirteenth century is unknown. About 1220 it was in the possession of the De Gaunts of Beverston, Maurice de Gaunt having then made a grant of land in the township to the Nuns of Clerkenwell. [See p. 32.] That Lord of Beverston forfeited many of his Manors to the Crown, and probably Woodmancote was one of them, for in 1325 it was held by Robert de Swineburne. It was purchased again for the Berkeley family by Thomas, Lord Berkeley, who also purchased Beverston from the Ap Adams. It was held by his son, Sir John Berkeley of Beverston, and by the descendants of that Knight, until 1557, when Sir John Berkeley sold it to Henry Lambert, a merchant of London. It continued for a century in the Lambert family, but they parted with it in 1670 to John Arundel, whose descendants again sold it, in 1736, to John de la Field Phelps, the head of a Dursley family, some particulars of which are given in the genealogical table below [1]

In 1847 St. Mark's Chapel of Ease was built on land given by Mr. Henry Vizard, whose liberality also was largely shewn in its endowment: but it has no special features of archæological interest that need description. It is part of the Rectory of Dursley, but has wardens of its own, of whom the following is a list:—

George Vizard	1847—8	John Hurndall, sen.	1851—8
Edward Bloxsome, jun,	1847—8	John Chas. Bengough	1858—9
Henry Vizard	1848—61	William Philip Want	1859—61
Henry Bishop	1848—9	Edward Wallington	1861—76
Edward A. Freeman	1849—50	John Vizard	1861—72
John Rotton	1840—1	William Cornock	1872—76

1 PHELPS of Dursley.

Thomas Phelps＝Marianne
buried at Dursley |
  14 Feb., 1647. |
         Thomas＝Elizabeth Williams
     buried 20 Mar., |
      1701. |
         Thomas＝Abigail Mayo
     buried 12 April, |
      1718. |
         Thomas＝Mary Arundell
     buried 29 April, |
      1735. |
         John＝Elizabeth Fowler
    J.P. County of |
    Gloucester, |
    buried 1755. |
         John Delafield Phelps＝Esther Gully
   High Sheriff in 1761 and J.P. |

John Delafield Phelps, J.P.   Rev. James Phelps＝Marianne Blagden Hale
d. s. p. Dec. 19, 1842.   buried April, 1829. |
                     William John
                 of Chestal, Dursley,
            J.P. High Sheriff in 1860.

ARMS—Quarterly First Per Pale Or and Arg. a Wolf salient Az. between semee of Cross-Crosslets fitchy gu., for PHELPS. Second the coat of FOWLER. Third the coat of FIELD. Fourth Arg. three pales gu. a Chief Peau, for GULLY.

CREST—On a wreath a Wolf's head Az. langued and erased gu. collared Or. thereon a Marblet sa.

MOTTO—*Frangas non flectas.*

DURSLEY AND SHAKESPEARE.

There is some reason for thinking that the great poet of England was once a resident in the town of Dursley, and that members of his family lived there down to recent times.

" Some passages in his writings shew an intimate acquaintance with Dursley, and the names of its inhabitants. In the Second Part of Henry IV., act v. sc. 1, ' Gloucestershire,' *Davy* says to *Justice Shallow*—' I beseech you, Sir, to countenance William Visor of Woncot, against Clement Perkes on the Hill.' This Woncot, as Mr. Stevens, the commentator, supposes in a note to another passage in the same play (act v., sc. 3) is Woodmancot, still pronounced by the common people " Womcot," a township in the parish of Dursley. This Township lies at the foot of Stinchcombe Hill, still emphatically called " The Hill " in that neighbourhood on account of the magnificent panorama which it commands ; and of which a correct idea may be formed from the sketch map given at the beginning of this volume. On Stinchcombe Hill there is the site of a house wherein a family named " Purchase," or " Perkis," once lived : and it is reasonable to conclude that Perkis of Stinchcombe Hill is identical with " Clement Perkes of the Hill." The family of Visor were also undoubted ancestors of the Dursley family known in more recent times by the name of Vizard.[1] *(See next page.)*

In addition to these coincidences, we must mention the fact that a family named Shakespeare formerly resided in Dursley and the neighbourhood. James Shakespeare was buried at Bisley on March 13th, 1570. Edward, son of John and Margery Shakespurre was baptized at Beverston on September 19th, 1619 [See p. 136]. The parish register of Dursley records that Thomas Shakespeare, weaver, was married to Joan Turner on March 3rd, 1677-8, and that they had children baptized by the name of Edward on July 1st, 1681,

Mary on August 28th, 1682, Thomas on March 1st, 1685, and Mary on December 27th, 1691. The Churchwardens' Register also shews that there was a mason in Dursley named John Shakespeare in 1704, and down to 1739, that Thomas Shakespeare had a " seat-place " assigned to him in 1739, and that Betty Shakespeare received poors' money from 1747 to 1754. Some of this family " still exist as small free-holders, in the adjoining parish of Newington Bagpath, and claim kindred with the poet."

To this it may be added that a pathway in the woods near the town is traditionally known as " Shakespeare's walk ; " and that Shakespeare's description of " a wild prospect in Gloucestershire," which takes in a view of Berkeley Castle

---

1 VIZARD of Dursley.

Arthur Vizard=Joan
Gent., Bailiff of |
Dursley in 1612. |
     Jerome=Mary
  ob. Jan., 1670. |
      Jerome=Mary Mynett
    ob. Dec., 1711. |
       John=Hannah Hughes
     ob. Ap., 1731. |
       John=Isabella Cornock
     of Stancombe,
     ob. Ap., 1752. |
      · William=Ann Phelps
     ob. 14 Feb., 1807. |
       John=Anna Maria Weight
     ob. 22 Jan., 1814. |
       John=Mary Leigh Scott

Mary=Rev. G. A. M. Litle   Thomas Trewren   Frances Alice   Arthur
                                      and
                                 Maria Cordelia

ARMS—Per fesse argent and gules a fesse ingrailed per fesse azure and or between three Esquire's helmets proper in the centre chief point a cross crosslet of the second.

CREST—On a wreath of the colours issuant out of Palisadoes or., a demi-Hind regardant vulned in the neck and holding between the paws an arrow the point downwards.

MOTTO—Cassis tutissima Virtus.

exactly answers to the view on which the eye still rests when the spectator is standing on Stinchcombe Hill, although cultivation has made it somewhat less "wild" than in Elizabethan or Jacobean days.

"How far is it, my lord, to Berkeley, now?
North.—I am a stranger here in Gloucestershire;
These high wild hills and rough uneven ways
Draw out our miles, and make them wearisome."
"But I bethink me, what a weary way
From Ravenspurg to Cotswold will be found
In Ross and Willoughby wanting your company," &c.
Enter to them *Harry Percy*, whom *Northumberland*
addresses:—
"How far is it to Berkeley? And what stir
Keeps good old York there, with his men of war?
Hotspur.—There stands the castle by yon tuft of trees."
[Rich. II. ij. 3.]

From these scraps of evidence—which are chiefly taken from a Note at page 21 of the Rev. Richard Webster Huntley's "Glossary of the Cotswold Dialect"—it is not unreasonable to conclude that Shakespeare may have lived among his friends in or near Dursley during the unaccounted-for interval between his removal from Warwickshire and his appearance in London.

Addition to foot note at page 9.

The Market Tolls were granted to Nicholas Wykes and his heirs by Letters Patent of Henry VIII., dated November 12th, 1528, and to Sir Thomas Estcourt in 1612. Both the Market House and Tolls were purchased in 1840 of Thomas Grimston Bucknall Estcourt, Esq., the then Lord of the Manor, by Mr. Henry Vizard, who by Deed of Gift dated Dec. 6, 1841, and enrolled in Chancery on April 11, 1842, conveyed the same to seven Trustees for the benefit of the town, but on Dec. 28th, 1849, the Markets and Fairs held in Dursley were declared free from Toll, by a resolution passed at a special meeting of the Bailiff and Aldermen.

The Market day is Thursday in every week. The Fairs were anciently held on St. Mark's Day, April 25th, and St. Clement's Day, November 23rd, but in recent times they have been held on May 6th and December 4th.

Addition to Berkeley pedigree at page 7.

ARMS—Arg. a fess between three martlets sa.

The Great Tower

Bewerton Castle

BEVERSTON.

THE little village of Beverston lies on the south-western
    decline of the high lands dignified with the name of
the Cotswold Hills, a few miles from the point where their
last slope dies away in the vale of Malmesbury. There runs
through it an old turnpike-road from South Wales and the
Stroudwater manufacturing district to Tetbury, Malmesbury,
and Cirencester, but this has long been superseded by a
railway which passes along the valleys from Gloucester
to Swindon, so that Beverston is now unknown except to
those who are familiar with the out-of-the-way places of
that part of Gloucestershire. The village itself consists at the
present time of twenty-eight houses, including the Rectory
and two farm-houses, but it was once of considerable size,
large enough to have a market of its own; and, according to
local tradition, nearly as large as the neighbouring town of
Tetbury. What little importance it formerly possessed has
entirely passed away, but the source of that importance is
still to be observed in the ivy-clad ruins of a fine old Castle
standing on the north side of the high road, and tempting
enquiry as to its history from the passer-by.

That history begins more than eight hundred years ago;
in the days before the Normans, those great builders of
castles, had gained any footing in England except as friends
and guests. The name indicates that the place originally
belonged to some gentleman or nobleman who owned the
name of Bever, for Bever's Ton is simply the township or

manor of Bever.[1] Who the owner of the name was, whether
English (so-called "Anglo-Saxon") or Norman, is a fact
yet to be drawn out of darkness of the pre-historic ages.
The name is still known in Gloucestershire, and is familiar
to the readers of Early English history as that of a chronicler
of the 13th century, Bever "of Westminster" or "of
London." The probability is, that the original Bever was
a Norman gentleman who had settled in England during the
twenty years or so which preceded the Conquest, when many
such gentry came over to better themselves under the protection of Emma, the Norman queen successively of Ethelred
and Canute, and subsequently under that of her son Edward
the Confessor. For it was the custom of these immigrant
gentry to build castles on the lands granted to them, and their
castles were not unfrequently called after their names.
[*Ang. Sax Chron.* A.D. 1052.] The settlement of Normans
in the district previously to the Conquest is easily accounted
for by the fact that Gloucester was a favourite residence of
Edward the Confessor.

---

[1] The name of Bever appears, oddly enough, as the name of a
witness to the signatures of the Squire and the Rector in the Tithe
award of the Parish, which is dated in 1804.

Leland, and those who have copied him, supposed the name of
"Beverstone," as they wrote it, to be derived from certain "great
blue stones" which tradition states to have been once quarried in the
parish. No trace now exists of such stones, but a field called "Broad
Stones" is situated about a quarter of a mile west of the Castle.
Another explanation of the name is that it was simply Burestan, or
"Stone Tower," and this is the way in which it is spelt in Doomsday.
The final "e" was seldom used until the latter half of the seventeenth
century. It is not used in the Episcopal records, and it is omitted on
several tombstones.

A learned Gloucestershire archaeologist, Canon Lysons, suggests to
me that Beuer, according to the Promptorium Parvulorum means a
drinking, and that thus Beurestan may mean a place for the growth
of beer, that is of Barley. It is said by old labourers that there used
formerly to be a "terrible lot" of barley grown on the Manor.

During the reign of Edward the Confessor Beverston is associated with the names of Earl Godwin and his sons by the mediæval chroniclers. It probably passed into the possession of Sweyn, Earl of Gloucester, on the outlawry of the Normans from England in A.D. 1052. [*Ang. Sax. Chron.* ad ann. 1052.] He was the most bitter of all the Godwins in his antipathy to the "Frenchmen" [Frencise men], and is said by the Anglo-Saxon Chronicle to have been restored by Edward to estates of which they had gained possession, of which Beverston may have been one.

In the national movement which that great Englishman, Earl Godwin, organized against the dangerous Norman favourites of Edward, three armies marched from the respective Earldoms of himself and his two sons[1] to a rendezvous at Beverston, where they met early in September, 1051.[2] It

---

[1] Godwin was Earl of Wessex, Sussex, and Kent; Sweyn his eldest son was Earl of Gloucester, Hereford, Somerset, Oxford, and Berkshire; Harold his younger son was Earl of East Anglia, Huntingdon, and Middlesex.

[2] "Then came Godwin the Earl, and Swegen the Earl and Harold the Earl, to Beverston, and many men with them, in order that they might go to their royal lord. [*Ang. Sax. Chron.* ad ann. 1048.]

"Godwin and his sons alone, who knew that they were suspected, not deeming it prudent to be present unarmed, halted with a strong force at Beverston, giving out that he had assembled an army to restrain the Welsh .... and a rumour prevailed that the King's army would attack them in that very place." [*William of Malm.* § 198.]

"Godwin and his sons, and their respective armies, came to Gloucestershire after the feast of St. Mary's Nativity" [Sept. 8th], "encamped at a place called Langtree, and sent ambassadors to the King at Gloucester, threatening war unless he gave up Earl Eustace and his companions, and also the Normans and Bolognese who held a Castle in Dovercliff. ... The King's army was so excited that if he would have permitted they would immediately have attacked Earl Godwin's army." [*Florence of Worc.* ad ann. 1051.]

The account given by Florence of Worcester is reproduced by Simeon of Durham, with the same date.

appears from the nearly comtemporary chroniclers and from
tradition that the armies united at some place near to Beverston and then formed an encampment at Uley Bury, the
Castle at Beverston being occupied as the head quarters of
the Earls. Uley Bury is a strong Roman encampment about
five miles west of Beverston on the road to Gloucester; and
is in the hundred of Longtree (of which Tetbury is the
principal town) although Beverston itself is in the hundred
of Berkeley. Rudder says that "some accounts expressly
say that they seized upon the Castle of Beverston" but he
gives no authority.

The policy of Edward and his advisers, and the for-
bearance of Godwin, led to the rapid dispersion of the army
of the latter, and to the retirement of himself and his sons
from England. He was pardoned and restored to his estates
in the following year, but died immediately after his return
to England. Sweyn was permanently outlawed, and was
murdered by a band of Saracens on his return from a pil-
grimage to Jerusalem. By the outlawry his estates were, of
course, confiscated to the Crown, and thus Beverston is
entered as Crown property in Doomsday book, which was
compiled in 1086, forty years after the three Earls had
assembled their forces there to menace the Normanized Court
at Gloucester.

This entry credits Edward the Confessor and William the
Conqueror with ten hides of land in the parish.—"In Bure-
stane x hid"—a quantity amounting to about 1200 acres.
The present area of the parish is 2139, of which 1715
are arable land. It is probably of the same extent as in
ancient times, but a large quantity of waste land has since
been enclosed which was not estimated in the acreage of the
Manor in the Doomsday Survey.

Beverston, however, formed only the eastern extremity of
the great Manor, which was co-extensive with the Hundred
of Berkeley; and not only this portion of that extensive Manor

but the whole of it had been forfeited to the Crown by the outlawry of the Earl of Gloucester. It seems originally to have belonged to a House of Nuns which occupied the site on which Berkeley Castle now stands, and it is not clear how it came into the possession of the Earl of Gloucester.[1] But the whole Manor being Crown land at the Conquest was afterwards granted by William I. to "Rogerus senior de Berkele," the representative of the ancient Lords of Dursley.[2] At his death, some time after A.D. 1091, the Manor descended to his nephew William, who was succeeded by his son Roger. The civil war, however, between King Stephen and the Empress Matilda involved both William and Roger de Berkeley in trouble, the father being imprisoned and the son deprived of his lands and of the old family Castle of Dursley.

On the accession of Henry II. [A.D. 1154], the whole of the lands of Berkeley were granted by the King to Robert Fitzharding, from whom descended both the families of Berkeley, of whom the elder branch was settled at Berkeley Castle and the younger at Beverston Castle.

This Robert Fitzharding was the son of a Danish prince who is said to have been the second son of a King of Denmark, contemporary with William the Conqueror. The old Chronicler, Wallingford, who wrote about 1214, alleges that it was an ancient custom of Denmark, before the Kings became Christians, to send all the younger sons of the reigning Sovereign out of the country, so as to avoid all disputes about the succession to the crown: that in consequence of

---

[1] The character of Sweyn, and a crime attributed to him, offers some confirmation of the story fathered on Earl Godwin himself (perhaps from a much earlier tradition) by Walter Mapes. [See *Atkyns, Rudder, &c.*]

[2] The title "de Berkele" occurs twenty years after the Conquest, in 1091. The seal of Roger at that date exhibits the figure of a Knight on foot, fighting with a leopard or lion which is grasping the Knight's shield with claws and teeth.

this rule Harding came to England and settled at Bristol on
lands given him by the Conqueror in the year 1069. Here,
in Baldwin Street, Robert Fitzharding was born, towards the
end of the Conqueror's reign, that is about 1085. When he
succeeded to his father's estate, in 1115, he removed his residence from Baldwin Street to a large stone house which he
built upon the Frome, but he is known to tradition as a burgess
of Bristol and not as a noble. It is a tradition of Bristol,
one backed by the historian Stowe, that the same street in
which Harding resided was also the residence of Prince
Henry, afterwards Henry II., during the years of his boy-
hood, and that he lived there under the charge of a tutor
named Matthews.

When the young Henry II. was nine years old, in the
year 1142, Robert Fitzharding founded the Abbey of St.
Augustine, which has been for nearly three centuries and a
half the Cathedral of Bristol. It was consecrated on Easter
Day, 1148, and the Founder with his wife Eva[1] were both
buried within its walls, between the Abbot's and the Prior's
Stalls, that is, in the middle of the western end of the Choir;
Fitzharding himself and his wife both dying in 1170.[2]

Robert Fitzharding had five sons and two daughters. The
eldest of the former, Maurice, became the ancestor of the
Berkeleys of Berkeley; the second son, Nicholas, was the
ancestor of the Fitz-Nicholls, now represented by the Poyntz
family; Robert, the third son, was the ancestor of the Gournays and Ap Adams of Beverston; Thomas, the fourth son,

---

[1] Eva is said to have been the niece of William the Conqueror;
being the daughter of "Sir Estmond" and Godiva the Conqueror's
sister.

[2] Robert Fitzharding's seal bears a curious figure of an animal
with body and legs like a horse, occupying the whole field. The head
is inverted between the fore feet, a very long tongue projecting
upward and a horn downward. [See figure in *Lysons' Glouc.*]

was Archdeacon of Worcester; and Henry, the fifth son, was, among many other benefices, Rector of Beverston.[1]

The old Berkeleys of Dursley Castle never recovered from their fall, but intermarriages in some degree remedied the injuries which the family suffered. Roger de Berkeley had a daughter, Alice, who was by the persuasion of Henry II. in later years married to Maurice the eldest son of Fitz-Harding, the Manor of Dursley being at the same time restored to De Berkeley, from whom it was inherited by his son Robert, who married a daughter of Fitz-Harding, and whose descendants held it until 1567. On the death of Robert Fitz-Harding, his son Maurice took the name of Berkeley, the great Castle of Berkeley having in the meanwhile been built by Henry II. (as a substitute for that of Dursley) on the site of the ancient Nunnery of Berkeley.

At the death of Robert Fitzharding, however, in the year 1170 that large portion of the great Manor and Hundred of Berkeley which lay round Beverston Castle, and which was probably held long before as a separate Manor, was entailed upon Robert, his third son; together with the Manors of Kingsweston, Aylberton, Over, Radewyke, and Northwicke; and also those of Berewe, Ingliscombe, and Weare, in the County of Somerset. From the last of these, which lay to the south of the Mendip Hills, near the town of Axbridge,

---

[1] Seven hundred years afterwards, the author became Rector of Beverston, whose family derive their origin—to be modest as to dates—from Gormo I., who was King of Denmark in A.D. 699. Gormo is reputed to be a descendant of Dan who founded the monarchy of Denmark about B.C. 1038, when David was King of Israel. But Sir Alexander Croke the historian of the Blunts, allows that "there is an unfortunate chasm" between the years of our Lord 401 and 699, so the present writer will not go beyond King Gormo, and contents himself with noticing the odd coincidence that two rectors of this little parish at an interval of seven centuries should each claim descent from the old royal house of Denmark. [See *Croke's Genealog. Hist. of Le Blounts.* vol. i. p. 17.]

this first Lord of Beverston, as an independent property, took the name of Robert de Weare.[1] His wife was Alice de Gaunt, great great grandaughter of the Conqueror's sister Maud, and daughter of Robert de Gaunt and his wife Alice Paganell or Pownall.[2] The husband and the wife were each of them, consequently, descended from a daughter of the house of Rollo.

Robert de Weare is the first, therefore, of the Lords of the Manor of Beverston to whom it can be distinctly traced; and he may be regarded as the founder, in 1170, of the family to which it afterwards belonged until the year 1331, when it was brought back by purchase into the elder branch of the Fitzharding Berkeleys. The estate thus founded was very large, and Robert is said to have lived in great splendour, attended by many knights and other retainers of good family, keeping up a baronial grandeur and magnificence similar to that of his elder brother the Baron of Berkeley. As his father had founded the Priory of St. Augustine at Bristol, so, on the opposite side of the Green, the Lord of Beverston founded the Hospital of St. Mark at Billeswick, for 100 poor men, otherwise known afterwards as the Hospital of St. Augustine, from the Augustinian Canons by whom it was partly occupied and its services maintained.[3] De Weare died before much progress had been made with his foundation, and it was completed by his heirs. But he was probably buried in its Chapel, and one of the cross-legged knights in stone who still lie in "the Mayor's Chapel," as it is now called, may be his memorial.

Robert de Weare left a son named Maurice, and a daughter who bore her grandmother's name of Eva. Maurice assumed the name De Gaunt from his mother[4] and married Matilda,

---

[3] A long account of Gaunt's Hospital is to be found in *Barrett's History of Bristol*, pp. 354-379. It was the foundation on which the famous Colston charities were built up.

[4] The Manor from which this name was taken seems to have been that of Gaunts, near Wimborne, in Dorsetshire.

BEVERSTON.

1. Descent of ROBERT DE WEARE.

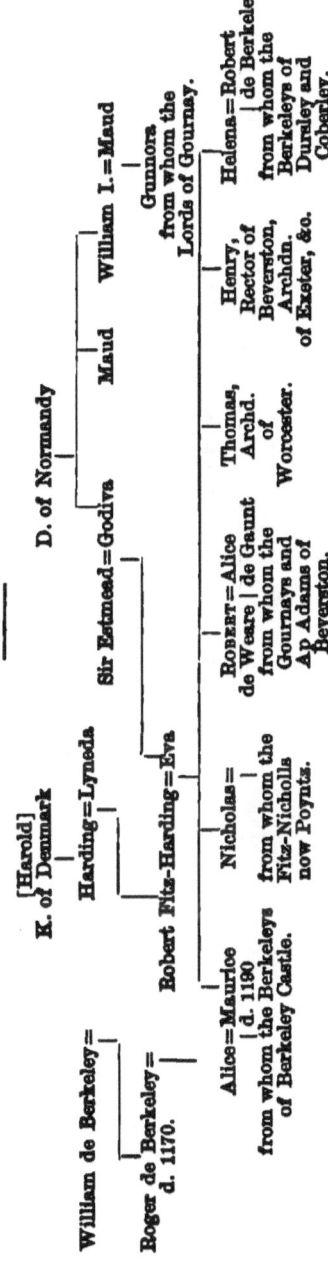

2. Descent of ALICE DE GAUNT.

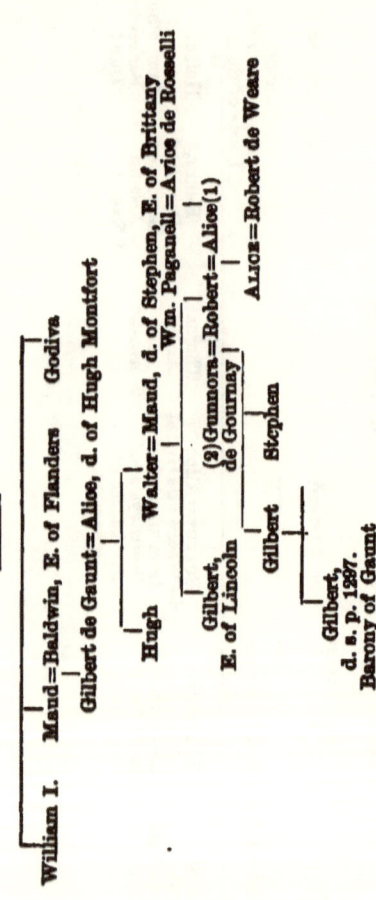

William I.

Maud=Baldwin, E. of Flanders   Godiva

Gilbert de Gaunt=Alice, d. of Hugh Montfort

Hugh   Walter=Maud, d. of Stephen, E. of Brittany

Gilbert, E. of Lincoln   Wm. Paganell=Avice de Rosselli

(2)Gunnora=Robert=Alice(1)
          de Gournay

Gilbert   Stephen   ALICE=Robert de Weare

Gilbert,
d. s. p. 1297.
Barony of Gaunt
Extinct.

Entries in Doomsday Book shew that the Paganells held lands in the neighbourhood of Beverston. "xliij. Terra Radulfi Pagenel. In Cirecestre Hund. Radulfus Pagenel ten. Torrentune ct Radulfus de, &c." . . . "In Langetrewes Hund. tenet Rog. de Jurei de Rad. Paganel." . . Longtree Hundred extends to within half a mile of Beverston, and "Trewsbury," near Daglingworth is perhaps analogous in spelling to the "Langetrewe" of Doomsday, Ralph Paganell held under the Conqueror 15 lordships in Yorkshire of which he was Sheriff, and 30 elsewhere.

the daughter and heiress of Henry D'Oilly, of Hookneston, in Yorkshire. She was a ward of the Crown, and permission to marry was only obtainable on condition that her husband should bring twenty knights to the king in time of war. Maurice de Gaunt was, however, one of the Barons who so long and so bitterly opposed King John; and who, in the selfish support of their order brought the King and the country to ruin. His estates were confiscated and granted to Philip d'Albini in the year 1215; and he so entirely forsook the national side in this quarrel that even after the death of King John he fought under the standard of Louis the French King (to whom the Pope had pretended to give the Crown of England), against the young King Henry III. At the battle of May 20th, 1217, which was afterwards named "The Fair of Lincoln," when the French army was gloriously defeated, Maurice de Gaunt was taken prisoner by the Earl of Chester, and it was only after a year's imprisonment that he was ransomed at the price of two of his wife's Yorkshire manors, those of Leeds and Bingley. When the kingdom was once more secure his lands were restored to him, but so much suspicion of disloyalty hung ' about him that when fresh troubles arose between the Crown and the Barons about the custody of the Castles he was again in danger of confiscation. Maurice appears at this time, A.D. 1225, to have been rebuilding the Castle of Beverston, and it was alleged that he was doing so without license from the Crown. On giving satisfaction to the king his estates were, however, confirmed to him by a deed dated two years later, in the 11th year of Henry III. The lower parts of the Castle are all of this date, massive Norman piers and groining still remaining in a perfect condition, . with external walls many feet in thickness.

About this time the lately founded Dominican Order, the Black Friars, or Preaching Friars, were rapidly establishing themselves in the principal towns of England, and Maurice

de Gaunt who had carried on to completion the foundation
established by his father at Billeswick, in Bristol, now
engaged in a similar great work on his own account, the
foundation of a Monastery for the Dominicans in the same
city. This building was erected on the Weir, northward
of the Castle, and a portion of the quadrangle (though of
later date) still stands to mark the spot, part (perhaps of
the original erection) being known as the "Bakers' Hall,"
and part being occupied as a Quakers' School. The Founder
died, while following Henry III. on his unsuccessful expe-
dition to France, on April 30th, 1230, and was buried
(according to the Annals of Tewkesbury) in the Chapel of
the Monastery:[1] but not a vestige of the Chapel remains,
the site being occupied by a. Quakers' Meeting House.
Although apparently twice married he left no children
behind him, and his Manors of Weston, Northwicke, Over,
Albricton, Radwicke, and Beverston, were devised by him to
his nephew, the three hundreds of Portbury, Bedminster, and
Harclive being left to Thomas, Lord Berkeley, his distant
cousin.

The nephew was Robert, son of Eva, the only sister of
Maurice, who died long before her brother, about the year
1216, at the end of King John's reign. She had married

---

[1] In the Itinerary of William of Worcester there are some extracts
from the Martiloge of this Priory. They seem to be in confusion as to
date, as Robert de Gournay and Anselm de Gournay who both died in
the 13th century are entered between deaths which are dated 1422 and
1429. Immediately following the entry which is dated 1422 there is
the entry, "Dominus Mauricius de Berkle, et domina Johanna uxor
ejus . . . jacet in choro in sinistra altaris, die primo octobris." [*Itin.
W. de Worc. ed. Nasmyth.* p. 233.] This may refer to Maurice de
Gaunt and his second wife, yet it is improbable that he should have
been called de Berkeley, the Beverston descendants of Robert Fitz-
harding having no reason for assuming that name.

Thomas de Harptree,[1] by whom she had two sons, Robert
and Hugh, the former of whom took the name of De
Gournay, and the latter of De Gaunt. Robert De Gournay
seems to have died very shortly after his succession to his
uncle's estates, in the same year 1230, if indeed he lived to
inherit them. Possibly they passed to the Crown as guardian
of his son Anselm, a minor The Martiloge of the Dominican
Friars has an entry which seems to shew that he died abroad:
"Cor domini Roberti de Gornay jacet in ista ecclesia, qui
obiit die 20 novembris." His widow, Avice de Longchamp,
died in 1268.

Anselm de Gournay has left as little record behind him
as his father. The Register of Gloucester Abbey shews
that he gave to St. Peter's a small gift of land and the
advowson of Beverston Rectory. "Anselmus de Gorney
dedit Deo et Sancto Petro Gloucestrie quinque solidatas"

---

[1] Of Harptree and Barew Gournay in Somersetshire. Some of
their Manors were held by the Berkeleys of Beverston as late as 1417.
[*Hutch. Dorset.* iij. 346.]

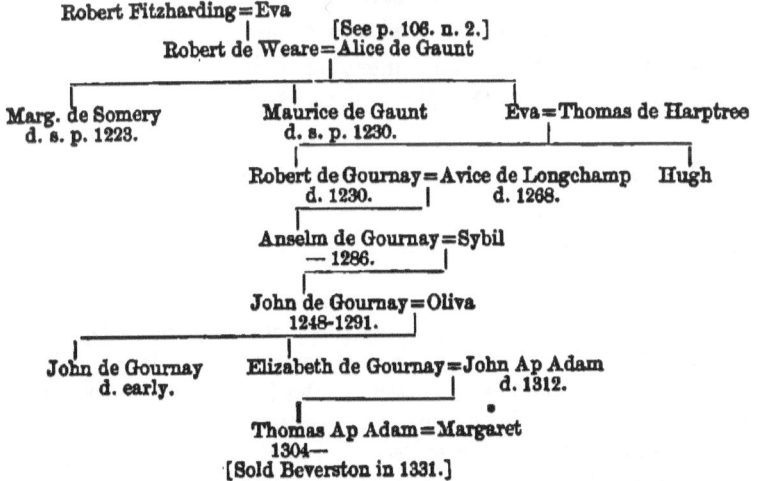

Descent of the GOURNAYS and AP ADAMS.
[See also p. 105. n. 1.]

Robert Fitzharding=Eva
           [See p. 106. n. 2.]
    Robert de Weare=Alice de Gaunt

Marg. de Somery   Maurice de Gaunt   Eva=Thomas de Harptree
d. s. p. 1223.   d. s. p. 1230.

               Robert de Gournay=Avice de Longchamp   Hugh
                   d. 1230.   d. 1268.

               Anselm de Gournay=Sybil
                  — 1286.

               John de Gournay=Oliva
                 1248-1291.

John de Gournay   Elizabeth de Gournay=John Ap Adam
d. early.   d. 1312.

              Thomas Ap Adam=Margaret
              1304—
          [Sold Beverston in 1331.]

⌊1¼ acre] "terræ in Beverstone, cum advocatione ecclesiæ ejusdem villæ, tempore Johannis Gamages abbatis." [*Hist. Mon. S. Pætri Glouc.* i. 65. *Record Off. vol.*] The grant of land was disputed by his son, but confirmed by Edward I. in the year 1287. [*Ibid.* iii. 20.] The advowson of the Rectory remained with the Monastery until the latter was merged in the Bishopric, when it went to the Crown, which has ever since presented to the living.

Contemporary with Anselm at Beverston was Maurice the fifth Lord at Berkeley. It is recorded that Lord Maurice was sixteen times in the field at the head of his followers and that he had the luxury of forty law suits.[1] He seems to have waged legal war for a long time with his Beverston cousin on the subject of weights and measures. The Grand Jury presented his Lordship for, among other social misdoings, distraining "Anselm de Gournay on the King's highway, and in Manors held *in capite*, because the latter would not take his measures of assize from his standard, whereas he ought to receive them from the King's Marshal." But in the year 1256 the King, Henry III., paid a visit to Berkeley Castle on his return from spending four days with the Prince Edward at Bristol: and on this occasion he pardoned Lord Berkeley "and his tenants their breaches of assize in merchandize and measure belonging to the King as supreme Clerk of the Market," and so probably the feud ended. Anselm's grandson obtained the grant of a market for Beverston from the Crown, a fact which suggests that Berkeley had exercised an authority over Beverston to which the inhabitants of the latter objected. Perhaps a relic of

---

[1] "This Lord, with a milk-white head in this irksome old age of seventy years, in winter termes and frosty seasons, with a buckrame bagge stuffed with lawe cases, in early mornings and late evenings, walked with his eldest sonne betweene the fower Innes of Court and Westminster Hall, following his lawe-suitès in his owne old person, not for himself, but for his posterity " [*Smyth*]. His pugnacity was not without excuse, for he was endeavouring to recover what his brother the Marquess had squandered away.

the grievance still exists in the custom which requires the Constable of Beverston to go on his knees in the Court Leet of Berkeley and in that posture take his corporal oath that he will seek the welfare and prosperity of the Lord of the Manor and Hundred of Berkeley: a ceremony performed amidst much laughter and not without reluctance on the part of Beverston.

Anselm de Gournay died in November 1286, and was buried in the Dominican Priory, the Martiloge recording "Dominus Ancelinus de Gurnay, qui jacet in choro, die 15 novembris." Of his wife nothing more is known than that her name was Sybil.

John de Gournay, son of Anselm and Sybil, was born in the year 1248, and lived to possess the estates after his father only five years. He married Oliva, daughter of Henry, Lord Lovel of Castle Carey, by whom he had a son, John, and a daughter, Elizabeth. The son died early, and thus on the death of her father in the year 1291, the lands passed once more to the female side. In the same year that she inherited this great property Elizabeth de Gournay was married to John, Lord Ap Adam of Gorste and Battesley within Tidenham, two.Gloucestershire estates being thus united.[1]

Lord Ap Adam put an end to the disputes with Berkeley respecting market rights by obtaining a charter for a market to be held in Beverston on Mondays. The rich barons of the Middle Ages attracted so large a number of retainers and followers around them that it was not uncommon for them to obtain such a privilege. But it is plain that there must at this time have been a considerable number of inhabitants, or a market could not have been maintained. At the same time the privilege was granted of holding an annual fair on the Eve, Feast, and Morrow, of the Assumption, that is on August 14th, 15th, and 16th; and the continuance of a fair for three days is also evidence that Beverston was much more

---

[1] "Thomas de Avening persona eccl. de Beverstan," 1292. [*Prynne's Records.* III. 592.]

than a road side village in those distant days. Lord Ap
Adam and his wife appear to have lived without children for
many years, but a son, Thomas, was born to them in the
year 1304. He himself died in 1312, and if his wife survived him it was but for a short time. He sat in the House
of Lords by summons from 1296 to 1309.

Thomas Lord Ap Adam, his young son, thus came to his
inheritance at eight years of age. He was either very unfortunate or very improvident, for his great estates began to
pass away from him as soon as he had reached the age when
they would be under his control. Before he had attained
his twenty-sixth year Beverston was almost his only manor.
Nor could his domestic relations within the bounds of his
narrowed property have been felicitous, for it is recorded that
he had a wife named Margaret, and that in 1332 he found it
necessary to bring a suit in Chancery against Thomas, son
and heir of Hugh de Gournay, for stealing the lady away
from Beverston, together with divers goods and chattels.
About the same time that he thus lost his lady Sir Thomas
Ap Adam also lost the last of his patrimonial Manors, for he
sold Beverston to Thomas, eighth Baron Berkeley; having
thus wrecked a noble inheritance before he had reached the
thirtieth year of his age, and being forced to retire to a small
estate which yet remained to him in Monmouthshire.[1]

---

[1] The descendants of Sir Thomas, last Baron Ap Adam (whether
by the runaway wife or another is not stated) are said to be as
follows: [*Burke's Ext. Peer.; and Record of House of Gurney.*]

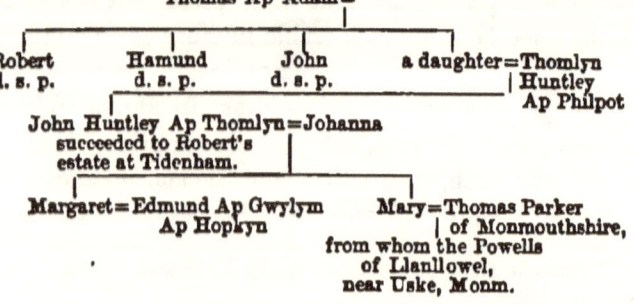

Thomas Ap Adam=

Robert   Hamund   John   a daughter=Thomlyn
d. s. p.   d. s. p.   d. s. p. | Huntley
    Ap Philpot

John Huntley Ap Thomlyn=Johanna
succeeded to Robert's
estate at Tidenham.

Margaret=Edmund Ap Gwylym   Mary=Thomas Parker
    Ap Hopkyn | of Monmouthshire,
from whom the Powells
of Llanllowel,
near Uske, Monm.

By this sale of Beverston Castle and Manor they became again merged, for a few years, in the vast estate of the Berkeleys of Berkeley. This change also brought back to Beverston the blood of the old Saxon Berkeleys of Dursley, for Lord Berkeley was descended from them on the female side as well as from the Fitzhardings on the paternal side. Since Robert Fitzharding's time, hitherto, Beverston had been in the possession of those of his descendants who were not inheritors of the old Berkeley blood. The mixed line of Fitzharding and Berkeley was now represented there for 265 years, from the beginning of the reign of Edward the Third until nearly the end of the reign of Queen Elizabeth.

Few traces remain of the earlier owners of Beverston, or their time. The substructures of the Castle have already been mentioned as being probably the work of Maurice de Gaunt in the early half of the twelfth century. The arcade of transitional Norman pillars which divides the Nave of the Church from the aisle, the doorway under the Porch, and a figure of our Lord with the resurrection banner in his hand, which has been inserted into the south wall of the Tower, are also of the same age. Of a rather later date are some stone coffin covers, incised with crosses, which have been built up (probably in the fourteenth century) into the south wall of the Nave, and the west wall of the Berkeley Chapel. The base of a circular tower of solid rubble masonry, 24 feet in diameter, was also discovered in 1873 in the Rectory Kitchen Garden, opposite to the west face of the great Tower of the Castle, and 37 yards distant from it. This seems to be a relic of the more ancient Castle, and shews that at some time the buildings extended much further than they do at present. Some large chamfered stones were also found under the Rectory lawn, and their position seemed to indicate the presence of a gate of a similar age.[1]

---

[1] The present Rectory has upon it the date 1729, and a much older house which was called the Rectory used formerly—forty or fifty years ago—to stand nearly where the School-house now stands.

Thomas, eighth Lord Berkeley, and third of the name of
Thomas, was directly descended from Maurice the son of
Robert Fitzhardinge, and Alice the daughter of the last
Berkeley Lord of Dursley, being thus the representative of
the elder branch of the Fitzhardings and also of the ancient
Berkeleys.[1]

All the Berkeleys had, at this time, joined the party of
the Queen and Mortimer against Edward II. Maurice, the
seventh Lord Berkeley, had been taken prisoner by the King's
army, and died a prisoner in Wallingford Castle, in the year
1326. His son and successor, Thomas, the purchaser of
Beverston, had also been imprisoned by the King at Berk-
hampstead, in the Tower, and at Pevensey Castle, for five
years before his father's death; but the latter event occuring
about the same time that the Queen's power had reached its .
ascendant, he and other rebels of distinction had been released
and restored to their estates.   On the capture of the King the
unfortunate Sovereign was committed to the custody of Lord
Berkeley, Sir Thomas de Gournay, and Sir John Maltravers;

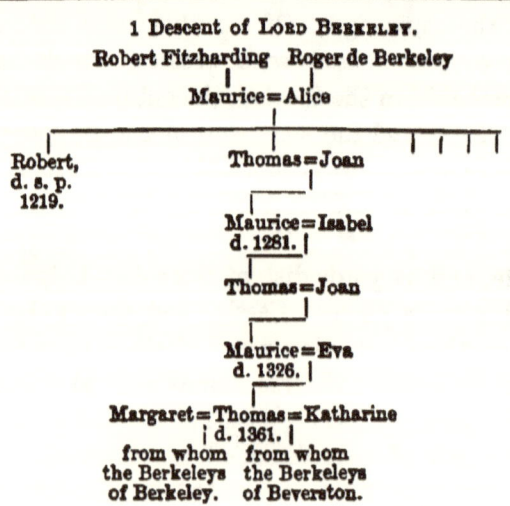

1 Descent of LORD BERKELEY.

Robert Fitzharding   Roger de Berkeley

Maurice = Alice

Robert,   Thomas = Joan
d. s. p.
1219.
                   Maurice = Isabel
                   d. 1281.

                   Thomas = Joan

                   Maurice = Eva
                   d. 1326.

Margaret = Thomas = Katharine
         d. 1361.
from whom   from whom
the Berkeleys the Berkeleys
of Berkeley. of Beverston.

and after having been imprisoned for some time at Kenilworth
and Corfe Castles, he was brought to Berkeley Castle on April
15th, 1327.   Lord Berkeley's treatment of his prisoner not
being sufficiently severe for the purpose which the wretched
Queen and her paramour Mortimer had in view, he was relieved of his office of gaoler, and then retired to his house at
Wotton-under-Edge, where he was residing,   or is said to
have been so, at the time of Edward IInd's barbarous murder, on September 21st, 1327.   In the reign of Edward III.
Lord Berkeley was put upon his trial for the King's murder,
and he was not finally acquitted until 1338.

Meanwhile he was improving his estates, farming on a
very large scale,[1] making enclosures, buying and exchanging
lands.   He was also a great fox hunter, remaining out four
nights and days together hunting foxes with nets and dogs.

Among his purchases of land were Lord Ap Adam's
Manors of Over[2] and Beverston, the latter in 1331.   The

---

[1] It is noticed of him that he used to frequent the fairs at Gloucester
and Tetbury, buying seeds for his farms and transacting the ordinary
business of a large farmer.   In 1334 he sheared 5775 sheep in Beverston for the Stroudwater woollen manufactories ; and he reared vast
numbers of pigeons, part of one of his great pigeon houses still standing near the Barbican of the Castle.

[2] Over had been in the possession of the Gournays and Ap Adams
as long as Beverston, and was purchased by Lord Berkeley in 1330 in
the name of himself and his wife Margaret.   In 1361 it was in the
possession of his widow Catharine, but it went regularly with the
Beverston estate until Sir William Berkeley was attainted in the first
Parliament of Richard III., 1483.   It was then granted to Thomas
Brian by whom it was conveyed to John Poyntz.   His son, Robert,
had a daughter Alice who married Sir Edward Berkeley, and thus
carried Over back again.

John Poyntz=
┌───┘
Robert=
┌───┘
Alice=Sir Edward Berkeley

The last of the Berkeleys of Beverston sold Over to John Daniel of
Bristol.

reign of Edward III. was an age of building, and among other work of his very active life Lord Berkeley rebuilt the Castle and the Church of Beverston, not destroying, however, the whole of the work of his predecessors in either building. Leland, writing about two centuries afterwards, says that he had been told by "olde Sir William" (who was the great great grandson of Lord Berkeley), that this rebuilding of the Castle was paid for by means of the ransoms which his ancestor obtained for the prisoners taken by him at the battle of Poictiers, which took place in 1356.[1] This story is not quite consistent with the fact that his eldest son, Maurice, being taken prisoner at Poictiers remained a prisoner in France until his father's death in 1361, because the 6000 nobles required for his ransom could not be raised.[2] But no doubt the greater part of the existing fabrics, both of the Church and Castle, are of the date thus assigned to them. Bigland says that in his time the arms of Lord Berkeley were to be seen in the East Window of the Chancel. The walls of the Church were also decorated with paintings of the Resurrection and Last Judgment, the Mass of St. Gregory, and St. Christopher, which were discovered and destroyed at the "restoration" of the fabric, when the interior face of the walls was entirely covered with a thick coating of Roman Cement.

The reconstruction of the Castle by Lord Berkeley left it a fine quadrangular structure, with—so tradition states—four Towers (though only two now remain) a Barbican, a large Banqueting Hall on the site now occupied by the dwelling house of the Castle Farm, and a Moat immediately under the walls of the Towers and Curtains. Perhaps also

---

[1] *Leland's Itin.* vj. 68. Leland tells a precisely similar story respecting Farley Castle, Somersetshire, which, he says, was built "by the prey of the Duke of Orleans, whom one of the Hungerfords had taken prisoner." [*Itin.* ij. 32, 33.]

[2] *Cooke's Berkeleys*, p. 24.

the circular Tower discovered in the Rectory Kitchen Garden was one of several by which an enclosing wall was guarded which would take in many external buildings, such as the barns, of which two still existing are handsome specimens of fourteenth century work. The western face of this Edwardian Castle still remains, consisting of a large square tower 34 ft. by 30 ft., at the southern end, a smaller one 24 ft. square set angularly at the northern end, and a curtain between them containing roomy galleries, the whole side extending to 123 feet. The distance from the outside of this face to the outside of the Barbican is 165 feet; the whole area of the Castle within the Moat may thus be reckoned at 2255 square yards, and the court yard must have been of small dimensions.

The great tower at the southern end of the west side consists of three storeys, and is 60 feet in height. The lower storey formed an entry and a guard room, the latter being lighted by a beautiful ogee headed window which remains extremely perfect, as may be seen from the bank of the Moat. The ascent from the entry is by a newell staircase in an octagonal turret, which seems to have been added on to the main tower in a very insecure manner. The large chamber above the guard room and entry was probably appropriated originally to domestic use, but turned into a Chapel early in the fifteenth century; two sedilia and a piscina having been added, which are elaborately carved in a shallow and rather debased style of art. Another large chamber occupies the tower above this, forming the third storey: and northward of this is the more ancient Chapel, which is situated in the curtain, and beyond which is another chamber nearly as large as that in the tower. There are double slits or squints on both sides of this Chapel, so that although it is not large enough to hold a dozen persons more than a hundred could be accommodated in the chambers on either side, most of whom could obtain a view of the altar through these squints, and all could distinctly hear the service which was going on . there.

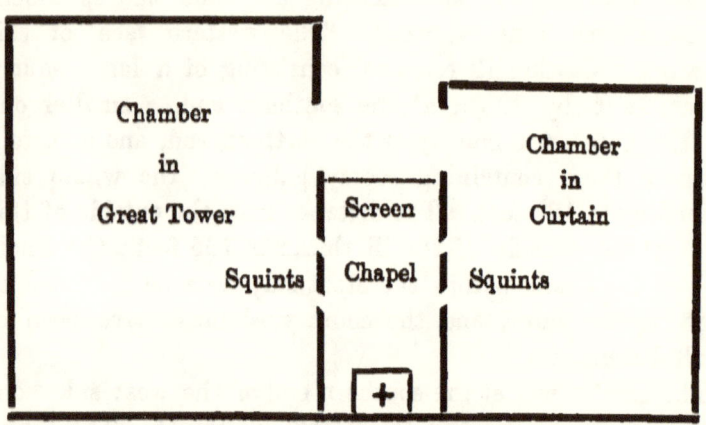

The only trace of the Great Hall is the mark of the weather table on the inner wall of the Curtain adjoining the great Tower. Below this is the roof of the present dwelling-house, which was built at the end of the seventeenth century. There is reason to think that the dwelling-house which preceded this, and which was burned down, was the Great Hall itself divided by floors and partitions. Half of the great Dormitory Hall at Durham was in a similar way occupied as a Canon's residence for several generations, and until 20 years ago, when the whole was added to the Library.

A noble gallery which, with the narrow passage between its western wall and the exterior wall of the Castle, occupied the second storey of the curtain is now roughly divided and used as store rooms for farm produce. A handsome stone chimney piece of 18th century workmanship shews how recently it was used. Beneath it on the level of the court-yard are vaulted offices, which are now used as dairy and brewhouse. Lower still is the only underground portion of the Castle, a gloomy "dungeon" which lies immediately under the west end of the upper Chapel. This vault, whatever its use may really have been, is entered by a door near the guard room.

The northern or angular Tower has nothing remaining of its interior divisions except the vaulting of the floor chamber which is used as a coal cellar. Above this vaulting the tower is gutted to the roof, which itself is modern. If there was ever a curtain on this northern side of the Castle not a trace of it remains, nor is there any of the other two towers which are said to have completed the square of the fortress. Such as they are, however, the remains of Beverston Castle are a noble memorial of the great Castle building age of the Edwards; and they shew that Lord Berkeley was a man of large resources and liberal taste.

Lord Berkeley was twice married; first to Margaret, daughter of Roger, Lord Mortimer, and mother of the ninth Lord Berkeley. She died in 1337, and was buried in a Chantry founded for the purpose in St. Augustine's Abbey, Bristol, and which is now known as the Berkeley Chapel, in the Cathedral. Ten years afterwards, in 1347, Lord Berkeley married for his second wife Catharine, daughter of Sir John Clyvedon, and widow of Sir Peter le Veel. Of four sons by the first wife, only one, Maurice, survived his father: and of four sons by his second wife only the youngest, John. Maurice became Lord Berkeley in succession to his father, while John was settled down in a younger son's inheritance at Beverston, becoming to a race of Berkeleys there what Robert de Weare had been to the Fitzharding branches represented by the De Gaunts, De Gournays, and Ap Adams. The father of both these Berkeleys, who may be fairly called the great Lord Berkeley, died on October 27th, 1361, and lies buried in the Parish Church at Berkeley. His widow acted as guardian to her son and manager of his Beverston Manor during his minority. She afterwards married a third husband, Sir John de Thorp, and seems to have survived him also, for dying at Wotton-under-Edge in 1385, she was carried to Berkeley and buried there by the side of her second husband, Lord Berkeley.

The young son of Lord Berkeley, therefore, afterwards Sir John Berkeley, inherited the Beverston estate as once more independent of the Berkeley estate, and the two have never again been united. He was born on January 21st, 1352, and was baptized on the second day after his birth, the Prior of Bath and Sir John Tracy being his godfathers, while the Lady Joan, wife of Sir Thomas le Boteler was his godmother. He was thus under ten years of age at his father's death. During the lifetime of his mother he remained unmarried, but after her death, when he was about thirty-three years of age he found a wife of seventeen in the daughter and heiress of Sir John Bettisthorne, of Bettisthorne or Bistherne, in the parish of Ringwood, Hants, on the south-western edge of the New Forest. By this marriage the large property of the Berkeleys of Beverston became still larger, and it is said to have then exceeded in extent that of the elder branch. Sir John Bettesthorne,[1] of Bettesthorne, Chadwick, and Gillingham,

---

[1] His wife is called Lady Goda by Smyth. He was knighted in the year 1386, when he must have been over fifty years of age. The brass on his tomb at Mere is engraved in *Hoare's Wiltshire, Mere*, pl. III. 12; and in *Boutell's Brasses;* as also in *Kite*, p. 22. The Bettesthornes are not traceable beyond John, the father [d. 1380] of Sir John; who came in for large estates at Shaftesbury and elsewhere through failure in the male line of the De Grimstead family. In 1404 Sir John Berkeley claimed in right of his wife the Manors of Plaitford, Alberstone, More, Alwardbury, Farley, the moiety of East and West Grimstead, and the advowson of the Church of More. At the same time he also held the Crown Moiety of the Manor of Shaftesbury, the other being held by the Abbess. [*Hoare's Wilts., Frustfield*, 49., *Hutchinson's Dorset.*, ij. 400.] Sir Maurice his son held the same Manors at his death in 1460. In 1641 and until 1650 "Sir Edward Berkeley's land called Benjafield" in the parish of Gillingham was sequestered. This seems to have been Sir Edward of Pille.

died on February 1st, 1399, and was buried on February 6th, at Mere in a Chantry Chapel belonging to his estate of Chadwick, afterwards known till the Dissolution as the Berkeley Chantry. The jurors on the inquisitio post mortem found that Elizabeth, wife of Sir John Berkeley of Beverston was his daughter and nearest heir, and was then aged thirty years or more. She thus brought Bistherne and all the other manors belonging to her father to her husband, and Sir John Berkeley did homage for these lands as hers in 1389 [*Esch.* 22, *Rich. II.*, No. 6. *Rot, Fin.* ib m. 11]. It is curious that among the waste land in the Manor of Bistherne there is a portion named " Berkele," although there does not appear to have been any connection between the families previously.

Sir John Berkeley occupied an important position both in Hampshire and Gloucestershire, and also in Wiltshire. He was at one time or another returned to Parliament for each of these counties, and was also Sheriff for one or other of them no less than nine times. For his native County he was Sheriff in the years 1393, 1398, and 1413. In 1396 he received a general pardon for having joined the rebellion of the Duke of Gloucester and the Earl of Arundel.

By Lady Elizabeth of Bettesthorne Sir John Berkeley had a son named Maurice and a daughter named Anne.[1] Their

---

[1] This daughter Anne is named in a grant of livery of his lands to Sir William Berkeley by Henry VIII., dated August 21st, 1522. Sir William is there said to be "kinsman and heir of John Berkeley and his daughter Anne." Another daughter was Eleanor, whose first husband was John Fitz-Alan, Lord Maltravers [d. 1423]. They had a son who was created Lord Arundel of Wardour (and was nominally 12th Earl of Arundel) and Eleanor received the courtesy title of Countess Dowager of Arundel. Her third husband was Sir Walter Hungerford of Heytesbury, by whom she had no children. [*Hoare's Wilts.*, *Heytsb.* 91, 221.] Hoare calls her daughter and co-heir of Sir John Berkeley. She married for a second husband Sir Richard Poynyngs. A third daughter, Elizabeth, was married first to Edward

mother appears to have died early, as Sir John married for a second wife Elinor, daughter of Sir Robert de Ashton, and for a third Margaret, widow of Sir Thomas Braose of Tetbury. Smyth says that he had fourteen sons and two daughters, but it does not appear that any more survived him than Maurice and Anne. He died in the year 1427, his last wife surviving him until 1444.

Sir Maurice Berkeley, the son and successor of Sir John, was knighted during his father's lifetime, and at the death of the latter was about thirty years of age. He married Laura the fourth daughter of Henry, third Lord Fitzhugh, and of Alice Neville, and sister to Robert Fitzhugh who was Bishop of London from 1431 until 1436. The mother of Lady Berkeley was daughter to the great Earl of Salisbury who was taken prisoner and beheaded at the battle of Wakefield, and sister to the still greater Earl of Warwick the " King-maker," the last of those wealthy and powerful Norman nobles whose arrogance sometimes aimed at enslaving the Crown itself. Her father, Lord Fitzhugh, appears in history under a gentler aspect. He held high office at court in the reigns of Henry IV. and Henry V., was entrusted with the care of Princess Philippa when she was sent to Denmark to become the wife of Eric XIII. of Sweden and VII. of Denmark, under whom the three Scandinavian Crowns were united ; and was Constable of England during the Coronation of Henry V. While in Denmark and Sweden in the year

---

Charlton, Lord Powis, and secondly to John Sutton, K.G., 4th Lord Dudley. Their grandson was the Edmund Dudley, executed with Empson by Henry VIII.: their great grandson, the Duke of Northumberland who acted as Regent in the minority of Edward VI.; their great great grandson the Lord Guildford Dudley who was the husband of Lady Jane Grey. The arms of Dudley and Berkeley of Beverston were formerly in a window of the Church of Deritend, a suburb of Birmingham. [*Dugdale's Warw.* 882.]

1406, Fitzhugh became acquainted with some Nuns of the Order founded not long before by a noble Swedish lady since known as St. Bridget, and on his return to England he made arrangements for carrying out an engagement he had entered into with them, to establish a branch of their Order in England, on his property at Hinton near Cambridge.[1] Eventually, however, they were established as one of the two latest Monasteries founded in England, those which Henry V. set up in 1415 in memory of his father at Sheen (now Richmond) and Isleworth. The latter, the Brigittine establishment, was the famous Nunnery of Sion, which was transferred after the Reformation to Portugal and still maintains itself as a community of English ladies; the name of the old Nunnery being retained for the Duke of Northumberland's house which stands upon its site Sion was endowed with many of the manors belonging to the Alien Priories, which were dissolved by Henry V. at the beginning of that war which ended at Agincourt: and among these were Avening, Nailsworth, Minchinhampton, and others near Beverston; together with Cheltenham, which was held of the Nuns of Sion on lease by Sir Maurice Berkeley the son of Laura Fitzhugh in 1464.[2]

Succeeding his father Sir John in 1427 Sir Maurice Berkeley became Sheriff of Gloucestershire in the years 1429, 1434, and 1435. He and his wife Laura had two sons,

---

[1] The Manor of Hinton eventually passed into the hands of Mowbray the first Duke of Norfolk. His daughter Isabel inherited it with many other Manors as her moiety of her father's lands. From her it passed to her son, the Marquess of Berkeley, and it was sold by Thomas Lord Berkeley, early in the reign of Henry VIII., to Robert Fewrother, Goldsmith (and Usurer) of London, for 800 marks, being then stated to be worth £32 a year. [*Smyth.*]

[2] For fuller particulars respecting Sion see the present writer's Introduction to his edition of "Oure Ladye's Myroure," a devotional work written for the Nuns of Sion about 1450: and now printed among the Early English Text Society's Works.

Maurice and Edward, both of whom survived him, and both
of whom eventually succeeded to the great estates left by
their grandfather Sir John in Gloucestershire, Hampshire,
and Wiltshire.

Sir Maurice Berkeley resided much at Bistherne, which
was probably a much pleasanter abode than his grim Castle
on the bleak Cotteswolds.[1] A singular tradition still lingers
at Bistherne respecting the slaughter of a Dragon, which is
connected with the name of this Sir Maurice by a document
preserved in the Evidence room at Berkeley Castle. The
local tradition is to the effect that a Dragon had his den at
Burley Beacon, about five miles from Bistherne, in a part of
Burley known as Bistherne Closes. Thence the creature
" flew " every morning to Bistherne for a supply of milk.
Here a valiant man built himself a hut, and with two dogs
lay in wait for the Dragon, keeping the dogs out of his sight
also. The innocent creature came as usual one morning for
his milk, when the hut door was opened, the dogs let fly at
him, and while he was thus engaged with them, he was
" shot " by the man. The dogs were killed on the spot,
apparently under the idea that they had become dangerous
through being bitten by the Dragon.[2] The Dragon slayer himself, says another version of the tradition (which seems to

---

[1] In 1455 " Mauricius Berkeley Miles " is one of the Commissioners
for Southamptonshire for raising money for the defence of Calais.
[*Acts of Privy Council*, vj. 240.]

On Ap. 16, year uncertain, " Mauricius Berkeley de Beverstone
Miles " is summoned as a Privy Councillor for May 21st. [*Ibid.* 341.]

[2] One of Lord Durham's ancestors slew a " Worm of Lambton,"
and was directed beforehand by a wise woman to cover his armour
with knife blades. He also slew his favourite hound immediately
afterwards, though the legend does not represent the latter as taking
any part in the encounter.

A great serpent is also heard of in the parish of Coberley in Gloucestershire, a parish in which a younger branch of the old Saxon
Berkeleys had their home until the fifteenth century.

come from nearer the fifteenth century), only succeeded in overcoming his foe by covering his armour with glass. The locality of the fight still goes by the name of "Dragon Fields."

The documentary version of this tradition is contained in the margin of a pedigree roll written previously to 1618, and preserved, as already said, in the Evidence room at Berkeley Castle. It is as follows :—

"Sᴿ Moris Barkley the sonne of Sᴿ John Barkley, of Beverston, beinge a man of great strength and courage, in his tyme there was bread in Hampshire neere Bistherne a devouring Dragon, who doing much mischief upon men and cattell and could not be 'destroyed but spoiled many in attempting it, making his den neere unto a Beacon. This Sᴿ Moris Barkley armed himself and encountered with it and at length overcam and killed it but died himself soone after. This is the common saying even to this day in those parts of Hampshire, and the better to approve the same his children and posterity even to this present do beare for their creast a Dragon standing before a burning beacon. Wch seemeth the rather more credible because Sᴿ Morice Barkley did beare the Miter with this authentick seale of his armes as is heare underneath one of his own deedes exprest bearing date yᵉ 10 of Henry 6. An Dni 1431."

This singular legend, the latest of the kind perhaps, is not without archæological memorial. It has already been mentioned that the "Dragon Fields" are still pointed out as the scene of the encounter. The village Inn of Bistherne (suppressed in 1873), likewise rejoiced in the sign of the "Green Dragon," green being the colour assigned to the dragon of the crest in a MS. at Berkeley on which the later bearing of Berkeley of Beverston is pourtrayed. The Beacon and Dragon both occur in a carving which remains on the front of Bistherne House, above the arms of Berkeley and

Bettisthorne, and with the date 1652. But a much older, and almost contemporary memorial of the Crest is preserved in the East Window of the adjoining Church of Sopley, between Ringwood and Christ Church, where there are two fragments of stained glass, the one containing the arms of Sir Edward Berkeley, the younger son of this Sir Maurice, and the other a representation of a burning Beacon, with the motto "So have I cause." The motto without the beacon is carved on a stone at Avon, in Sopley parish, the stone being built into a smithy which represents that at which Sir Walter Tyrrell shot his horse during his flight from the New Forest after shooting William Rufus. Both Beacon and motto appear also on a brass of a kneeling knight and lady which is said to have been brought from Netley Abbey to Romsey Abbey, and to be of sixteenth century date. [*Archæologia* xv. 302.] The Beacon is, further, the Crest of the Marquess of Northampton, who is descended from Werburga, the great grand-daughter of Sir Maurice Berkeley, and the supporters of the Northampton arms are dragons.

Upon the whole it seems likely that this Dragon legend is founded on some fact. It may have been some wild beast not now known in England which was encountered on the borders of the Forest by Sir Maurice Berkeley. Or perhaps it was some huge serpent against whose coils broken glass was used as a protection, and a local correspondent suggests that the Forest adder would probably grow to a very large size if it ever had a chance of living for a few years. Or "Dragon" may be the form which some mad animal took in popular legend, the danger of whose bite is indicated by the slaughter of the dogs and the rapidly following death of the knight himself.

To come from misty legend to clear historical fact, it is known that Sir Maurice Berkeley died in the year 1460.

He is supposed to have been buried in the chapel of the
Dominican Priory at Bristol, of which the Register, as
quoted by William of Worcester, contains an entry " Dominus
Mauricius Berkley, miles, obiit 26 die novembris." In the
nineteenth century a gentleman who had slain a Dragon
would be a national celebrity, and we should certainly
provide posterity with full particulars respecting him. The
fifteenth century, at least in 1460, had no printing presses,
and was much more sparing than we are in the use of the
pen. Yet men who slay Dragons of any kind are so useful
to their country, that one cannot but wish history had told
us more clearly the particulars both of the noxious Dragons
and of the brave knights who slew them.

The next Berkeley of Beverston was also a Maurice, son
to the dragon slayer and Laura Fitzhugh. He was born in
in the year 1434, and was married in very early life to Anne
daughter of Reginald West, Lord de la Warr. Sir Maurice
served as Sheriff of Gloucestershire in 1463 and 1471, and
was Knight of the Shire for the same county in the Parliament of 1469.[1] In the year following he was joined with
Lord Berkeley in a Commission for raising troops in Gloucestershire on behalf of Edward IV. in the contest which ended

---

[1] Lord Stourton, Sir Maurice Berkeley "Knight of our body " and
Sir John Cheyney "Esquire of our body," were appointed Commissioners by King Edward IV. to arrange a dispute between the
Corporation and the Bishop of Salisbury respecting an oath which
the former were accustomed to take to the latter. In the end the
Commissioners decided that the Episcopal claim was a just one,
but the Crown smoothed over the difficulty by apppointing the Bishop
a Commissioner to receive the oath on behalf of its august Self:
this final decision being dated December 19th, 1461. [*Hutchinson's
Dorsetshire*, **ij**, 400]

As will be seen, there was a close connection between the Stourtons
and the Berkeleys of Beverston, and their arms stand side by side in
the chancel screen of Mere Church. [*Hoare's Wiltsh. Mere*, 10]

with the battles of Barnet and Tewkesbury. He died at the age of forty in 1474, but yet appears to have survived his wife. Both of them were buried in the Lady Chapel of Christ Church, Hampshire, that Chapel having been founded by Sir Thomas West, ancestor of Lady Berkeley. This second Sir Maurice, left, as his father had done before him, a son and a daughter, the one being named William and the other Katharine.

Katharine Berkeley was married, in the first instance, to John, Lord Stourton, by whom she had no children. Her second husband was Sir John Brereton, to whom she gave an only daughter Werberga or Warborough, who became the ancestress of the Marquesses of Northampton.

Sir William Berkeley, born in 1451, was Sheriff of Hampshire in the years 1476 and 1480; and also of Somersetshire and Dorsetshire in 1477. He was Esquire of the body to Edward VI., and is said to have held other and greater employments at Court. His wife was Lady Katharine Grey, daughter of Lord Stourton, his sister and he thus marrying brother and sister. Sir William Berkeley was mixed up with the rebellion of the Duke of Buckingham against Richard III., and on the discomfiture of the party fled to the Earl of Richmond in Brittany. [*Polydore Vergil*, 200.] He was among those who were attainted in the first Parliament of Richard III. [*Rot. Parl.* vj. 245], and doubtless remained abroad during the whole of that reign. In 1485 the Earl of Richmond secured the Crown as Henry VII., and restored Sir William Berkeley of Beverston to his estates, but he did not live to return to them, dying of sweating sickness about the same time that Henry settled himself on the throne.[1] He died without children, and probably abroad, his wife surviving him.

---

[1] A cousin of the same name, Sir William Berkeley of Stoke Gifford, but mostly called of Weley Castle, Worcestershire, took the oppo-

The younger son of Laura and Sir Maurice, and uncle of the Sir William just spoken of, had held the Hampshire estates during the life of his elder brother Maurice, and of his nephew; and was Sheriff of Hampshire in the year 1471, and member for the County in 1468. On the death of his nephew in 1485 Sir Edward Berkeley succeeded to Beverston and the other Gloucestershire estates, but those in Hampshire passed away to his niece Katharine, the wife of Sir John Brereton. Their daughter Werburgh was first married to Sir Francis Cheyney, by whom she had no children, and secondly to Sir William Compton, Groom of the Bedchamber to Henry VIII., by whom she was the ancestress of the Northampton family.[1] The Bistherne estates were thus separated from those of Beverston, and in 1634 were settled on Sir Henry Compton, younger son of Lord Compton and first cousin of the first Lord Northampton, from whom they passed to the husband of his female descendant, who took the name of Compton.

Sir Edward Berkeley thus migrated from Bistherne to Beverston, where doubtless he had been born, and in 1493

site side, and after a prosperous career during the short reign of Richard III. was attainted by the Parliament of that King's successor in 1485. All his estates were granted in tail male on March 2, 1486, to Jasper, Duke of Bedford, the uncle of Henry VII. but with remainder to Sir William; and as the Duke of Bedford died childless the proper owner soon regained them. [*Record Off. Materials illustr. reign of Henry* VII. 335.]

Camden states that there was a custom peculiar to Gloucestershire that when the estates of condemned persons were forfeited to the Crown it was only for a year and a day, after which they were restored to the proper heir. Bishop Gibson remarks on this that the custom was lost by desuetude in his time. [*Gibson's Camden's Britannia*. 231, 246.]

[1] The pedigree of her descendants down to Henry Compton of Bistherne [ob. s. p. 1724,] and his wife ...... Willis of Ringwood, is given in *Hoare's Wiltshire, Frustfield*, 49.

he became Sheriff of Gloucestershire.[1]   His first wife was
Christian Holt, daughter and heir of Richard Holt, Esquire,
of ——. They had an only daughter to whom the name
of her Fitzhugh grandmother, Laura, was given, and who
was eventually married to Sir John Blunt, afterwards third
Lord Mountjoy and Governor of Guisnes.[2]   The second wife
of Sir Edward Berkeley was Alice daughter of Sir John
Poyntz; by whom he had three sons, Thomas, Maurice, and
William. He is said by Smyth to have been employed in
great offices of trust, but what these were is not stated. He
died in the year 1505, and his widow Alice in 1509, two
of his three sons ultimately succeeding to Beverston.

The eldest of these three sons, Sir Thomas Berkeley, married into the great Durham family of Neville, his wife being
Elizabeth daughter of the second Lord Abergavenney. Her
arms are impaled with those of Berkeley of Beverston in a
fragment of coloured glass that remains opposite to the Beacon
crest in the East window of Sopley Church, perhaps marking
some benefaction to the Church or the foundation of a

---

[1] On September 12th, 1485, Sir Edward Berkeley's name is in the
list of Sheriffs for Southamptonshire. On December 5th of that
year there is an indication that he was leaving Bistherne, Thomas
Westbury receiving a grant for life of the office of Bailiff or Forester
[Verderer] of Burley in the New Forest " with wages, &c., such as
Edward Berkeley had in the same office." [*Materials illustrative of
reign of* H. VII. *Rec. Off.* p. 195.] Yet on Dec. 11th, 1485, there is
a similar grant to Edward Berkeley, Esq., with wages of 6 pence a
day out of the issues of the County. [*Ibid.* 212.]

[2] Her descendants were as follows :—

Laura Berkeley=John Blunt, 3rd Lord Mountjoy

William 4th Lord Mountjoy.	Rowland d. s. p. 1509.	Laura d. 1480.	Sir Thomas Tyrrell=Constantia
			from whom the Tyrrells of Heron, Essex. [This is the Sir Thomas Tyrrell of whom Sir Thomas More says, that being Master of the Horse to Richard III. he was sent to murder the two Princes in the Tower.]

Chantry there, or perhaps as one of the alliances of the Lady Werburgh Compton who was then in possession of Bistherne in the neighbouring parish of Ringwood. Lady Elizabeth died in the year 1500 leaving no children. Her arms are, however, impaled with a coat, which is not that of Berkeley, in an old window now in the hall at Chavenage, and probably removed there from Beverston Castle. Sir Thomas was living in 1521, when he was Sheriff of Gloucestershire, and at his death he left behind him three married daughters, and a son aged six years, who became the King's ward, but who died in his youth.

Maurice, the second of Sir Edward's three sons, had died without children on September 9th, 1513. On the death of the young John Berkeley, therefore, the Manors of Beverston, Over, &c., went to William the third son of Sir Edward. Livery of his lands was granted to Sir William Berkeley by the Crown on August 21st, 1522, in which there is a clause stating that it is granted notwithstanding a false Inquisition which had been made at Gloucester in 1509. This refers, perhaps, to some transaction connected with the death of his mother, Alice, the widow of Sir Edward, who died in that year. Sir William Berkeley married Margaret, daughter of the great William Paulett, Marquis of Winchester and Lord High Treasurer to Edward VI. and the Queens Mary and Elizabeth. He died in the year 1552, leaving two sons, John and Edward, and several other children.

The sedilia in the lower chapel of the Castle appear to be of the date of Sir William Berkeley, and he is the "old Sir William" named by Leland as giving him the information that his ancestor Lord Berkeley had repaired the Castle of Beverston with the ransom of his Poictiers prisoners.

Sir John Berkeley, the son and successor of "old Sir William," married Frances, daughter of Sir Nicholas Poyntz of Iron Acton, by whom he had one son and three daughters.

He was one of the Knights of the Bath who were created at the Coronation of Queen Elizabeth on January 13th, 1558-59. His wife, Frances, died at Beverston, the Parish Register containing the entry, "1576. ffrances Barkeley the wife and ladie of Sir John Barkeley, Knight, and lord of Beverston, was buried the xxvijth day of August 1576, A.R.R Elizabeth. 18°."[1] He married again, but Smyth says of the second wife that she had no children and that her ungoverned life made her unworthy of a memorial in the few pages which he has dedicated to the Beverston branch of the Berkeleys. This second wife of Sir John Berkeley seems to be the lady referred to in a Domestic State Paper dated December 3rd, 1623. This is an answer put in by Dame Elizabeth, widow of Sir Michael Hicks and her son Sir William Hicks to a petition presented by Dame Alice, widow of Sir John Berkeley of Beverston. In this petition Lady Berkeley set forth a claim to an annuity of £20 a year from the Manor of Beverston, and the answer denies that the Manor was ever subject to such a payment; adding that if ever there was such a charge Dame Alice had made it void by her own act and bond. [*St. Pap. Dom. James* I.] Although Sir John was a man of ability and respectability he succeeded in ruining his property,

---

[1] His name occurs in the Parish Register in the year 1573, in the following entry. "John Brewer ye sonne of William Brewer was baptized ye xxijth of November. Godfathers Sir John Barkeley, Knight, and Richard Marloe." In a later year 1575, there is an entry stating that William Bartlett, servant to Sir John Berkeley, Knight, was married to Ann Bristol on May 19th. Also nine months later [o.s.] 1575 "ffrances Bartlett ye daughter of William Bartlett was baptized ye xth of March. Godfather Jo: Pierce. Godmothers ye Ladie ffrances Barkley and Isabel White."

1580 Mr. Edward Barkley was Godfather to Edward Bartlett on Aug. 10th, Mr. John Barkley to John Collman on Oct. 5th, as he had been to Agnes Brewer on Oct. 26th, 1579.

by what means is not known. He died in 1581, but there is no record of his burial in the Parish Register.

Of his three daughters Joan the eldest became a Benedictine Nun of St. Peter's, Rheims, at the age of twenty-five, in the year 1581. She was very instrumental in establishing the first English Nunnery abroad, one that was founded at Brussels, but removed to Winchester at the French Revolution. Of this Belgian Nunnery Joan Berkeley became Abbess on November 4th, 1599, and she died in office on August 2nd, 1616, at the age of sixty-one. Of the second daughter the Parish Register gives us one glance—" 1595. Tho. Simmons clericus and Katharine Barkeley gentlewoman were joyned together in marriage ye xxviijth day of Aprill 1595." A similar glance is also obtained of the third daughter,—" Jasper Merrick m^r of artes and minister and Margaret Barkeley gentlewoman were coupled together in matrimonie ye xxist of August anno predicto," that is in 1595. Mr. Simmons was Rector of Cowley, Glouc., and had a son Thomas to inherit the blood of the Berkeleys. Mr. Merrick was Rector of Great Barrington, and had a daughter named Sybil. But the fortunes of this once wealthy family had fallen very low when two daughters of the house, in such days as those of Elizabeth, were permitted to marry two country. Rectors, men who held positions of no wealth or distinction in their profession, and appear never to have risen higher.

The only son of Sir John, who was also named John, married Mary,[1] the daughter of John Snell, Esq. In the

---

[1] "Marie Berkeley, gentlewoman," was godmother to Marie Bartlett in 1586, and to Marie Turner in 1591. "Mistress Katharine Barkeley," was godmother to Sara Pope in 1583. Margaret Barkeley, gentlewoman, was godmother to John Nicolas in 1590. It seems to have been a kindly habit for members of the family to become Sponsors for the children of their married servants; there being as many as eleven entries of their names in such a capacity between 1573 and 1591.

year 1597, after sixteen years' possession of Beverston he sold the Castle and Manor, the last of his family's lands and possessions,[1] to Sir John Poyntz. Twenty-three years afterwards, in 1620, Sir John Berkeley[1] went to Virginia, perhaps at the invitation of Lord Delawarr the Governor, and with the object of retrieving his fortunes in a new country of which Englishmen had already great hopes. But the Berkeleys of Beverston had got on the ebb tide of fortune, and Sir John had only been in Virginia a few months when he formed one of a party who were massacred in one of those encounters with the Indians which led to the loss of so many among the early settlers there.

This last of Berkeleys who ever possessed Beverston Castle had five sons and four daughters. The eldest son, Maurice, married Barbara, daughter of Sir Walter Long, and had a son named Edward, with other children. One of the daughters was named Frances, and her baptism led to the last local record of the association between her family and their old Castle, the entry in the Parish Register being that in 1596 " ffrances Barkeley the daughter of John Barkeley of Beverston, Esquier, was baptized ye xxixth daye of Auguste. Godfather Jasper Merrick, gent. Godmothers Emē Estcourt of Shipton, gent., Elizabeth miles of Elmestree, gent." [2] But no further trace has, at present, been discovered of the descendants of this great family since they left their ancient home at Beverston.

---

[1] The Berkeleys of Beverston are said to have possessed 22 Manors in Gloucestershire. Beverston, Over, Cam, Woodmancote, King's Weston, Cromhall, Ailberton, Bentham, Charfield, Compton Greenfiat, are among those which are attributed to them.

[2] He is spoken of by Smyth as "Sir" John, but as late as Aug. 29th, 1596, when his daughter Frances was baptized, he is called "John Barkeley of Beverston, Esquier," in the Parish Register. In three cases where he stood Godfather he is called Mr. John Berkeley, these being in 1578, 1579, and 1591.

135

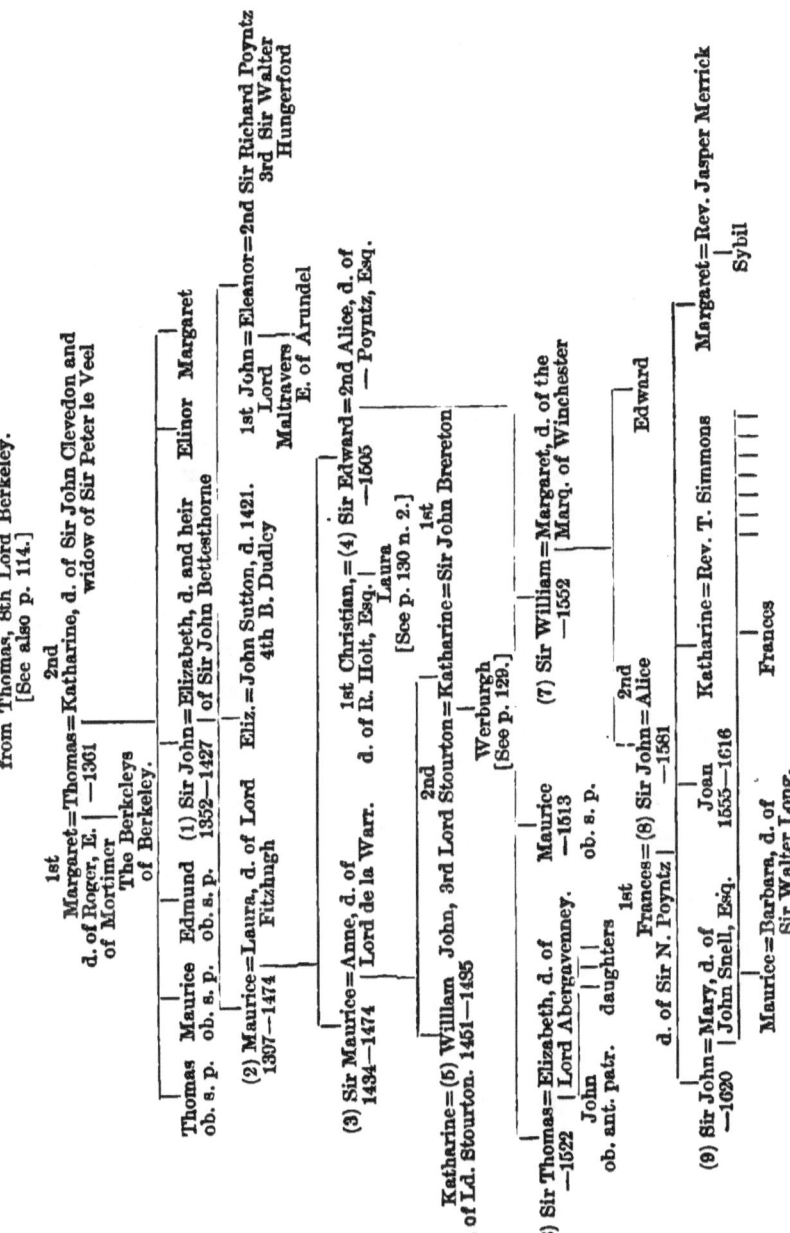

Descent of the BERKELEYS of Beverston
from Thomas, 8th Lord Berkeley.
[See also p. 114.]

From the hands of Sir John Poyntz[1] the Beverston estate soon passed into those of Henry Fleetwood, Master of the Court of Wards, and a great estate monger, who got into trouble, however, for deficiency in his accounts." [*Fosbrooke's Glouc.* i. 412.] He was no doubt a money-lender and mortgager who got hold of lands cheaply by fore-closing on embarrassed borrowers. He is set down in a subsidy of 1608 as " of Beverston." After holding it for a short time Mr. Fleetwood sold the estate to Sir Thomas Earstfield, but he bought it back again and then sold it once more to Sir Michael Hicks, Knight, a barrister, and Secretary to Lord Burleigh; whose eldest son became Sir William Hicks, Baronet, of Beverston, in 1619, and lived until 1680. His descendants held the Estate until the year 1842 when it was sold to R. J. Holford, Esq., of Weston Birt, and are now represented by Sir Michael Hicks Beach, whose Baronetcy is still styled " of Beverston." During the earlier half of the seventeenth century the Castle of Beverston was still the residence of its owners, Smyth saying that in his time— about 1630-40—it was kept in good repair and was " often inhabited by the Lord thereof."

Of the residence of Sir William Hicks at the Castle there is, however, no local memorial, unless some entries of baptisms belonging to families unconnected with Beverston may be considered as those of children of visitors to him. The most remarkable of these is the baptism of a Shakes-peare about four years after the death of William Shakes-peare. This is as follows, the year being 1619 :—

" Edward Shakespurre the sunne of John Shakespurre and Margery his wife was baptized the 17th day of September.

| Godfathers | { | Edward Eastcourt |
| | | Francis Savage |

| Godmother | { | Mary Eastcourt " |

---

[1] On October 21st, 1600, " Anne Poyntz, gentlewoman," was god-mother to Tobie Nicolas. [*Par. Reg.*]

Francis Savage and Mary Estcourt were married to each
other in 1621; but Mr. Sotheron Estcourt, who is well
acquainted with the history of his family, is unable to trace
any connection with [Shakespurre]."[1]

Twenty years afterwards, the name of Estcourt again
appears in the Register, for "Nathaniel the sonne of Mr.
John Estcotte and Elizabeth his wife was baptized June 29th
being St. Peter's Day, 1641." Walker, in his "Sufferings
of the Clergy," gives the name of "Escourt——D.D." as the
ejected Rector of Beverston cum Kingscote: [*Walker's Suff.
Clergy.* 237.] but Richard Hall the younger was Rector from
1638 until 1684, and his signature is appended to a document in the Register which is dated 1653-4. Hall was,
however, Vicar of Coaley, and his three parishes may have
necessitated the assistance of Dr. Estcourt at Beverston,
though the latter could not have been Rector.

One other name of a distinguished family appears also as
that of a probable visitor at the Castle, "Thomas the sonne
of Thomas Hyde, Esq., and Bridget his wife" being
baptized on January 24th, 1632. This was probably one of
the great Lord Clarendon's family who were connected with
Wootton Bassett about 14 miles distant from Beverston.

But the Castle had become the residence of farmers at least
as early as 1640, for "Nicolas Shipway farmer, of the Castle,
was buried August 27° 1640" while "John Shipway of the
Castle and Elizabeth Webbe the daughter of Daniel Webbe
the elder both of this parish were marryed September
21° 1640" not having allowed the shadow of the cypress long
to hinder the budding of the orange blossoms.

Soon however the sweet perfume of orange blossoms was
to be replaced by the grim odour of gunpowder, and the

---

[1] It is curious that Hathaway, the maiden name of William Shakespeare's wife, is a not uncommon name in the Beverston register, and
is still borne by several farmers at Kingscote and elsewhere in the
neighbourhood. [See also DURSLEY.]

peaceful pursuits of Farmer Shipway and his household to give way to those of a military garrison. When Gloucestershire came to take so large a share in the miserable rebellion against Charles I., the King took possession of Beverston Castle as a commanding post on the edge of the disaffected manufacturing district which lay in the cloth weaving valleys between it and Gloucester.[1] Malmesbury, Tetbury, and Wotton-under-Edge, were also fortified posts, but Beverston seems to have been the only isolated Castle then existing in the district. How early in the Civil wars the Castle was thus taken possession of by the Crown is not known, but the Parish Register records that "Daniel Backhouse, a souldier of the Castle was buryed the 23rd of Novemb: 1643;" that "Thomas Prichard a souldier of the Castle was buried the 15th of Decemb: 1643;" that "John Eires of Horsley a souldier of the Castle was buryed the 19th day of February 1643" (or 1644 New Style); that "Richard Austen, a souldier of the Castle was buryed the 11th of November 1644;" and that "Thomas Manwayring, Mareschall of the Castle was buryed the 16th of December 1644." A very great mortality had fallen upon Beverston in 1643 and 1644, the usual average of annual burials being 3, and the number rising to 22 in 1643 and 11 in 1644; among the thirty-three being 15 women, 5 infants, and several old persons.[2] It may have been, therefore, that the five deaths

---

[1] The King passed through Tetbury on his way from Bristol to Gloucester, on August 8th, 1643, and dined there: but the route he took was by Cirencester and Painswick. [*Iter. Carol. Gutch's Collect.* ij. 431.]

[2] One of the women, "Agnes the wife of William Wright was miserably burnt to death in her home April 8th, and was buryed that same night following. 1644." [*Par. Reg.*] She had been married in 1639.

There is a tradition in the village of a terrible visitation of small pox, and a field near Charlton is still known as the Small Pox field

thus recorded among the garrison of the Castle were part of this mortality, and that they do not indicate fighting before its walls.

Beverston Castle took no unimportant part, however, in the actual warfare of those terrible times, and its ruined condition is to be dated from them. As the war went on, the northern parts of Gloucestershire fell more and more into the hands of the rebels, and as Beverston "commanding the rich clothiers of Stroudwater," hindered the southward carriage of the manufactures by which these disloyal clothiers became rich, it was a great object to get it out of the hands of the King. Early in 1644, therefore, Colonel Massey, the rebel commander at Gloucester, marched thence to Beverston with a party of 300 foot and 80 horsemen. The horse soldiers were sent on to Tetbury, where Horatio Cary the governor, with his whole regiment, were put to flight by them, with the loss of fourteen men slain or taken prisoners. Beverston was not, however, so easily managed.

"Colonel Massey"—says an old Puritan Minister who wrote an account of the rebel doings in Gloucestershire— "brought up his men and two sakers against Beverston Castle, where, having surrounded it, he planted his guns within pistol shot of the gate, and gave fire several times. Fifty musketeers ran up to the gate at noon-day and fixed a petard, which nevertheless failed in execution." Doubtless the drawbridge was duly drawn up against the stone rabbet which is still to be seen in the walls of the Barbican, and the petard could only be lodged near the gate by throwing it across the Moat. But besides this the defenders

---

from a hospital having been erected there near to a ready supply of water. Such a visitation occured in Tetbury in 1711. But John Ludlow, sexton for about twenty years preceding 1875, says that there are indications of a great mortality in the shape of "many corpses heaped together" at the western side of the Church Tower.

in the upper part of the Barbican were well prepared for the assault. "Those from within threw grenades amongst our men but hurt none, who although thereby forced from the gate, yet they ran up the second time, being open to the full shoot of a secure enemy and brought off the petard with much gallantry." It does not seem as if such fighting was very dangerous work when out of fifty men in front of the gate none could be hit by the garrison. But it is gratifying to find that the defence was effective enough at this time to drive away the assailants. "The design was not feasible for a quick despatch; for the gate was barricaded within," having a formidable portcullis,[1] the groves for working which up and down still remain. Then "the night came on, and those remote parts did promise no security to so small a party: likewise the state of the city required them nearer home; wherefore after twelve hours the party was drawn off" retreating towards Wotton-under-Edge. [*Corbet's Hist. Milit. Governm. Glouc. p.* 61. ed. 1647.]

The Governor of Beverston Castle at this time was Colonel Oglethorpe. Corbet says that he had made himself "odious to the country by strange oppressions and tyranny," the Puritan way, no doubt, of recording that he had done his duty faithfully as an officer of the Crown, and did not let the Dissenting republicans have everything their own way among "the rich clothiers of Stroudwater." But discord arose within the Castle through the appointment of Sir Baynham

---

[1] This portcullis remained until about 70 years ago, and the drawbridge until a later date: but the Moat in front of the Barbican, and westward as far as the northern Tower is now filled up, probably with the stones of the curtain wall on that side. About half of the Barbican has disappeared, including the upper chambers and the vaulting between the portcullis and the drawbridge. Cocks and hens still find a roosting place, however, in the northern guard-room.

Ruins of the Barbican.

Beverston Castle.

Throckmorton[2] to supersede Oglethorpe in the command; and it seems to have been considered that the latter was treated unfairly by his removal from the post which he had so effectually defended. The King was often ill advised by those about him in such matters, and this was not the only case in which the Royal and National cause lost ground that might have been kept through similar want of tact. In the middle of May Throckmorton was on his way to take the command of Beverston, when an unfortunate event happened which was cleverly made use of by Massey as a means of getting the Castle into his hands. While he was engaged in securing Herefordshire to the rebels who called themselves the Parliament, but had no constitutional claim to the title, Massey " received advertisement that seven of his soldiers had taken Colonel Oglethorpe, the governor of Beverston Castle and six other of his troopers, and brought them to Gloucester." [*Staveley's Eben-Ezer, a full and exact account of . . . . Colonel Massey's victories. Published June 4, 1644. p. 330 of Washbourn's reprint.*] Corbet says that Oglethorpe was in "a private house courting his mistress," but the contemporary account just quoted does not refer to any such circumstance. However that may really have been Massey evidently considered that he had made a very important capture, for " coming to Gloucester May 21" [1644] " in the

---

[2] Sir Baynham Throckmorton was connected with the Berkeleys thus:—

    Maurice Lord Berkeley=Isabel
        1425—1506 |
                    Anne=Sir William Dennis
                      |
            Sir John Berkeley=Isabel
            of Stoke Gifford |
                    Sir Richard Berkeley=Elizabeth
    ┌──────────────────┴──────┐
    Henry   Elizabeth=Sir Thomas Throckmorton
                 Berkeley | of Tortworth, Bart.
                 Sir William=Cicely, daughter of Sir Thomas Baynham
                            |
                    Sir Baynham Throckmorton

evening" he "despatched the business he came about, and
then finding, by examination of some of the said prisoners,
that there were some distractions happened upon taking the
governor of Beverston Castle touching the government
thereof, and the rather because the King had granted the
same unto Sir Baynham Throckmorton while the said
Oglethorpe was governor, the said noble governor of Gloucester resolved to take the opportunity to perform some worthy
exploits." [*Ibid.*] He could not at once make up his mind,
however; for to take Beverston he would have to give up a
very important work in Herefordshire, and Corbet's account of
Massey's doubts shews how very important a position Beverston Castle occupied from a military point of view. He speaks
revilingly of Oglethorpe (which leads a just mind to think the
Royalist Colonel had something more of excellence than usual
in his character), and says, that "when once taken he was
not so high and stern before but now as vile and abject. By
which means the Governor" Massey "was made sensible of the
weakness of the Castle, but much divided in his own thoughts
whether to leave the country that came on so fairly to a self-
engagement, and neglect the contribution already levied"—
that is in Herefordshire—" but not yet paid in, or desert the
hopes of a gallant service : till at last, considering the great
command of the Castle, that the gaining of it would free the
Clothiers of Stroudwater from the bondage and terror of that
government, and might prove a great detriment and annoyance to the enemy in stopping or disturbing their passage
from Oxford to Bristol, he turned his thoughts to the business, put on and resolved to try for it." [*Corbet's History,
&c.*, 91.] At two o'clock the same night, therefore, this
prompt general posted off to Ross, and commanded his foot
over Severn at Newnham Passage, whilst the horse marched
through Gloucester. By a forced march occupying the night
and day he rendezvoused within three miles of Beverston on

Thursday the 23rd. From this halting place he quickly
marched on to Beverston. The garrison were taken completely by surprise, and being deceived by some plausible
messages sent in to them by Massey, the officer in command
during Oglethorpe's absence surrendered before midnight.
[*Staveley's Eben-Ezer*, 330.] The same garrison which under
Oglethorpe had made so effective a resistance was now induced
to give up the Castle at once to Massey, "upon condition
that both officers and common soldiers, leaving their arms,
ammunition, bag and baggage"—the arms and ammunition, according to Staveley, amounting to 50 muskets and
four barrels of powder—they "should freely pass to whatsoever garrison of the King's themselves desired, only four
officers had the privilege to take each man his horse. So
that" adds Corbet "without loss or danger we were possessed
of Beverston Castle, to the great content and satisfaction of
the country round about." [*Corbet's Hist., &c.*, 91.] The fact
seems to have been that a panic had seized the garrison
through their loss of Colonel Oglethorpe, and that the state of
affairs was so misrepresented by Massey (who was notorious
for this kind of stratagem) as to lead those in command to
consider it useless to make any attempt at retaining possession
of the Castle for the Crown. Corbet, however, asserts that
"it was lost unworthily on the enemy's part, who might have
held it with ease. Of so great simplicity was he conscious
that commanded the garrison, as to ask the place whither our
forces intended the next march, expressing his doubts of
Malmesbury, and fear of being taken the second time.
Nevertheless they required a conduct thitherward and were
guarded by two troops of horse, and that very day our forces
fell before it." [*Ibid.*] Captain Reid "a faithful man in the
service of the Parliament" [*Eben-Ezer*] was left as Governor
of Beverston whilst Massey and his troops marched the same
night to Malmesbury. After some sharp fighting and a good

deal of bloodshed (the marks of the cannon balls are still visible on the west front of the Abbey) Malmesbury was, in two or three days, taken; and among the prisoners were those who had retreated thither from Beverston.

A week after this gallant surprise of both places, on May 31st, 1644, the House of Commons " Ordered, That the town of Malmesbury, and the Castle of Beverston, as to the government of. them, shall be left wholly to the disposal of Colonel Massey." [*Eben-Ezer*, 336.] Colonel Henry Stephens was the Governor of Beverston appointed by Massey under this authority, and was doubtless a relative of Nathaniel Stephens the then owner of Chavenage House, a mile east-ward of the Castle. Tradition connects this Elizabethan Hall with the names of Cromwell, Lord Essex, and Ireton, three upper rooms having those names affixed to their doors as memorials that they were once occupied by the three Republican Generals. Another tradition also brings Charles I. in royal robes, but headless, with a black coach drawn by black horses, to fetch the departing soul of each Lord of Chavenage at his death, as a punishment for the treason of Nathaniel Stephens during his life.[1]

Shortly after his appointment Colonel Stephens left Beverston without orders, for the purpose of leading three troops of his own regiment and some from Malmesbury to the relief

---

[1] At a sale of the contents of Chavenage in 1870 " Cromwell's hat " was one of the curiosities offered by the auctioneer. The house is an interesting old mansion, with a large Hall, the windows of which are filled with a curious mixture of mediæval glass (probably brought from a neighbouring Priory and from Beverston) and Dutch glass of a much later date which contains several Merchants' marks. At one end of the Hall is an Organ gallery, and from thence there are communications with several bed-rooms which are hung with tapestry. A chapel outside the house contains some quaint kneeling figures of Elizabethan or Jacobean Stephenses; and the spread eagle, the Stephens' crest, appears as a finial on two gables of the Mansion.

of Rowden House, between Devizes and Malmesbury. By his imprudence he was turned from besieger to besieged, a force of 400 horse and foot being cooped up in Rowden House, by a bold dash of the Royalists. Beverston was thus placed in danger of recapture but was relieved by a party of horse soldiers from Gloucester. [*Corbet's Hist. &c.*, 125, 127.] The Castle does not seem to have borne any part in the further troubles of the time, Gloucestershire falling almost entirely into the hands of the rebels. Yet on July 14th, a Sunday, in 1644, Charles I. marched by the Castle at the head of 7000 troops, horse and foot, on the road from Gloucester to Bath and thence westward to Cornwall, resting on the night of the 13th at Saperton House, Sir Henry Pool's, and on that of the 14th at Badminton, then Lord Herbert's of Ragland. [*Iter. Carol. Gutch's Collect. Curios.* ij. 434. *Symonds' Diary*, 30.]

The traditions of the village assert that the time of the " siege " was a very terrible one for Beverston people : point to fields which were occupied by the besiegers ; and declare that many of the garrison as well as of the assailants were slain. But it seems to have been rather a rapid surprise than a siege, and it is more than likely that every one on both sides escaped from its dangers scot free. Peace seems at least to have returned to Beverston within a very few months, for " Mary Chambers the daughter of Mr. William Chambers of the Castle, and Elizabeth his wife, was baptized on October 7th, 1644," within less than half a year after it had been taken by the Roundheads.[1]

---

[1] The two succeeding entries, on November 16th and December 19th, are of the baptisms of "Anne the natural daughter of Mary Neeme" and "Sarah the natural daughter of Constance Myll:" and they are, perhaps, a memorial of garrison times in Beverston.

There were no christenings entered between December 27th, 1644, and August 14th, 1646. This may arise from the irregularities of the " Parish Register " whose appointment is thus entered.

Bigland says that the Castle was burnt down "soon after the siege," and that a large dwelling-house which was built within its walls was burnt down about 1691, being replaced by the present Farm House. [*Bigland's Glouc.* j. 177.] There may have been two such destructive fires within half a century where there is no record of any in 500 years before; but fire would not have destroyed the massive walls which must have stood on the Northern and Eastern sides. It is more likely that some kind of dismantling process went on at Beverston as at Berkeley when Castles were no longer permitted to be fortified, after the Restoration. Perhaps the old Hall, fitted with floors and turned into Mr. Shipway's Farm-house, was really burnt down in 1601: and then large quantities of the squared stones from the remaining walls would naturally be used in building the existing house. The interior rubble of such walls gradually crumbles down, and has doubtless been used to fill up the Moat on the North and

---

"Wee the Parishioners of Beverston whose names are hereunto subscribed doe certifie that we have made choice of Peter Wood to be our Parish Register according to the Act of Parliament

Ric: Hall Minister
Daniel Webbe
Timothy Webb } Churche
Edmond Allen } wardens

Anto Kingscote /   John Shipway
William Ivons } Overseers
Joseph Webb } of the poor
John Brown } Constables "
Ralph Nicholas }

This document is undated, but Anthony Kingscote died in Aug., 1654.

Richard Hall, minister, was doubtless one who, from the repose of a good Benefice, could see good on both sides, for he reigned during the whole time of the Presbyterian system as well as during that of the Church; being Rector from 1638 to 1684. His father, Richard Hall also, was Rector from 1617 until 1638, and both lie side by side within the altar rails.

East sides and for other purposes about the Castle and the Village. It is evident that no care has been taken to preserve any part of the Castle except what was useful for the domestic purposes of a farm house; and hence it is more surprising that so much has been preserved than that so much has disappeared.

The earliest view of the Castle which is known to the writer is one among Buck's large collection of engravings of the Churches, Castles, Monasteries, &c., of England, and which is dated on the plate itself, in the year 1732. It is not at all accurate, but shews the Moat full of water all round the Castle; and a portion of the north wall not now existing. The next view is one engraved in *Grose's Antiquities*, [vol. v., or Suppt. vol. i.] 1785. In this the Western side is shewn, much as it is now, but with unblocked windows and without its surroundings of trees. A view from the Barbican side also forms No. IV in *Hearne's Antiquities of Great Britain*, published in 1807. A view of the Church, with the Castle beyond, is to be found in *Bigland's Gloucestershire*, i. 175, published in 1791. Buck's view is engraved on a smaller scale in the " History of the House of Gurney."

ECCLESIASTICAL BEVERSTON.

There is no reason to think that the parish of Beverston is otherwise than contemporary with the Manor of Beverston: but the earliest notice of it with which the writer is acquainted dates about the year 1170, when Henry, the fifth son of Robert Fitz-harding, was Rector. He was one of the great pluralists of the feudal times, being Archdeacon of Exeter and Rector of all the churches within the honour of Berkeley. Such an array of responsibilities was not enough, however, to satisfy the spiritual cravings of ambitious minds among the Norman clergy, and the Venerable Henry Fitz-harding was also Treasurer of Normandy. [*Smyth.*] He could thus have very little time to spare for his parishioners at Beverston; but as he was unable, probably, to speak a word of their language, this circumstance may not have been of much consequence to them. No doubt the Norman clergyman did as so many of his successors in the parish did in the eighteenth and nineteenth centuries, spent nine-tenths of his Tithes at a distance, and paid a resident Curate who could talk to the people in their own tongue, with the remaining tenth.

About the year 1280 Anselm de Gournay made over the Patronage of the Rectory to the Abbey of St. Peter at Gloucester, together with an acre and a quarter of land, just enough to give them a footing in the parish. [*Hist. Mon. Glocest. Rec. Off.* ed.] Probably all succeeding rectors were Monks of Gloucester.

In 1292 THOMAS DE AVENING was Rector, but whether (like a recent successor) he was also Rector of Avening, does not appear. [*Prynne's Records*, iij. 592.]

There is a grave stone just outside the Chancel on which is incised a beautiful Calvary Cross, and which may be the memorial of a mediæval Rector. All that can be made out of the inscription is " . . . Holcombe qui Obiit . . deo . . Decembris Anno dni millimo mcccclxiiij cujus anime . . amen."

At the suppression of St. Peter's Monastery in 1540, the Advowson of Beverston was transferred to the Crown, and was not restored to the Church of Gloucester when it was converted into a Cathedral Church in 1541. Previously to the latter date the parish of Beverston had been in the Diocese of Worcester.

WILLIAM JENNINGS was Rector in 1554, having been presented by Queen Mary. [*Bigland's Glouc.*]

THOMAS PURIE became Rector in 1563, and continued so for the long period of 54 years. In 1571 he was made Prebendary of Gloucester, and remained so for forty years, resigning in 1610. He was of a Gloucester family well known in that city during the sixteenth century. Walter Purie, his grandfather, was a benefactor to the Church of St. Mary le Crypt: his father, Thomas, was Sheriff in 1541, Mayor in 1550, 1560, and perhaps in 1580. On August 24th, 1564, this "Thomas Purie the elder, of Gloucester," was godfather to "Thomas, the son of Thomas Purie, Clerk," as appears by the second entry in the Parish Register of Beverston. He is buried in St. Mary le Crypt. A later Thomas was Member for Gloucester in 1666, and his son Thomas, born on July 16th, 1619, was Mayor during its siege by the forces of Charles I.

Purie was contemporary with Sir William, Sir John, and Mr. John Berkeley, and also with Sir Michael Hicks the first of that family who was called "of Beverston." He had a family of seven children; and, after an incumbency of more than half a century, one of his last acts was to baptize a grandchild. Among the godfathers and godmothers of his children (never residents of Beverston) were William, Henry, Tobie, and Mary Sandford of Stonehouse, and Winifred Pointz of Alderley.

His eldest daughter, Susanna, married Richard Woodruffe, Vicar of Elmstree and afterwards of Arthington (?), on May 31st, 1591. His second daughter, Alice, when she was only seventeen years old, married Robert Wiere of Beverston, on October 2nd, 1589, his former wife, Joan Wiere, having died on June 11th, 1588. They continued to live in Beverston as late as 1613, when their daughter Katharine Wiere was married to Robert Downe alias Buckler. The third daughter, Margaret, born in 1579, married two clergymen in succession, her first husband, married on April 20th, 1604, being William Blewett, "mr of artes and minister of the worde of Gode at Long Newton;" her second, "Richard Allen, mr of artes and pastor of the parish of . . . . . , . Diocese of Wells," whom she married on May 4th, 1613. Mr. Blewett was living on October 7th, 1610, when he was godfather to Elizabeth, daughter of John and Margaret Purie, so that his wife did not long continue in her widow's weeds.

Katharine Purie, the wife of the Rector of Beverston, whose name often appears in the Register in the kindly office of godmother to the children of parishioners, died on December 1st, 1604. A handsome slab, evidently copied from the Holcombe stone, but without the cross, covers her grave on the north side of the Chancel, the following inscription being carved around its margin in black letter:—"Here lieth the bodye of Katharine Purye the wife of Thomas Purye minister of the worde in this place, who dyed the 1 day of Decemb: in the yeare of the Lorde 1604, and of her life the 67."

Above, on the north wall of the Chancel is a more lengthy

and curious inscription of the true Elizabethan character ;
as follows :—

Aᵒ 1604.

Decē. 1ᵒ Ætat 67ᵒ

Epicediu¹ Katharinæ Pury

Quæ defuncta iacet saxo tumulata sub illo,

Bis cathara, haud ficto nomine, dicta fuit.

Nomen utrumque sonat mundam, puram, piamqe :

Et vere, nomen quod referebat, erat,

Nam puram puro degebat pectore vitam ;

Pura fuit inundo, nunc mage pura Deo.

Πάντα καθαρὰ τοῖς καθαροῖς

Omnia pura puris.

Tit: i: ver: 15:

---

¹ This rather rare word means Funeral *Dirge* as distinguished from
monumental *Epitaph.* It was probably used to distinguish the verses
from the actual Epitaph on the slab below. The verses may be
translated thus :—

She whom, deceased, this stone doth now o'erlay
Was twice named Cathara in no feigned way.
Each name Pure, Pious, Clean-lived, signifies
And she was truly what each name implies :
For with pure heart pure ways of life she trod,
Pure was she here, now far more pure with God.

The following particulars of the Purie family (except the name of
Walter) are taken from the Register.

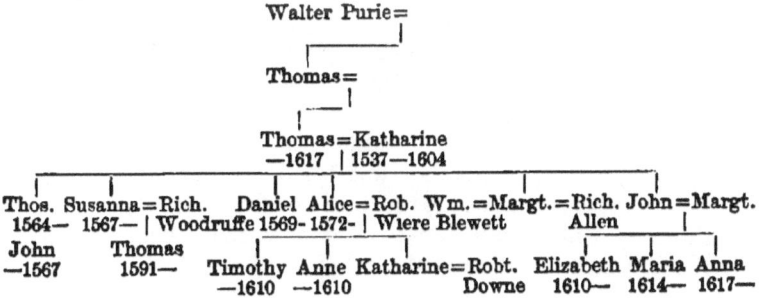

Purie (so he writes the name himself) kept the Parish Register with the greatest exactness and neatness during the whole time of his Incumbency, his very plain writing not being changed in character during the whole fifty-four years.[1] For more than fifty years he entered the names of all godfathers and godmothers of the children he baptized, a practice not long continued after his death. On August 30th, 1617, he entered the baptism of his grandchild Anna in his usual firm and clear hand as far as the word godmothers and then stopped. " Marye Halle and Marye Myles " are written in another hand, perhaps that of " John Smith, minister," who had lived in the parish for several years and seems to have acted as Purie's assistant.[2] It looks as if the hand of the old Rector had suddenly stopped through illness, for although on the day but one after, September 1st, 1617, he entered the burial of John Wright, the following entry is that of his own burial, on October 5th, 1617, five weeks later. He must then have been about 80 years of age, or perhaps more ; for the 54 years of his Incumbency were not likely to have begun until he had been several years ordained. Strange to say there is no inscription to his memory.

The pages of the Register bring one into contact with the

---

[1] There are no particulars of additional interest recorded, such as are met with in some registers. But Purie always mentions Holy Days when the date of the entry coincides with any. Thus in 1580. " Mdm That there was a crisome child of Nicolas Barnes buried ye xijth day of May, being Ascension Day 1580." A " chrisom child " is an infant who dies within a month after christening, while the anointing of its Baptism is still fresh upon it. Near the porch of Durham Cathedral there is a beautiful little tombstone of one who died a few years ago. Another was buried at Beverston in 1586. " They are without fault before the throne of God."

[2] Probably Smith was a Puritan clergyman who would not hold a cure. He is buried under one of the high tombs in the Churchyard.

handwriting of this Elizabethan Rector of Beverston, and
with a scrap or two of his personal history during the fifty
years that he was so: the pages of Foxe the Martyrologist
give us one of his letters, and a glance at his early history.

A hot-brained youth named Julius Palmer, fellow of Magdalen College, Oxford, was expelled from that college at the
age of twenty, in the latter part of Edward the Sixth's reign,
for insulting Dr. Haddon the President, and for what Foxe
calls "other Popish pranks." For a short time he became a
tutor in the family of Sir Francis Knollys, but on the
accession of Queen Mary he succeeded, "waiting as a dog for
a bone," in obtaining restoration to his fellowship. This
had the effect of changing his mind to such an extent, that
although "If he could have suppressed the word of God in
King Edward's days, such was his malicious zeal, he would
sure have done it;" the kindness of Queen Mary's Papist
Commissioners made him rebound from one extreme to the
other, and "in the end he became of an obstinate papist, an
earnest and zealous gospeller." As he had been expelled by
the Protestants in 1552 so in 1555 he was in danger of being
expelled by the Papists, and he therefore left the College
voluntarily, obtaining a grammar school mastership at Reading. Here some dispute arose between him and one Thomas
Thackam respecting a similar appointment in Gloucestershire;
and when Palmer was at length apprehended, and eventually
burned (at twenty-three years of age) at Newbury on July
6th, 1556, Thackam was bitterly charged by him with having
contrived his death because he had, at his earnest request,
taken a seditious letter, (of the contents of which he knew
nothing,) to the Mayor of Reading! Foxe recorded this
charge in his "Acts and Monuments" in 1570, and Thackam,
then a clergyman at Northampton, wrote "an Answere to"
the "Slaunder," consisting of thirty-three folio pages, [*Harl.
MSS.* 425, 10] in which he indignantly repudiated it, as

he also did at a personal interview with Foxe, and among other things declared that he had given Palmer money to keep him from starvation. In a later edition the martyrologist half withdrew what he had said about him. But he only half withdrew it, because in the meanwhile he had sent Thackam's "Answere" to Beverston with a request that Pury would peruse it. The following is the Rector of Beverston's reply:—

"Right reverend and beloved in the Lord,

"I have received your letters, together with Thackam's answer, which I perceive you have well perused, and do understand his crafty and ungodly dealing therein, that I may not say, fond and foolish. For he doth not deny the substance of the story, but only seeketh to take advantage by some circumstances of the time and place; wherein yet may be ther was an oversight, for lack of perfect instructions, or good remembrance at the begynning. He confesseth that he delivered a letter of Palmer's own hand to the maior of Reading, which was the occasion of his imprisonment and death; only he excuseth himself by transferring the crime *a seipso ad martyrem*. Briefly, his whole end and·purpose is to give the world to understand that the martyr was guilty, as well of incontinency, as also of wilful casting away of himself. O impudent man! The wise and godly reader may easily smell his stinking heart. He careth not, though he outface the godly martyr, and the whole volume of martyrs to save (as he thinks) his own honesty and good name. Howbeit I cannot, but God will, confound him to his utter shame, and reveal his cloked hypocrisy to the defence of his blessed martyrs, and the whole story. Though many of them be dead that gave instructions in times past, and now could have boure witness, yet, thanks be to God, ther want not alyve, that can and wyl testify the truath herein to his confusion. No dylygence shall be spared in the matter, as shortly, I trust, you shall understand. In the mean while Thackam nede not be importunate for an answer. He reporteth himself to the whole towne of Reading; therefore he must geve us some space. The God of truth defend you, and all other that maintain his truth, from the venomous poyson of lyars. *Vale in Christo, qui Ecclesiæ suæ te diu servet incolumen.* From Beverston in Glocestershire, May vi.

Yours in the Lord
Thomas Purye, minister.

"To the right reverend in God. mr John Fox, preacher of the gospel in London, be these dd. at Mr Daies the printer, dwelling over Aldersgate, beneath S Martins." [1]

The information obtained by Pury for Foxe was contained in a letter from "John Moyer, Minister," dated from "Crosly this 18. of May" and addressed "To his assured Friend and Brother in Christ, Mr. Purey Preacher at Beverston," and is printed in Foxe's "Appendix of such Notes and Matters as either have been in this History omitted, or newly inserted," [2] but it contains nothing that throws more light on the matter in controversy, or that is of interest in these pages. There is also a "Reply to an indiscreete Answer made by Thomas Thackam sometime of Reading against the story of Julius Palmer, martyr," which may have been written by Pury, consisting of sixty-four folio pages. [*Harl. MSS.* 425. 11.] This may have been written by Pury, the handwriting being like his, but it is full of petty accusations and abusive language, and adds nothing to the story.

It is of more interest to observe that Foxe appends to his original account of Palmer some Latin verses which play upon his name in a manner precisely like that of Pury in his

---

[1] Strype's Memorials Eccl. III. i. p. 584. *ed.* 1822.
[2] Foxe's Acts and Monuments, viii. 721. *ed.* 1849.

Epicedium on his wife. Palmer himself had written an "Epicedium," Foxe says, on Bishop Gardner.

> "De Martyrio Palmeri, hexasticon
> Palmerus flammas Christi pro dogmate passus,
> Impositum pondus, ceu bona palma, tulit.
> Non retrocessit, sed, contra, audientior ivit,
> Illæsam retinens fortis in igne fidem.
> Propterea in cœlum nunc Palmifer iste receptus
> Justitiæ Palmam non pereuntis habit.
> Justus ut Palma florebit." [1]

This play of words,—to the effect that Palmer suffering for the faith of Christ bore the weight of his sufferings like a good Palm tree, and thus as a good Palm bearer received the victor's Palm branch—seems to mark the pen of the good man who made so much out of his wife's name :—and so also does the Scripture quotation at the end, " the Righteous shall flourish as the Palm Tree." We shall not be far wrong, probably, if we conclude that Pury was responsible for the whole narrative given by Foxe, and that he was one of Palmer's friends when they were all sowing their wild oats at Magdalen College. As will be seen in the account of Dursley, we are indebted to a Thomas Thackam who flourished there in 1566 for much of what we know respecting its early Elizabethan history. Was the next door neighbour of Thomas Pury the Thackam of whom he wrote, or his father?

The next Rector was RICHARD HALL [1617-1638]. His signature appears at the foot of the Register, and his wife's name, Elizabeth, now and then stands as godmother to a parishioner's infant. The Register also records two of his gifts to the Church and Parish. "1636. The pulpit cloth and cushion, and altar cloth of green cloth with green silk fringe

---

[1] Foxe's Acts and Monuments, viii. 219. *ed*. 1849.

were given by Mr. Richard Hall, Rector of Beverston, at his own charges." "1638. There was given to the use of the poor of the parish of Beverston three pounds by Elizabeth Hall the widow of the said Richard, to be employed from year to year by the Rector and Churchwardens successively for ever on Friday before Whit-sunday." The altar cloth, pulpit cloth and cushion, probably disappeared at the time when Puritanism was in the ascendant and their ecclesiastical colour would be odious to those in power. The poor money has also disappeared, being odious, doubtless, to those charged with its payment.

Richard Hall died on June 30th, 1638 and was buried on July 1st, in front of the Altar, where lies a stone with the inscription " Sub hoc saxo jacet corpvs mri Rich. Hall Rectoris istius ecclesiæ. obiit 30o Junii 1638."

Another RICHARD HALL, son of his predecessor, succeeded [1638-1684] of whose family history the following particulars may be gleaned from the Register.[1]

Mrs. Hall (Hester) was buried on June 29th, 1655. Her husband survived her 29 years, dying on August 2nd, 1684, and being buried on August 3rd on the south side of his father's grave. The inscription on his grave-stone is as follows, but is nearly effaced by the foot of the priests his successors passing to the Altar: " Svb hoc saxo reqviescit corpvs Richardi Hall hvjvs ecclesiee Rectoris qvi postqvam in hacce triginto octoqve annos honeste ac fideliter mvnere sacerdotali perfvnctus esset mortalitatem deposvit vicesimo die Augusti, Anno Dom. 1684, Ætatis svæ 73." Purie and

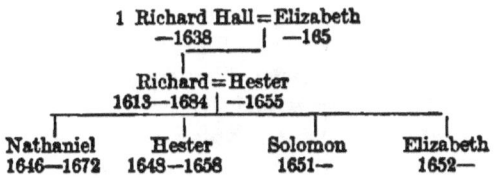

1 Richard Hall = Elizabeth
—1638 | —165

Richard = Hester
1613—1684 | —1655

Nathaniel   Hester   Solomon   Elizabeth
1646—1672 1648—1656 1651—   1652—

the Halls held the Rectory among them for no less a time than 121 years. The younger Hall remained at his post during the Rebellion, but whether or not be conformed to the Presbyterianism then established there is nothing to shew. But the phrase " munere sacerdotali " on his grave-stone, does not look as if he was a Puritan.[1]

The Halls, father and son, were succeeded by ANDREW NEEDHAM [1684-1711], of whose family the Register records as follows :—

```
                 Andrew Needham = Ann
                     1642—1711    |

         |                |                 |
      William          Mary           Sibilla = Rev. James Cornelius
     1687—1692       —1703  —Nov. 30, 1700 |
                                         James
                                      Nov. 23, 1700—
```

Mr. Needham failed in health some time before his death, and his place in Church was supplied by a Curate named Daniel Capel, who was afterwards Curate of Cam and Dursley for many years, and is buried in Dursley Church. Mr. Needham died on August 6th, 1711, and was buried in front of the Altar to the south of the Halls on August 9th. The inscription over his grave is as follows: " In Spe Beatæ Resurrectionis Positæ sunt hic Reliquiæ Viri admodum Reverendi Andreæ Needham, A.M. Hujus Ecclesiæ necnon adjacentis Capellæ de Kingscote per Annos ter-novem Pastoris. Qui satur Dierum et maturum Cœlo huic Mundo placide, non invitus, Valedixit, sexto Die Aug:

Anno $\left\{ \begin{array}{l} \text{Salutis Nostræ MDCC[XI]} \\ \text{Ætatis Suæ LXIX ”} \end{array} \right.$

---

[1] His signature stands at the head of those affixed to the appointment of a parochial registrar of which a copy is given at page 146, note 1. In the year preceding his death is a curious entry of the name of a child transformed from Hester to Easter on account of her baptism taking place on Easter Tuesday. " 1683 Easter Wickes, daughter of William Wickes and Hester his wife was baptized the 11th day of April being Easter Tewsday. Godfathers, John Shipway, sen., of this Parish, and John Sandford of Stanley St. Leonards, Godmothers, Elizabeth Bridges of this Parish, and Ann Browning of Elmstree.

Mrs. Needham survived until January 6th, 1726, when, at the age of 86, she was laid beside her husband. Their two daughters and a son lie under three separate stones southward of Mrs. Pury's; Sibilla, Mrs. Cornelius, having died in childbirth. No Rectors of Beverston, or any of the members of their families, have since that time been buried in the parish.

For a long series of eight non-resident Rectors began with JOHN SWINFEN [1711-1728], the successor of Mr. Needham. He was also Rector of Avening, where he was buried. During his Incumbency eight marriages are registered in which both men and women resided at Avening. This may indicate that he sometimes lived at Beverston and required his Avening parishioners to come over to him when they wanted his services on week days: but the marriages of strangers abound in the registers until quite recent days. From 1696 until the end of the century only 4 out of 12 persons married at Beverston belonged to the parish; and in the preceding 4 years all were strangers.[1]

THOMAS SAVAGE was the next Rector [1728-17..]. Of his appointment there is this record in a newspaper of the time. " His Majesty has been pleased to grant to the Rev. Mr. Savage the Rectory of Beverston with the Chapel of Kingscot in the Diocese of Gloucester, void by the death of the Rev. Mr. Andrew Needham" [*London Evening Post. May* 7-9. 1728]. This is curious, for it altogether passes over the incumbency of Mr. Swinfen, as if Mr. Needham, whose death had occurred seventeen years before, was the last Rector named in the official list of Crown appointments.

---

[1] "Ould Thomas Croom" of the Castle was buried on September 24th, 1716: but his "sperrit" used to haunt the Castle and its precincts. He "walked" through having removed a neighbour's landmark; and his "sperrit used to go rowlling and rattling about as big as a 'oolpack." It was seen of that size by an old woman who told the story in John Ludlow's hearing when he was a boy, early in the nineteenth century. At last the spirit was laid under the old yew tree not far from the bridge over the moat.

Mr. Savage was one of the Tetbury Savages. He probably forsook the old Rectory House which stood on the site of the present School House, and substituted for it another house nearer the Castle which had been occupied by some of those "well-to-do" families whose names occur in the early Registers. That house, the present Rectory, bears traces of considerable antiquity, but over the garden door of it are the initials of Mr. Savage ⎡T. S. 1729⎤ indicating that some considerable alterations ⎣_____⎦ were made by him. He himself is believed to have resided in the house at Tetbury belonging to the late Mr. Josiah Paul.[1]

The next six Rectors were appointed through political interest: and all "farmed" the Parish, placing a Curate in Charge, and residing on other benefices.

. The Hon. Allen Bathurst [....-1767] was Rector of Saperton, and was appointed to Beverston by the interest of Lord Bathurst. He was son of the first Earl Bathurst, and brother of the great Lord Chancellor of the name, who is also known as the friend of Pope. Mr. Bathurst was born in 1729, and died at the age of 38 in August, 1767, being buried in Saperton Church, where there is a tablet to his memory.

CHARLES JASPER SELWYN [1767-1794] was presented through the interest of a relative who was Member for Gloucester. He was Rector also of Blockley in Worcestershire [1761-1794]. His family was of Maston and has since given the distinguished Bishop of New Zealand and Lichfield to the Church, as well as Lord Justice Selwyn and the Canon of Ely of the same name; all of them being his great-nephews.[2]

---

[1] The two Bells were put up during the Incumbency of Mr. Savage. They are by Rudhall of Gloucester, the large one being dated 1737, and the smaller one having the inscription "COME AWAY MAKE NO DELAY."

[2] Mr. Selwyn's great grandson, Captain Selwyn, R.N., is the present head of the family. [See Cam] He was buried at Batsford,

Augustus Thomas Hupsman [1794-1796] the next Rector was also Vicar of Berkeley and was nominated to Beverston by the interest of the Earl of Berkeley. He was buried at Cranford.

During the Incumbency of these last four Rectors the Parish had been in the charge of the Rev. Thomas Hornidge who was also Vicar of Coaley and of Norton in Wiltshire. He held the Curacy for exactly the same time as Mr. Pury had held the Rectory, 54 years; and seems to have been regarded with much affection by the parishioners. The following particulars of his family are all that can be gathered from the Register :—

Thomas Hornidge=Sarah
1720—1796 | 1721—1795

John	Thomas	Sarah=John Green	William	Anne
1749—1815	1751—	1753—1788	1756—	1758—

Mrs. Hornidge died on January 17th, 1795, and her husband on June 25th, 1796. A large slab with their initials and those of their son John, covers their grave on the North side of the Chancel floor; and above it on the North wall is a marble tablet with the following inscription. "Below this

two miles from Blockley, but in the county of Gloucester, and on the northern slope of the Cotswolds. The following is the inscription on his grave :—

Beneath this stone
are deposited
the remains
. of
The Reverend
Charles Jasper Selwyn,
33 years Vicar of Blockley
in the County and Diocese of Worcester,
Rector of Beverston and Kingscote
in the County of Gloucester,
and Prebendary of Sarum,
who died the 10th day of Sept., 1794,
in the 67th year of his age.

monument in the same grave are deposited the remains of the
Rev. Thomas Hornidge, Clerk, B.A., Vicar of Coaley, in this
County, and of Norton, in the County of Wilts, and also
resident Curate of this Parish from the time of his ordination
in the year 1742 to the time of his death: And of Sarah his
wife. The latter died on the 17th January, 1795, aged 74,
and the former on the 21st June, 1796, aged 76."

JOHN SAVAGE [1796-1803] was also Rector of Weston
Birt and was appointed to Beverston by the interest of Earl
Camden. He lies buried at Tetbury, where there is a marble
slab to his memory on the south wall by the Altar. His
Curate was the Rev. George Hayward, of whom only this is
recorded in the Register :—

George Hayward = Charlotte Elizabeth

| George Christopher [Afterwards Rector | John St. John |
| born Oct. 30, 1797   of Nymphsfield.] | bapt. Jan., 1801 |

THOMAS PETTAT succeeded Mr. John Savage [1803-1839].
He was Rector of Hatherop. An old man, a regular Church
goer, who lived through most of that time, says that he
never saw Mr. Pettat in Beverston, and never heard of
any one who ever saw him there.

During his Incumbency an Enclosure Act [43 Geo. III.
ch. 144] was obtained for re-adjusting the lands of the
Parish and for commuting the Tithes in kind to a Rent
Charge. The subsequent Award is dated June 30th, 1804.

The Curate during the whole time of Mr. Pettat's Incumbency was the Rev. William Scott Panting, who was also,
during part of his 36 years residence at Beverston, Curate of
Lasburough and who kept a school for boys at the Rectory.[1]

[1] For many years Mr. Panting oscillated every Sunday between
Beverston and Kingscote, holding a service in each Church alternately
in the Morning and the Afternoon. When the Beverston service was
in the Morning a reminder was given to the Parishioners by the
ringing of the Church Bell at 8 o'clock. Those who wished to go to
Church twice a day walked over to Chavenage ! This with a double

ALAN GARDNER CORNWALL was the last of the eight non-resident Rectors. [1839-*Aug 5th.* 1872] He was appointed by the interest of Lord Ducie, and was Chaplain in Ordinary to the Queen: also Rector of Newington-Bagpath with Owlpen.

During Mr. Cornwall's Incumbency he and Sir Michael Hicks Beach built the School (most of the stone for which came from an old house which stood on the Glebe opposite to its site) and the present Lord of the Manor built the School House. The Church was restored a generation ago in a very liberal spirit by the Lord of the Manor, but unfortunately the Architect employed knew but little of Church architecture, and so he destroyed old mouldings, chiselled over carvings, removed a beautiful screen from the Chancel Arch, stuccoed over the interior of the Church with plaster and crowned his work with a roof of wonderful design bounded by a deep moulding of Plaster of Paris, painted to imitate wood, at the wall plate. His bench ends are ornamented with carvings in putty, placed in circles which convey a distant idea of " poppy heads : " and cast-iron is used for the tracery of seat mouldings in the Chancel.

During Mr. Cornwall's Incumbency the following Curates succeeded Mr. Panting at Beverston.

Frederick Ford	1840-1841
Thomas H. Vyvyan	-1841
Henry Wybrow	1842-1843
Thomas J. Lingwood	1843-1848
H. Knowles Rawdon G. Green	1849-1850
James Hamilton	1851-1854
Edward Mc Lorg	1855-1865
· Richard Hibbs	1865-1867
W. H. Kemm	Aug. 1869-Mar. 1873.

Parish from which the non-resident Rector received at least £600 a year. The Curate received £40 a year.

JOHN HENRY BLUNT [1872-   ] was the first resident Rector for about a century and a half. Although known as a Conservative he ' was nominated to the Crown by Mr. Gladstone at the time the latter was head of a Liberal Ministry. Before Mr. Blunt was instituted the Chapelry of Kingscote was formed into a separate Parish under an Order of Council issued some twenty years before.

CHURCHWARDENS SINCE 1743.

William Tugwell	1743—1751	William Robins	1803—1814
Lewen Tugwell	1743—1778	Jacob Hayward	1815—1853
John Powell	1751—1781	William Kilmister	1853—1854
William Tugwell	1778—1788	Robert Long	1854—1864
John Simpkins	1781—1785	Robert Kilmister	1864—1866
Jonathan Wickes	1785—1799	Charles Long	1866—1874
John Hayward	1788—1790	James Garlick	1873—
Lewen Tugwell	1790—1793	William Warner	1875—
John Hayward	1793—1805		

PARISH CLERKS.

John Philpott	—1728
Jonathan Wickes	—1799 also Churchwarden from 1785 to 1799
John Stockwell	—1803
Giles Long	1803—1810
John Frape	1810—1838
John Ludlow	1838—

C A M.

This ancient clothing village stretches along in a curve from the foot of the Long Down westward and northward for nearly two miles, dividing into Upper Cam and Lower Cam at the Railway Station, and standing, for a good part of the distance, on the Cam brook or "river." The parish was once of considerable importance as a place for the manufacture of cloth : a manufacture recently revived on an extensive scale, and with modern machinery instead of the ancient hand-looms. Some eight or ten generations ago Smyth wrote of Cam with such glowing enthusiasm that he must have regarded it as a sort of Happy Valley of the Cotswolds. It was "a Township soe evenlie partaking of Hill and Vale, with an wholesome Aire to both, and so equally furnished of Timber and Wood for Buildinge, Fire, and all Bootes in Husbandrie ; with Arable, Meadow, and Pasture Grounde, for the Feed and Breed of all Sorts of Cattell ; with Fish, Fowle, Perry, Cyder, and the like, that it would abundantly suffice for the Maintenance and Well-beinge of its own Inhabitants without Supply from any other, in any needful Thing which the Hart of Man would moderately desire." Who would not wish to have lived in Cam in those days ! The neighbourhood bore so high a character for fertility that " As for pasturage," says Fuller, " I have heard it reported from credible persons that such is the fruitfulness of the land nigh Slimbridge, that in spring time let it be bit bare to the roots, a wand laid along therein over night will be covered with new grown grass by the next morning" [*Fuller's Worthies*, 349.]. The canny King James capped this asser-

tion by declaring that he knew a field in Scotland where, if a
horse was turned in on a Sunday it would be in vain even to
look for him on the Monday !

Why this favoured village was called Cam is obvious to all
who believe that Gloucestershire names are akin to those of
Wales. The stream which passes through the midst of it is
a crooked stream, the roads of the parish are crooked roads,
the heights around are crooked in their sky-line, and " Cam "
in Welsh means nothing more nor less than " crooked " itself.
If Mr. Planché had seen the valley and its curving stream
before he had dipped his pen into the Cornish Camel would he
not rather have written of our little Cam than of it

> " Who can wonder crooked river,
> Once that thou hast found thy way in
> Thou shouldst use thy best endeavour
> Such a paradise to stay in."

But a little lower down the Cam river than the village of
Cam the name " Cambridge " is found, and as Slimbridge is
the name of the adjoining parish it is not unlikely that
Cambridge was originally the full name and Cam an abbrevi-
ation. Now the name of Cambridge is to be traced as far back
as a thousand years ago, when it is mentioned in association
with the Danes ; and it appears to have been at the time of
the Danish occupation of East Anglia that " Grantabricg "
began to be known as Cambridge, and the Granta as the
Cam. " There is a river at Macedon and there is also,
moreover, a river at Monmouth " said Fluellen " 't is so like
as my fingers is to my fingers, and there is salmons in both :"
and though there are no " salmons " in either Cam at this day
the names of the two rivers are " so like as my fingers is to
my fingers," and in each case seem to point to a Danish
rather than a British origin. " Upthorpe," the name of an
ancient manor in the Gloucestershire parish, has also a ring
of the East Anglian tongue about it ; while " The Thing,"

which was the old name of a house lately destroyed at Cam
Green seems to carry us as directly back to a Scandinavian
Council chamber as ".The Mote" of Downton near Salisbury
carries us back to the Witenagemote.

The earliest historical trace of the locality is in connection
with a defeat sustained there by the Danes in the year 903.
Ethelward, the early English chronicler, says that in that
year " the tempestuous hosts of the barbarians" laid waste the
·lands of the Mercians " as far as the river Avon," which then
as now formed "the boundary between the West Angles"
· of Somersetshire "and the Mercians" of Gloucestershire.
" They passed thence towards the west of the river Severn and
obtained no small booty by their ravages.   Afterwards they
returned homewards, rejoicing in the riches of their spoils,
and crossed in regular order over a bridge on the eastern bank
of the Severn which is commonly called Cambridge.[1] Here
the troops of the Mercians and West Angles suddenly met
them in battle array, an engagement immediately followed
and the English obtained the palm of victory on the plain of
Wodensfeld, the Danish army being driven to flight by the
darts of the English   These events are recorded as occurring
on the fifth day. of August" [A.D. 903], " and their three
Kings, named Halfdene, Eowyls, and Igwar, fell in that
tumultuous fight."   Where the plain of Wodens-field may
·have been there is nothing to show, but as it is probable that
many names of places which begin with the syllable " Wood"
were originally names beginning with the name of the god
Woden, it is a not unreasonable conjecture that Woodchester
Park, about two miles east, is the ancient battle-ground of
Woden's-field, having also been previously the " castra" of a
Roman detachment from the adjacent camp on Uley Bury.

[1] The battle of Quatbridge near Bridgenorth, with which that of
Cambridge has been confused, was fought some time before the
death of King Alfred, in the year 896.

2 N

When Cam appears in history as a parish it is as part of the
original, or great, Manor of Berkeley, and the representative
of Fitz-Harding is therefore Lord of the Manor.   But lands
were held in Cam for at least three centuries by a family of
Hardings of whom there is no record in the Fitz-Harding
genealogies given by Smyth.   The descent of the heirs and
heiresses of this family was as follows :—

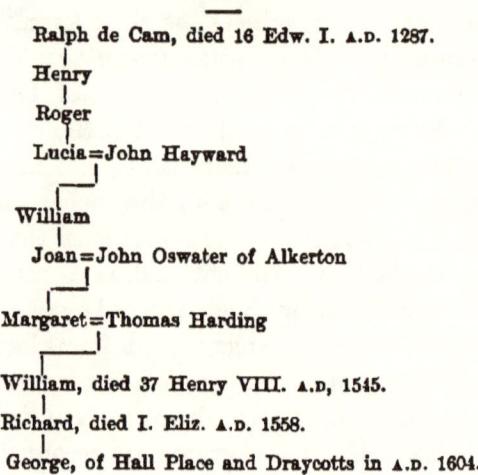

HARDING of Cam.

Ralph de Cam, died 16 Edw. I. A.D. 1287.

Henry

Roger

Lucia=John Hayward

William

Joan=John Oswater of Alkerton

Margaret=Thomas Harding

William, died 37 Henry VIII. A.D, 1545.

Richard, died I. Eliz. A.D. 1558.

George, of Hall Place and Draycotts in A.D. 1604.

Hall Place was sold by George Harding, whose principal
Manor was then at Coaley, to a Herefordshire family of the
name of Hopton.   In 1689 William Hopton, Gentleman,
appears as selling the " Vennings," more recently called the
" Manor House," to John Phillimore; the sale being mentioned in the marriage settlement of John Phillimore the
younger.   A later member of the family, Mrs. Frances
Hopton, gave her Draycott Estate for the support of a school
for the parish, and her other lands in Cam to a relative
named Hadley.   Most of the parish is now the property of
Lord Fitzhardinge.

ECCLESIASTICAL CAM.

The Benefice of Cam belonged in the twelfth century to the Abbey of Reading, having being granted to it by Matilda the queen of Henry I. But the Abbey of Gloucester had a prior claim which the monks maintained successfully against those of Reading, and it remained in their possession until the Dissolution of the Monastery, when it was transferred to the See of Gloucester. The patronage still belongs to the Bishop of the Diocese, but the great tithes, which constitute the Rectory of the Parish, are in private hands.

The earliest record of the Church is that it was enlarged by Thomas Horton, the 18th Abbot of Gloucester. It was rebuilt by Thomas Lord Berkeley, the rebuilder of Beverston Castle and Church, about the year 1340. In that year Lord Berkeley is also said by Smyth to have founded chantries in the Chapels of Newport, Wortley, and Cambridge in Gloucestershire, making special arrangements for the masses and prayers there to be said, and for the regulation of the lives and conduct of the Chaplains; forbidding them to take money of any or to be servant to any but God in spiritual matters and to himself in temporal concerns: enjoining them to live chastely and honestly, and not to come to markets, alehouses, or taverns, nor frequent plays or unlawful games: and "all this," adds the historian of the Berkeleys, writing in 1618, "he did in so devout and holy a manner, that unless he had been a disciple of Wickliff who now lived, he could not have come nearer to the doctrine of the Church of England in these days."

The Church is said to have been originally dedicated in the name of St. George, and a story is told by Atkyns of a clothier who stole a statue of the saint from the porch and

carried it in his waggon to Colebrook where it was set up as
the sign of an inn. The present dedication is that of St.
Mary, but in the modern restoration of the Church a very
good sculptured boss of St. George and the Dragon has been
placed in the stone vaulting of the porch to commemorate
the old tradition.

As it now stands the Church consists of a Nave and Aisles
of work dating principally from the fifteenth century, but
with modern roofs ; of a very fine Tower belonging to the
same date ; and of a modern Chancel, in the decoration of the
interior of which colour has been judiciously used on the
ceiling. The Chancel arch is supported on corbels and three
short columns, and a wooden screen no doubt occupied the
opening. But as the latter is much narrower than the
Chancel itself the wall on either side has been pierced with
lights, or " squints," for the purpose of giving the congregation in the Nave and Aisles a more complete view of the
service going on at the Altar. Before the restoration of the
Church there were two such lights on either side, but a third
has been added on the south side, and has increased the
screen-like effect of the whole. The Font is a circular bowl
of early date, ornamented with a beautiful string-moulding
of nail heads, and standing on a modern base of five columns.
The pulpit and altar-table are interesting specimens, of late
Jacobean work. On the walls of the Church, and in its floor,
are many costly marble monuments, which show the former
prosperity of the local manufacture.

Among the monuments on the south wall there is one on
which were formerly the arms of Selwyn :—Argent, on a bend
cottised Sable three annulets Or. An inscription remains
" In memory of three Children, viz. :—William William and
Sarah (of Jasper Selwyn of this Parish Gent: and Eleanor
his wife) whose Remains were in this Isle deposited: of the
1st on the 18th September 1726, The Second the 1st of July
1727, And yᵉ third the 22nd of Dec. 1730." Two other

sons, both named John, were baptized on April 30th, 1735, and July 27th, 1736, but there are no further entries. The name has become famous in Church and State in modern times, in the persons of Sir Charles Jasper Selwyn, the Lord Justice of Appeal, the venerable Bishop of New Zealand and of Lichfield, and the learned Canon of Ely. [See also p. 160.]

The most notable features in the exterior of the Church are the parapet of the Nave roof, which is similar to that around the choir of Tewkesbury Abbey, and the beautiful Tower, which, although small, is equal in proportion and general character, to the famous towers of Somersetshire. At the foot of the south east buttress of the tower is an admirably carved dragon, almost " as large as life," a ram's head and a bull's head occupying similar positions on the western buttresses. The heads of a king and bishop are no doubt intended to represent the contemporary monarch, perhaps Edward III., and the then Bishop of Worcester, perhaps John Thoresby. Two well-carved gurgoyles may also be observed, the one a horse's head, and the other a demon playing on a pipe. The spandrils of the arch surmounting the western door contain shields bearing the cross of St. George and the arms of the Berkeleys.

One of the steps which lead to the belfry of the tower is formed of a portion of an early fifteenth century grave stone, on which are still to be traced the floriated arms of a cross and the fragmentary inscription

𝕽 𝕬 — 𝕬 𝕸 𝕴 𝕾 𝕾 𝕰

This was probably a memorial placed above the grave of one of the Harding ladies whose Christian name was Amice.

In the churchyard there are many tombs of the Phillimore family of which some account is given further on. Near to these at the east end of the Church there is also a table tomb of considerable archæological interest. Its date is 1685 and it is supposed to stand over the grave of one Perrott who died in that year, and the manner of whose death is commemorated by a sculpture on the side of the monument. This sculpture represents a man driving a plough, the costume of the man and the form of the plough being carved with a force and detail which make them valuable as contemporary illustrations. The chain by which the horses were drawing the plough has suddenly snapped and part of it is flying back above the plough towards the head of the ploughman : there being also a single link of the chain close behind his head. On the sides of this panel are two other panels containing the usual skull, hour-glass, and cross bones of the period. The tradition connected with this sculpture is that it represents the death of a farmer who was ploughing on a Sunday, and who was killed by a part of the plough chain thus striking his head : the accident being regarded as a judgement upon him for breaking the fourth Commandment.

On the north-west side of the Church is a tombstone bearing the following inscription, " In memory of Joseph White of this parish, Thatcher, who died the 12th of June 1837 aged 103 yrs. This stone is erected by the Right Honourable Lord Segrave to perpetuate so remarkable an instance of longevity." The baptism of Joseph White is not traceable in the Parish Register.

There was once a Hospital for a Master and several brethren at Cam, an institution similar to the Charter House in London, or St. Cross at Winchester, but on a smaller scale. It was founded by Robert Lord Berkeley at the end of the twelfth century, and was given to Gloucester Abbey by Thomas Lord Berkeley in the year 1224. At the Dissolution of the Monasteries the endowment and buildings of this benevolent institution were made over to some nobody named Hodges, a public charity being thus confiscated to private use.

THE VICARS OF CAM.

RICHARD SMITH   1569—1581

HUGH PARSONS   1582—1598, buried at Cam on May 16th, 1598.

JOHN CHURCHMAN   June 19th, 1598.—June 19th, 1614.

JOHN PHILLIPS   1615—1618.

WILLIAM SMITH   1618—1629.

FRANCIS HATHWAY   1630—1633.

DOSITHEUS WYER   1633—June, 1635.

JOHN KNIGHTON   1635—1636.

THOMAS DAVIS   1636—1640.

OBADIAH HIGGINS   1640—1648.

TOBIAS HIGGINS, Jan. 1st, 1638—1652, buried at Cam on December 2nd, 1652.

WILLIAM HARDINGE, 1653—1664. The Parish Register records that on March 2nd, 1663—1664 there "was buried that painfull and faithful Pastor and servant of Jesus Christ m^r William Hardinge the ablest gospell preacher that ever Cam parish enioyed." There was also formerly the following inscription engraved on a brass plate, and placed on the North wall of the Chancel :—

" Hic jacet in occiduo cinere
GULIELMUS HARDINGE
In Artibus Magister, Theologus tam Doctrinâ
Quam pietate eximius, concionator felicissimus,
Pastor fidelis, maritus amantissimus, parens
indulgens : post varia studia, quibus fideliter
nec infeliciter incubuit, instinctu et impulsu
Spiritus Sancti, monitu et hortatu amicorum,
ordines sacros amplexus, et curâ pastorali
hujus Ecclesiæ Camæ indutus anno sui Jesu
1654, Decanatumque Durslæi Ruralis Decanus :
vitæ officiis et omnibus curis,

Morte exutus die Dominico
Mane ultimo Februarii, Anno
Domini 1663, ætat. 39.
In Memoriam hujus Reverendi Viri,
Chara pariter et pia uxor Dorothea
Hoc posuit Monumentum.

His widow, ten years younger than himself, was laid by his side at the age of 68 in 1702."

JOHN BARNSDALE, August 11th, 1664—1680-1. Was buried at Cam on February 9th.

THOMAS STRATFORD, April 16th, 1681—1707-8. Was buried at Cam on March 3rd. His monument is against a pillar with the inscription, " Before this Place lies the Body of Thomas Stratford, Vicar of this Parish 25 years. He died March 1, Anno Dom. 1707, ætatis suæ 64."

EDWARD TURNER, 1708—1718. The following inscription to his memory was formerly against the South Wall of the Chancel : —

" Near this Place lieth the Body of EDWARD TURNER, Vicar of Cam, and also sometime Vicar of Dursley. In both these Places, among other good deeds for which his Zeal was eminent, he procured a Charity School. ' He died Feb. 13, 1717, aged 44 years, leaving a mournful widow and nine young children to the all sufficient care of Providence.

Hester his Daughter died March 19, 1717,
aged 3 years 10 months.

DANIEL CAPEL, 1718—May 1st, 1737. He was also Curate of Dursley, in the Church of which Parish he lies buried ; there being a monument to his memory on the East End of the North Aisle, surmounted by the Capel arms, and stating that he died at 50 years of age.

PETER SENHOUSE   May, 1737—1763.

BENJAMIN WEBB   1763—

..   ..

WILLIAM FRYER   1801—1835.

WILLIAM CHARLES HOLDER 1835—Nov. 6th, 1837. His monument is on the wall of the North Aisle and is surmounted by a model of the School in white marble.

GEORGE MADAN   1838 —1852.

B. F. CARLYLE   1852—1862.

EDWARD CORNFORD   1862—1874

F. T. PENLEY   1875—

CHURCHWARDENS SINCE 1835.

Samuel Pearce	1835—6	John Harris	1841—61
Thomas Gabb	1835	Samuel Long	1861—6
J. T. Cam	1836—8	John Harris	1861—8
Samuel Gabb	1836	James Till Barton	1867—8
Stephen Robinson	1837—40	A. B. Winterbotham	1869—71
Thomas Morse	1839	George Harris	1869—75
Henry Dartnell	1840	Ignatius Dark	1872
Thomas Gabb	1841—61		

The Parish Register.

It is often found that Clergymen and Parish Clerks have registered other things than Births, Deaths, and Marriages, in the very important volume or volumes in which these are recorded. Sometimes the Clergyman has had an historical mind and has given curt notices here and there of public events; or he has attached personal memoranda to the names registered, and in both cases he has probably rendered a service to posterity. The Parish Clerk's memoranda have usually been of a personal character, recording that such an one was "a vagrant," another "a sectary," or "presbriterian," and a third "a igorant man." There is not much of this in the Cam Register, but there are yet some peculiarities which are of interest.

The Register is all written in contemporary hands, but the present title, in a beautiful Church text reads as follows:—

o 2

" A register of all chrisnings weddings and burialls which have bene in the parish of Cam since the yeare of our Lord 1569. Renewed by Maurice Trotman and Henry Alye churchwardens for the yeare of or Lord 1621." [1]

It is quite certain that the renewal here spoken of was not that of copying into the present book the records of an older register; but it may possibly mean that the book was re-bound in 1621. The register is undoubtedly an original one, and few are found of an earlier date.

The earlier entries, for twelve years, were all made by Richard Smith, the first Vicar after the Reformation. Having a taste for epigram he headed each of the three portions of the Register with a Latin couplet The first of these is an exhortation to each one who is baptized in Christ to put on Christ, lest original or wilful sin should burden and press down the soul.

" Christenings

" Indue te christum qui baptizaris in ipsum :

Ni proprio premeris crimine, seu patrio."

The second seems to be a commentary on the wise man's saying that " a virtuous woman is a crown to her husband," and his exclamation " give me any wickedness but the wickedness of a woman." There is nothing better, it de-clares, than a good woman, nothing worse than a bad one: the one excels in every thing that is good, the other in every thing that is evil.

" Weddings

" Nil melius muliere bona, nil est mala peius :

Omnibus ista bonis præstat, et illa malis."

The third is a sententious declaration that death destroys all distinctions among men, dragging those who are the most

---

[1] In the Christenings part of the Register, p. 19, "Mr. John Try" is written over an erasure as the Churchwarden's name in 1621. In the Wedding part, at p. 77, Henry Alye signs his own name.

dissimilar into one common condition, making the master
equal with the servant, and levelling the sceptres of Kings
with the mattocks of labourers.

" Burialls

" Mors dominum servo, mors sceptra ligonibus æquat:
Disimiles simili conditione trahens."

Five pages of the Register, pages 63-68, are occupied
with a list of Parish Officers; namely, Churchwardens from
1599, Overseers from 1614, Tithingmen and Constables from
1639, Surveyors of Highways from 1646, all going on to
1685. The list is continued in the first twenty-six pages of
the Churchwardens' account book down to 1739.

At page 84 of the Register there is also a carefully compiled Table giving a summary of the Baptisms, Weddings,
and Burials registered from 1569 to 1679. Opposite the years
1641 —1648 is the memorandum, " No Weddings registered
all these eight yeares. Few Christenings or Burials registered all these eight yeares in the heate of the warre. And
in the yeares 41, 45, 46, no Burials at all Registered. Part
of the time of the Civil warre which was not quite ended
till 1660." This is in John Barnsdale's writing, who began
every year from 1665 with the entry of the year of Charles
II. reign and ended it with a summary of the Baptisms,
Marriages, and Burials, repeated in each register.

A similar Table to the above, but of Burials alone, occupies page 124. It reaches from 1570 to 1668 : and as there
was some room to spare it is filled up with the following
verses :—

" Est homo flos, gramen, cinis, umbraq., pulvis et aura :
Somnus, bulla, vapor, ventus, inane, nihil.
Cursus Fortunæ rotatur imagine Lunæ :
Crescit, decrescit, constans consistere nescit.
Man is a Flour, a Shade, Grasse, Ashes, Dust, and Aire ;
A Bubble, Vapour, Sleepe, Wind, Toy, Nought,
though now so fair.

Much like ye Moone, so rolleth Fortune's Wheele:
It waxeth, wanes, unconstant doth it reele."

About this time one of the four Lecturers of Dursley was named Fortune, and there were also Fortunes of North Nibley who intermarried with the Phillimores of Cam. Whether the poetical Vicar had them in view when he wrote the second of these couplets is not on record. Nor has the pen of scandal recorded whether any further meaning than appears underlay the following entry in 1697. "Moses a poor childe left by an unknown party at Lower Cam was baptized Aug. 7th, and being casually found was named Fortune." Of the fortunes of poor Moses Fortune in later life no trace is to be found in the Register. But Moses Fortune was not the first unfortunate child thus treated in Cam; for in 1680 is this long entry: "Ignotus a poore child left by an unknown party at Lower Cam, on a Leaping Stone before Thomas Pope his gate in the Streete was baptized at Cam Nov. 21st, and from that stone surnamed Stone, but since found to be the son of Hannah the daughter of James Clerk Baker in Berkeley." Had she brought the child all the way from Berkeley to lay it at "Thomas Pope his gate."? At any rate the poor little waif was sent back again, for a memorandum is inserted among the burials that "Ignotus Leapingstone who had been baptized at Cam on Nov. 21st, had been buried at Berkeley on Dec. 15th, next ensuing."

The year 1668 was remarkable for the number of deaths which occurred in the Parish. The average number for 85 years only amounted to 12, though it occasionally rose above 20: but in 1668 as many as 41 deaths are recorded. A note is appended saying, " This hath been the greatest yeare of mortality so far, of any these last Hundred yeares," but no reason is assigned, nor is there any accumulation of numbers at any particular time of the year, to indicate an epidemic.

In a later volume of the Register the most remarkable
entry is that which records that six young people of one
family were all baptised together on March 24th, 1779,
namely "James, Robert, John, Esther, Sarah, and Hannah,
sons and daughters of Henry and Dorcas Hill."

The Scripture names used in this family may remind us
before parting with the Register of Cam to notice the very
common use of Scriptural Christian Names during the middle
part of the last century. Before the Great Rebellion they
were not more frequently used than at the present day; nor
afterwards until after the first third of the eighteenth century
had passed. About the middle of the century thirty are
found at one opening of the Register in which the whole
number of entries only amounts to sixty; including the
burials of persons christened at a much earlier date: and
the following are found within a space of about one generation :—

Michael	Joseph	Samuel	Josiah
Gabriel	Benjamin	Jesse	Daniel
Abel	Dinah	Abner	Mordecai
Seth	Tamar	Jonathan	Esther
Enoch	Moses	David	Shadrach
Noah	Aaron	Abigail	Meshach
Abraham	Job	Bathsheba	Susannah
Sarah	Keziah	Nathan	Judith
Isaac	Jemima	Solomon	Tobias
Rebekah	Joshua	Agur	Nehemiah
Jacob	Deborah	Uriah	Simon
Israel	Boaz	Obadiah	John
Rachel	Ruth	Elijah	Nathaniel
Zilpah	Jephtha	Elisha	Peter
Reuben	Samson	Jonah	Philip
Simeon	Eli	Zachariah	Bartholomew
Levi	Hannah	Hezekiah	Matthew

Andrew	Stephen	Aquila	Phœbe
Lazarus	Nicholas	Priscilla	Eunice
Mary	Cornelius	Epaphroditus	Rhoda
Martha	Paul	Dorcas	Lois (9 times).
Joanna	Luke	Lydia	
Matthias	Timothy	Tabitha	

This general adoption of Scripture Names seems to have been influenced by Methodism. In one family there occur within the space of one generation those of Seth, Isaac, Joseph, Hannah, Samuel, Bathsheba, Solomon, Nathan, Daniel, and Susannah: and another branch of the same family may be taken separately for the purpose of illustrating the point more particularly in the form of a genealogical table.

In this case the Methodist influence is clearly shown, Whitfield and John Wesley being in their glory in Gloucestershire from Rachel's birth to that of Lydia.

Some other peculiar names to be found during the same period are Julian, Marmaduke, Leander, Guy, Benedict, Philadelphia, Mirandah, Battah, Purina, Celia, Robertiana, Christian, Grace, Patience, and Prudence.

The writer can add out of many within his own experience that of a labourer's child whom he had to christen " Calliopeia Rosa Selina:" and of another baby respecting which the answer given by the mother when he said " Name this Child" was, " Aint he a dear little lump, Sir!"

BURIAL IN WOOLLEN.

Legislation in matters connected with the Church has often taken an odd turn since it got so much into the hands of Parliament. The wisdom of the House of Commons once provided that Lent should be carefully observed throughout the land for the encouragement—not of piety but—of the fisheries. It levied a heavy duty on the marriages of Bishops and Archbishops. It imposed a duty—the stamp is still to be seen with its rose and crown and "III PENCE" in some of our Parish Registers—on the registration of every Baptism, Marriage, or Burial, under a penalty of £5, the Clergy being privileged to receive two shillings in the pound for collecting the tax! [23 *Geo.* III. *ch.* 67.] But perhaps no such odd legislation was ever so enduring and vexatious as that which required the burial of man, woman, and child in Woollen for the encouragement of the woollen and paper trades. The Parish Register of Cam contains unusually full material for illustrating the operation of this vexatious law; and as it has been nearly forgotten, except by antiquaries, though it was in force until within a few months of the Battle of Waterloo, the reader may be interested in an account of it.

The first law on the subject [18 *Car.* II. *ch.* 4], was passed in the year of the Great Fire of London, 1666, but as the Legislature had neglected to provide efficient means for putting it in force it was never obeyed. Eleven years later, therefore, another Act was passed, [30 *Car.* II. *ch.* 3.] repealing the former, imposing a penalty, and encouraging informers by the offer of an ample reward. The preamble of this Act states that its predecessor "was intended for lessening the importation of linen from beyond the seas, and for the encouragement of the woollen and paper manufactures of this kingdom, had the same been observed." But "in respect there was not a sufficient remedy thereby given for the discovering and prosecution of offences against the said Act," it had become necessary to replace it by one of a more stringent character. This second Act was further amended by another of two years later date, entitled "An Additional Act for burying in woollen" [32 *Car.* II. *ch.* 1.].

.The law, as thus settled in 1677 and 1680, enacted that no dead body should be buried in any material that was not made from sheeps' wool, under a penalty of £5. It required that, within eight days after burial, if it had not been done earlier, an affidavit should be "sworn and sealed" before a Justice of the Peace declaring that the person buried "was not put in, wrapped or wound up, or buried, in any shirt, shift, sheet, or shroud made or mingled with flax, hemp, silk, hair, gold, or silver, or other than what is made of sheeps' wool only; nor in any coffin lined or faced with any cloth, stuff, or any other thing whatsoever made or mingled with flax, hemp, silk, hair, gold, or silver, or other material than what is made of sheeps' wool only." If this affidavit was delivered to the Clergyman he had to make an entry to that effect in the registration of the burial. If it was not delivered to him within eight days after burial the Clergyman was required to inform the Churchwardens and Overseers of the Parish, who forthwith were to take out a warrant for the recovery of £5 penalty from the responsible survivors; the money to be obtained by distress if it was not paid at once, and to be divided between the informer and the poor of the parish.

For the purpose of carrying out the provisions of the Act in Dursley and in its neighbourhood some directions were given by John Smyth, Esq., a local Magistrate, who was probably the son of Mr. Smyth the Historian of the Berkeley family; and a copy of these is written on page 143 of the Cam Register. They are as follow :—

"Directions given by John Smyth Esqr &c. to the Town of Dursley.

The Title of the Register Book mentioned in the Act to be made anew in every parish for burying in woollen only.

A Register of the Parish of Dursley in the County of Glouc. of such as have bin Buried in woollen, pursuant to the Act of Parlmt.

The Certificate to the Minister within 8 dayes.

A. B. Buried in woollen only the   day of Aug. 1678, as appeareth by the Affidavit of C. D. E. ff. sworn before John Smyth Esqr. one of his Maties Justices of the Peace &c: the   day of Aug: aforesaid.

To follow this Certificate, enter this Burial thus in the Register Book.

J. S. daughter of G. L. yeoman, Buried in woollen, prout Lex postulat, the   day of Aug: 1678, as by the Affidavit of E. ff. G. H. appeareth sworn before John Smyth Esqr. &c: the   day of   1678.

The Ministers Certificate to the Churchwds and Overseers of the Poore, when no such Affidavit is brought to him within 8 dayes.

I Edward Towgood Minister of Dursley do hereby certify to the Churchwds and Overseers of the Poore of Dursley aforesd that Marrian the wife of Willm Chamberlain of Dursley aforesayd Clotheworker was Interred in the Church yard of Dursley aforesayd the 7th day of this Instant August; but no Certificate thereof that it was done in woollen only pursuant to the Act of Parlmt hath been brought unto me within dayes 8 of the sayd Interment. In witnesse whereof I have hereunto sett my Hand the   day of   1678."

These authoritative directions of one of his Majesty's Justices of the Peace had no sooner reached Cam than they were put in practice by the Vicar of Cam of that day, John Barnsdale, a man of great exactness as the Register shows,

and one ready to show a good example of obedience to the
law—as most of us are when the law is to our advantage.

Travelling back to page 129 of the Parish Register we
find John Barnsdale carefully putting a new Title to his
register, but it is amusing to see the three sceptical words
with which he ends it, and which show that he expected
the law would be disobeyed.

"Here followeth the Register of such as have been Buried
at Cam in the County of Glouc. in woollen, pursuant to
ye late Act of Parliamt, Caroli IIdi Tricesimo: or should so."

Perhaps he and one of his principal parishioners had been
talking the matter over, and he knew what to expect: for
certain it is that the very first entry discloses a law abiding
Vicar and a law resisting parishioner. Antiquaries may be
grateful to both, for this is probably the most circumstantial
account on record of the practical operation of the Act.

"William, ye son of Willm and Jane Phinimore of Cam
was buried in the Church-yard of Cam aforesaid, the
sixteenth day of August, 1678. But no certificate thereof
that it was done in woollen only, pursuant to the Act
of Parlmt was brought unto the Vicar officiating in the
sayd Parish, within 8 dayes of the sayd Intermt, with the
Affidavit of two credible witnesses.

Whereupon Aug: 24th instant the sayd Vicar gave
notice thereof in writing under his hand to ye Chchwdns
and Overseeres of ye Poore of Cam, who, Aug: 26th
instant had a warrant granted them by John Smyth Esqr.
one of his Maties Justices of ye Peace &c: for Levying
the fforfeiture of ffive Pounds on the Goodes and Chattels
of Willm Phinimore before mentioned.

Whose Goodes were accordingly endeavoured to be dis-
trained upon: but without distresse made he payd ye same,
viz one moiety to ye use and benefit of the Poore of Cam:
namely to Mary Hitchins wid., Sarah Sawby wid., John

Perrot's wife, Daniel Dowsell's wife : Thomas Wood's wife, 10s. apiece. And the other moiety thereof was on the same day, viz Sept 6th, payd to yᵉ use of John Barnsdale Vicar of Cam, who informed."

One may hope that no uncomfortable feelings disturbed the future intercourse between Mr. Phinnimore and his Vicar. The very next burial entered is that of Daniel Phillimore Senior, late of the parish of Berkeley; and John Phillimore of Cam, sen. yeoman, aged 91, was buried in 1680 : but it does not appear that Mr. William Phinnimore required any further service of the kind for his immediate family before the time came when this entry also had to be made, " Mr. John Barnsdale, late Minister of Came, was buried in the Chancell in the Parish Church of Came aforesaid in sheep wooll only february the 9. 1680, as appeareth by the Affidavit of William Cornock of Cam aforesaid, broad-weaver and Joan Killemister of the same singell wooman sworne before John Smyth Esqʳᵉ yᵉ 9th Instant 1680." On Aug. 10th 1684 Robert son of William Phillimore " was buried in woollen only in witness whereof Mary Lacy and Jane Phillimore sware and sealed Aug. 17. 1684."

But the law was, in fact, so vexatious that many persons preferred to disobey it first, if they were allowed, and pay the fine of £5 afterwards : though it is said that constables would sometimes enter a house and require the linen shroud to be removed from a corpse prepared for burial ; and that at the end of the Burial Service the parish clerk would call out " who makes affidavit ? " and that such unseemly interference with people at the saddest time of their lives took place quite up to the close of the last century. There were, however, *doctrinnaires* even in those days ; and one of them wrote, so late as 1800, that it was an excellent law which saved 200,000 lbs. annually " from untimely corruption in the grave" and passed them "to the hands of the manufacturers of paper." [*Monthly Mag.* 1800.] But the law gradually fell into desuetude in many places and bore so unfairly upon those on whom it was still enforced that in 1814 it was repealed [54 *Geo.* III *ch.* 108]; penalties already incurred, but not paid, being remitted.

Meanwhile those who disliked being put to rest in the grave like ordinary mortals had somehow contrived to drive through the Act of Parliament boldly.

" 'Odious! in Woollen! t'would a saint provoke!'
Were the last words that poor Narcissa spoke
' No, let a charming chintz, and Brussels lace,
Wrap my cold limbs, and shade my lifeless face :
One would not, sure, be frightful when one's dead—
And—Betty—give this cheek a little red.' "

The lady of whom Pope wrote these caustic lines [*Moral Ess. Ep.* j.] was a famous actress named Oldfield, who was buried in Westminster Abbey, in the year 1731, in " a Brussels lace head-dress, a Holland shift with tucker and double ruffles of the same lace, and a pair of new kid gloves."

On the other hand there are parts of the country, as the North of England, where there is a prejudice against using any other material than woollen for burial; and new flannel shrouds ornamented with black ribbons are there almost universal. Whether this feeling springs from the custom originated by Act of Parliament, or whether it has a more ancient origin, is worth enquiry.

The Churchwardens' Book.

This is not of so much interest as the Parish Register, nor so valuable for its historical memorials as the Churchwardens' book of the adjoining Parish of Dursley.

It begins with the date April 21st, 1726, and ends on May 10th, 1842 : and the first entry consists of the following

piece of parochial poetry; the first four lines being on the
front, and the rest on the back of the Title page.

" Vain world! Thou nought but frequent changes rings
Time wears out Registers of Men and Things.
The old grows useless, and neglected lie
Its fate consigns it to obscurity."

" Man's gay and active days does soon decline
His meridian sun has but a short shine
Cyphers may almost sum up his short span
So vain and fleeting is the life of man
His time does hasten with rapidity
To be absorbed in Eternity."

Following the title page there is a valuable " register of
Officers in yᵉ parish of Cam from 1690 to 1739 " which
occupies twenty-six pages. Here are registered the names of
the Churchwardens, Overseers, Supervisors (or Highway Surveyors), Constables, and Tythingmen. A still earlier list is
written at the end of the earliest register of Christenings,
which carries back the list of Parish Officers to the year
1599: and perhaps there are few parishes which can boast of
such a list for so long a period as two and three quarter
centuries. In the list of these officers the names of Tyndale
and Huchens frequently occur as they do in the Parish
Register of the adjoining parish of Stinchcombe; and, as is
well known William Tyndale, the translator of the New
Testament into English in the reign of Henry VIII., used
the name of Hutchens as an *alias*, a fact which seems to
confirm the tradition that he was connected with this district
of Gloucestershire.

There are not many entries of interest in the Churchwardens' accounts, but the following may be thought worth
record in type.

1725   " For goeing to Gloucester to stop process when
            presented by Nathˡˡ Pope.   3s 6d

1727 "Mary Terret shall have a Shift and a Horse load Coal."

1730 "For setting stones at yᵉ Tower to prevent playing att Balles. 2s. 6d.

"for apillpot Candelstick £1. 1. 0.

1731 [*J. Parker's*] "Part of the expense in going aprocessioning £1. 2. 0.

[*Nath. Pope's*] Part do do £.1. 0. 0.

In 1737 there is a similar entry of "Expenses for processioning £1. 4. 0."

1732 "The Accompt of Jnᵒ Phillimore and Wᵐ Roach Churchwardens of the Parish of Cam for Our Fathers for the Year 1732."

"Paid for a support in the Middle Ile of the Church for two boxes for briffs 4s."

From this it appears that Briefs were sometimes responded to by the people putting their money, or not putting it, into boxes similar to alms boxes. This may have been the way in which the penny was gathered from the parishioners of Ormsby for the rebuilding of Dursley steeple [see page 43].

1734 "For a Shift for Edith Spencer 3s. 4d.

1735 "For A Bed and Wool for Oaty's Son and Dafter 7s 6d.

1736 "Samˡ Harding's Money for the Expence of Thoˢ Oaty Familly with the Small pox. £10. 2s.

"Paid for a new Bible £3. 6. 0."

"pd for Six foxes 3s 6d." In 1738 four foxes were paid for, in 1740 four more, in 1741 six,—but the price reduced to 3s 0d.—and in 1744, shocking to relate, there is an entry "To Cash pd Mr Gyde's Huntsman for a Fox 1s. 0d."!! In 1745 four more are entered, not it is to be hoped to the Huntsman, at 2s 0d, and four "polecats" at 1s 4d.

These latter entries are curiously mixed up with payments

for " 2 Bottles of Wine [1] and one loaf 5s 0d," and a new
Prayer Book for the clerk, 15s 0.

1750 " Pd Wm Davis for 3 Tabels for the Benny Facktions
    £1. 5. 0 "
    " Pd fcr for drawing and gilding the frames
    £4. 13. 10."

1765 April 8th, " Mary Phillimore of Upthrop " was ap-
    pointed Churchwarden for Upper Cam, with
    William Keen, but Samuel Phillimore seems to
    have acted.

1768 April 4th, Mrs Mary Randolph was appointed Over-
    seer for Lower Cam.

So advanced was the question of " women's rights " in Cam
even a century ago.

1782 New dial for clock   £4. 9. 8
    Painting ditto   3. 10. 0
    Mending and cleaning ditto   11. 0
1809 New face to clock and making
    altarpiece   12. 14. 2½
1808 Painting the Dial   5. 15. 6
1813 Mending the Clock   6. 0. 0
1817 " Paid Mr Daw's Bill for
    the King's Arms and Dial "   15. 9. 0

The Clock dial was evidently a serious charge upon the
Church Rates.

1813 Oct 12. Paid at Citation for prayer for Wellington's
    Victory. 4s 0d.

1814 7 loads of Stone from Hampton Common £17. 3. 4
    Hauling ditto   £10. 10. 0
    This was for the repair of the Church Tower,
    the whole cost being £31. 19. 1.

---

[1] It is observable that "Taint" and "Tent" Wine are entered at
an even earlier date than this, showing that the use of this Wine for
the Holy Sacrament is an old custom.

1823   The Church was new pewed at a cost of £269, subscribed by 30 persons, the Vicar's subscription being £21.

Taint Wine £7. 11. 0

1824   " Rd Miles fetching the D: Bass from Nicholls " 1s 0d.

3 Strings to the Double Bass   £1. 4. 0

1825   Mending the Double Bass   £1. 0. 0

1826   Expenses with the double bas   5s. 0

1828   Tuning and repairing the organ   11s. 0

At the end of the book is the following entry, which it is a pleasure to put upon permanent record. A similar gift was made to Cowley near Oxford about the same time by Bishop Coleridge.

" June 10th in the Year of our Lord 1823 On which day the Revd Wm Fryer, Vicar of the Parish of Cam, presented to the Parish a Sacramental Cup and Cover or Salver, to be used for private Communion, by the Vicar, as occasion may require for the time being for ever. And on the Decease of any and every such Vicar, the Churchwardens of the said Parish of Cam will be and are hereby empowered to demand of the Heirs, Executors, or Administrators of every such Vicar the aforementioned Cup &c. And on the appointment of a new Vicar shall present the same to him, to be used, as previously noticed, and on no other occasion, unless they might be *particularly* wanted when the holy Sacrament of the Lord's Supper shall be administered in publick.

Wm Fryer Vicar

Thos Morse   ⎫

W Long   ⎬ Churchwardens

Thos Gabb Overseer

Benj. Drew

Thos Hadley

Stepn Robinson

Chas Whittard Junr Vestry Clerk "

SPARROWS AND CHURCHWARDENS.

In the days when the present writer was sowing his ecclesiastical wild oats in a Fen Curacy, the archæological zeal which time has long tempered led him up a very long ladder (during restoration work) to a beam which crossed the Nave of the Church some fifty feet above the floor. There he found the old oak timber pitted with largish holes, and from out of the holes he extracted some lumps of lead. He was making a collection of all curiosities found in the Church,— and not a few real ones had been found,—for preservation at the Vicarage,—and these lumps of lead were placed in a pill box duly labelled, according to received tradition, "slugs from the guns of Cromwell's soldiers, shot at the Royal Arms." Not long afterwards on inspecting the recently discovered treasures he found the inscription corrected by his commanding officer to "shots from old John Wilkins' gun when slaughtering the sparrows." Whether the old sexton was a bad shot and fired much lead ineffectually at each sparrow, or whether sparrows abounded inside the Church and attached themselves fondly to that special beam is not recorded: but it is certain that the anti-sentimental Wilkins theory is supported by general evidence of the hostility to sparrows which was formerly borne by Church officers.

And in these days when Acts of Parliament are called for to protect small birds, and handbills setting forth the penalties to be paid for disobeying the law are posted up in every Church School, it is worth while to show what is on record respecting small birds and their treatment a generation or so ago in the parish of Cam.

The sparrows lived as peacefully in Cam until 1819—so far as the Churchwardens' accounts show—as if they had been birds of Paradise : but for the eleven years that followed they had a hard time of it, and if they attempted to pick up a living anywhere within the parish boundaries, it must

P 2

have been under the influence either of great ignorance as to
the principles of Cam boys and Cam Churchwardens, or of
such courage as makes brave sparrows like brave men march
to the mouth of a gun in the course of duty.

Here is the account of their treatment, as it may be gathered
from the Churchwardens' book.

Years.	No. of Sparrows heads.	Money paid.		
1819	532	£1	2	2
1820	1859	3	17	1½
1821 1822	1432	2	19	8
1823	640	1	5	10
1824	1543	3	4	4
1825	1411	2	18	10
1826	224		9	4
1827	1520	3	3	4
1828	3571	7	8	9½
1829	3842	5	15	3½
1830	3345	3	6	9½
1831-7	2701	2	18	0¾
Total	22,620	£37	9	6¾

In those days a sparrow was considered to be worth a
halfpenny: or rather perhaps his "room being" thought
"better than his company," that was the sum which a
Churchwarden thought good to pay out of the Church Rates
to get rid of him. But in 1829 when the Reform Bill was
looming in the distance the value of the sparrow suddenly
fell to a farthing. As soon as it was certain that it would
pass the Cam farmers felt that they would want their money
for other purposes than sparrows' heads, and so in 1831, the

payments nearly ceased. From that time until the accession
of Queen Victoria only about one-tenth of the number of
birds were paid for compared with preceding years: and
when our Lady Sovereign raised all virtues to the throne
that of humanity towards small birds began to prevail, so
that the price of a sparrow has never since appeared in the
Church accounts of Cam.

It was not nice for them to appear in Church accounts at
all.   One would rather the birds should find themselves a
·house of refuge in the Church than that it should be associated with their destruction.

And while the farmers were thus expending the Church
Rate the grubs must have laughed from the furrow into the
faces of their ploughmen : and the wireworms must have
sung merrily ,as they bored into the very hearts of their
turnips.

THE BELLS.

If a family of Church Bells could chime out to us their
recollections, what stories they might tell even in a country
parish like Cam, that has never been remarkable for great
events.

Sometimes, it is true, they would tell us, they have had
duty to do on great occasions.   They never failed to ring out
on the Fifth of November, so long as there was a general
belief that

"There can be no reason
Why Gunpowder treason
Should ever be forgot."

They were once as regular also in commemorating the 29th
of May.   But they had scarcely rang out their harmonies on
that day in 1763, before discord arose on the subject among
the Parishioners.   A Vestry Meeting was called on June 1st
at which·" it was agreed not to pay anything for the future

for ringing on the 29th Day of May, and it was likewise agreed that what was paid to the ringers ye 29 of May last shall not be allowed." But this temporary discord soon passed away, for the ringers were paid their usual five shillings for the day in 1764, and in nearly if not all succeeding years. Much less persistent was the memory of that battle at Culloden in 1746, which extinguished all the hopes of the Stuarts, for although the bells rang "in remembrance" of it in 1747 and 1748, it seems afterwards to have been quite forgotten, at least in the Belfry. Later on the Cam family rang their part in the national bell-harmony of joy for the great victories of Wellington. Coronation days were not forgotten by them : sad national tolling days set the deepest toned among them to send forth his solemn wail once a minute that it might mingle in the great chorus of sorrow : and when England's Princess came home with her husband wonderful indeed would it have been if any bells had been unwilling to join in the universal marriage peal.

But the ordinary associations connected with the Church Bells of a village are chiefly of a domestic character. Our Bell-family would tell us stories of generations who listened to their summoning voice as they chimed the hour of prayer year after year and age after age ; of those whose childish hands had clapped together with laughing joy as they heard the merry chimes ; who had walked sunnily forth from the Porch when mature years had made the wedding-peal theirs ; who—later still—had followed their elders to the same Porch as the great tenor tolled out the last peal for them ; and who themselves in time came to their last peal also and heard the sound of Bells no more, unless bells make part of the sweet music of Paradise.

" From the Church tower where they dwell,
Tolls to prayer the passing bell,
When, with dull and solemn tread,
Mourners bear to Church their dead,

Muffled voices sad and low
From those bells sob out their woe.
Merry marriage chimes are ringing,
Mirth on all sides round them flinging;
From the Church door softly glide
Happy bridegroom, blooming bride,
Young and old around them press,
Kindly gaze, and fondly bless.
By those chimings gently shaken
Hope and memory awaken;
Youth hath bright and blissful gleamings
Of such joy in future dreamings;
While the oldest in the train,
Think that they are young again.

Happy bells! the heart rejoices
In their dear familiar voices,
Loved for all their tender sadness,
And their full out-spoken gladness;
Nor the less beloved when they
Call us on the Holy Day,
Or at other week-day times
Bid to prayer with cheerful chimes."

But the Bell family of Cam is not one of very ancient date,
for they only came into existence five human generations ago,
which is nothing in the family history of Bells,—one at
Claughton in Lancashire being dated 1296, and many as old
existing. There are five of them now, but the bell cage was
intended to hold six when it was put up—as an inscription on
it states—by "Thomas Church and John Milsom Churchwardens, 1679," and so, probably, their ancient predecessors
were really six in number, but were replaced by five only
when the present ring was cast in 1710. Tradition has it
that the sixth bell was translated to Stinchcombe, and perhaps tradition may say true.

Like a very large number of Gloucestershire bells those of Cam owe their parentage to the Rudhalls, bell founders of Gloucester, who continued to supply Churches with excellent bells until 1826, when the old and famous name gave place to one now almost as famous in belfries, that of Mears.

The inscription on each of the five bells tells the story of its own birth as follows:

1] JOHN HALLING ABRA: RVDHALL BELL FOVNDER 1710
[Diam. 3ft.]

2] ABRA: RVDHALL CAST VS ALL 1710 [Diam. 3ft. 2in.]

3] A: R: 1709. PROSPERITY TO OUR BENEFACTORS AND RINGERS
[Diam. 3ft. 3in.]

4] A: R: 1710. LET VS RING FOR PEACE [Diam. 3ft. 3in.]

5 Tenor] COLONEL HOPTON BENEFACTOR A: R: 1710
EDWARD TURNER MINISTER.
PEACE AND GOOD NEIGHBOURHOOD. [Diam. 3ft. 6in.]

In addition to which inscription each bell bears an ornamental border, of a design found not uncommonly on other bells, as well as those of the Rudhalls.

In older days the inscriptions upon bells were almost invariably of a religious character. So near to the time of the above as 1681 some of the bells of York Cathedral were inscribed with "Jubilate Domino," "Exultate Deo," "Gloria in Excelsis Deo:" while a little earlier, in 1627, is found on another bell of the same Church:—

"Sweetly tolling men we call
To taste on food to feed the soul."

and in 1599,—

" I will sound and resound to Thy people, Lord,
With my sweet voice to call them to Thy word."

When Cam bells come to be re-cast again, here are five hints for those who shall have to think about inscriptions for them.

Eighteenth Century Orthodoxy.

At the end of the Churchwardens' book there is a contemporary copy of a bequest in which the Vicars of Cam have an interest, and which is worth reprinting here [1] as an illustration of Churchmanship in the middle of the last century.

" Richard Tyler, late of the city of Bristol, Gent., pursuant to the will of his brother John Tyler, Gent. (both Natives of Berkeley), in the year 1749, gave an Estate, situate in the Tything of Hinton, for the following uses, as appears by a deed enrolled in Chancery in the year 1750 : viz. Thirty Shillings to be equally divided between the Clerk and Sexton of the Parish Church of Berkeley, for ringing the Bell and attending Divine Service as hereinafter directed. The remaining part of the yearly profits to be divided between the Ministers of Berkeley, Cam, Wotton-under-edge, Cromhall, Tortworth, Dursley, and Thornbury, for reading Morning Prayer, and preaching seventeen sermons annually in Berkeley Church on the following Days, and during Lent, on the following Subjects :—

1. The Lent Fast.
2. Against Atheism and Infidelity.
3. The Catholic Church.
4. Excellency of the Church of England.
5. The Defence of the Divinity of our Saviour.
6. Baptism.
7. Confirmation.
8. Confession and Absolution.
9. Errors of the Church of Rome.
10. Against Enthusiasm and Superstition.
11. Restitution.
12. Attending Public Worship.
13. Frequenting the Holy Communion.
14. Repentance.

[1] It is to be found in Bigland's Collections, 157, and in Fosbroke's *Berkeley Manuscripts*, 66.

Sermons on the first seven subjects to be preached in the first year, beginning on Ash-Wednesday, 1750, and on the remaining other seven in the following year, and so alternately and successively for ever. One of the said Sermons to be preached by each of the above named Ministers on every Wednesday in Lent, Four of other Ten by the Minister of Berkeley, and the remaining Six by the respective Ministers of the other parishes aforesaid, on the first Wednesday in every succeeding month, within the compass of the year."

THE PHILLIMORE FAMILY.

An ancient family whose name has become historical, that of Phillimore, was long settled at Cam, where many of their tombstones are to seen in the Church and Churchyard, and where their name appears in the Parish Register about 250 times between 1571 and 1825.

The earliest trace of them in Cam or its immediate neighbourhood is found in the Records of the Manor of Stinchcombe. In 1522 John Fynamore received from the Crown a Lease of a Water Corn Mill called Corriett's Mill, — afterwards joined with a Gigge Mill and a Fulling Mill under the same roof,— to hold for his life and that of his wife Alice (lately the wife of John Tyndale), John and Thomas Fynamore his sons by Agnes his former wife, and William Fynamore his son by Alice his present wife. John Fynamore himself died in 1532, Alice his widow in 1535. The next trace of the family is found in a Will which is preserved in the Probate Office at Gloucester [1] This is the will of William ffyllymore of Coaley (the next parish to Cam) which was proved on Aug. 12th,

---

[1] Foxe the Church Historian records the story of Henry Finmore, Filmer, or Finnemore,—for he spells the name in each way—who was Churchwarden of Windsor, and a friend of Marbecke the famous adapter of the old Church song to the Book of Common Prayer. Finnemore was burned to death under the Act of the Six Articles on July 3rd, 1543. [*Foxe's Acts & Mon.*, v. pp. 488, 993. ed. 1846.]

1558, and by which his personal property is left in part to
Thomas and Jane ffylymore his father and mother. This
Jane was probably the Joan Phinnimore, widow, whose burial
is entered in the Register on Oct. 31st 1575. Between
1571 and 1604 there are many entries of sons and daughters
born to George, Richard, and John Phinnimore, who appear
to have been three brothers, clothiers, from whom the subsequent members of the family were descended. In the Stinchcombe deeds the name is spelt Fynamore, Fynymore,
Fynemore, Phinnymore, Fyllimore, and Fylymore. It is
first spelt "Phillimore" in 1640, and from that time both
forms of the name occur during thirty or forty years, the
later one alone being used after about 1680 in the Cam registers, though the early one is still common in Gloucestershire
and elsewhere. President Fillmore traced his American
ancestry back to a John Phillmore who was living about the
year 1710, and thought that John Phillmore was derived
from an English family named Phillemore : so that Cam has
probably given a President to the United States.

The principal residence of the family appears to have been
a house which stood on the site now occupied by the Chapel
of St. Bartholomew, and which in its later years was converted
into an Inn under the sign of the Berkeley Arms. Here, it
is said, were many portraits of the Phillimores which had
been left in the house as fixtures, but which were destroyed
by the rough frequenters of the Inn when they were in their
cups. Another of their houses was Nash Hall now a farm-
house known as The Knapp.[1] In this house there still
remains as one of the fixtures a fine picture of sixteenth

---

[1] "Mr. Samuel Phillimore of the Knapp" is mentioned in the
Churchwardens' accounts for 1777. There is a grim tradition at the
Knapp that a body lies buried under the stone steps which lead down
from the hall to the cellar, and that the spirit of the deceased rises
whenever grass grows on the steps. Boiling water used to be poured
upon the steps to prevent the grass from growing.

century date which is said to be one of the family portraits.
It represents a naval officer's half-length left profile, with
cravat and ruffles of the Caroline period: and in the back-
ground on his right is a three masted ship, with Spanish
colours, which seems to represent some famous capture
made by him. The picture is in its original frame of black
and gold, and appears to be the work of a superior artist
of the school of Lely. Another house of the family was
The Vennings, called more recently The Manor House.
This was bought of William Hopton by John Phillimore in
1689, and left by him in 1611 to his second son John. This
house,—which was given to an old servant in the early part
of the present century,—retains two memorials of its former
occupants, the one a merchant's mark of John Phillimore, with
the date 1706 :

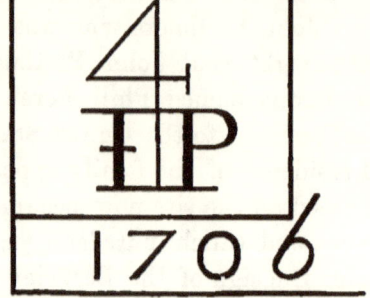

the other, the

initials of John Phillimore and his wife Mary on the head of
the porch, with the date 1712. This John Phillimore was

the eldest representative of Richard the second of the three
brothers above named, and is now represented by W.
Phillimore Stiff Phillimore, Esqre., of Snenton near Nottingham, and of Wresden in Uley.

A younger brother of the preceding John Phillimore was named Joseph, and migrated to London, where his son Robert became established on property at Kensington, and, by marriage with Elizabeth Jephson an heiress, on an estate at Kendalls in Hertfordshire. From him were descended the Phillimores of Kendalls, the eminent ecclesiastical Judges, Dr. Joseph Phillimore and his son Sir Robert Joseph Phillimore, and Sir John Phillimore a naval officer of high repute in the last generation [1]

The last of the Phillimores who remained in their old locality were Mr. John Phillimore of Symond's Hall, Uley, and the Knapp, Cam, and his sister, Mrs. Purnell of Kingshill, Dursley. Mr. Phillimore died in 1825 and Mrs. Purnell in 1826, when the Cam Estate and £14,000 were left to John Phillimore Hicks, Esqre., the lands at Uley and Owlpen, with £15,000 to Robert Kingscote, Esqre., a near neighbour of ancient family, and some £40,000 to other legatees.

The following table gives a correct view, it is believed, of the connection between the Cam Phillimores and those whose names have been mentioned above as distinguished members of the family in modern times. [2]

In addition to the alliances indicated in the table the Phillimores of Cam have intermarried with Gloucestershire families of Fowler, Dorney, Hicks, Wallington, Purnell, Holbrow, Small, Austin, Stiff, and Jenner.

---

[1] It is worth mentioning that the Gloucestershire village which is so honourably associated with the great law names of Selwyn and Phillimore was also the native place of an industrious author of some note, Edward Trotman, who wrote an abridgement of Sir Edward Coke's eleven volumes of Reports, and was buried in the Temple Church on May 29th, 1643.

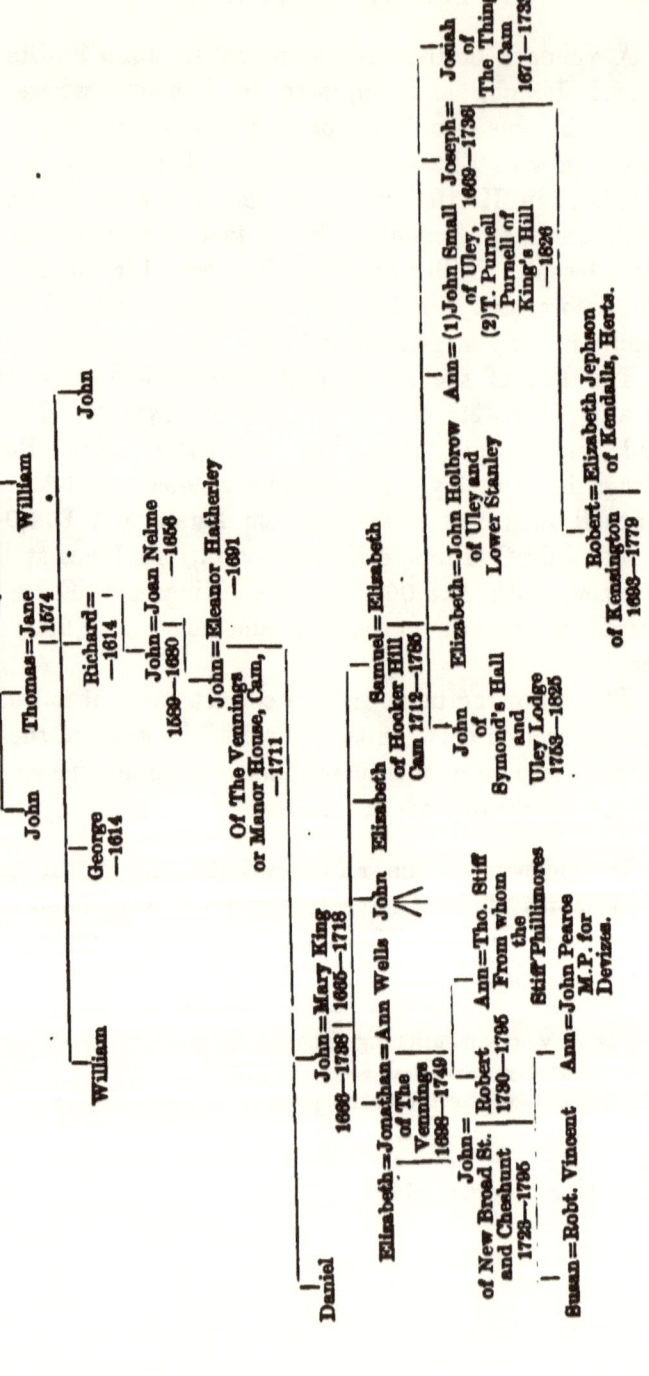

2 PHILLIMORE of Cam, &c.

ARMS. Sable three Bars or in chief, as many Cinquefoils or. CREST. Out of a Tower a falcon rising wings elevated, proper.

In Cam Church there is also a monument on which the same arms are represented with the Cinquefoils argent.

In Papworth's Ordinary and in Berry's County Families both Bars and Cinquefoils are argent; and the Crest is sometimes a dove out of a castle, and in other cases an eagle displayed gules.

STINCHCOMBE HILL.

This is the name given to a broad T-shaped peninsula of high ground running out westward at right angles from the line of the Cotswolds, near Dursley and Cam. The length of this projection is about three miles, and though the ridge which forms it is at first only thirty yards across and fringed with trees, it expands at last into a fine open down, the "Hill" proper, with Drakestone Point (the highest part, 750 feet above the sea) as an offshoot to the South.

The view, though perhaps not finer than some others in Gloucestershire, has features of peculiar interest. The Hill is not so high as Broadway or even as Nibley Knoll (within two miles), nor does it give so wild a prospect as May Hill or Stanton Hill. But for three-fifths of the circle the horizon is not less than twenty miles distant, while the nearer landscape is full of beauty and variety. And what is more important, at every point of the distance the eye rests on something which is worthy of attention. Perhaps the point which distinguishes this view most strongly from others in Gloucestershire is the long and broad course of the Severn across it, which can be traced from a few miles below Gloucester till it is merged in the Bristol Channel. Without it the valley would be comparatively colourless : its presence adds a beauty to the scene which need only be beheld to be appreciated.

The rough Outline-view which accompanies these pages will perhaps serve to direct attention to what is best worth seeing. The point from which it is taken is a small cup-like hollow about a dozen yards south-west of the flagstaff on Drakestone Point. It should be clearly understood that where the outline

of the Hill is denoted by a dotted line, the Hill is supposed
to be transparent for the sake of introducing objects which
can be seen from other parts of the Down. It will be best to
follow the view from south to westward, starting from the
conspicuous monument on Nibley Knoll, marked 1 on the
map.

The Monument (1) was erected a few years ago to commemorate William Tyndale (1483—1536), the English
Reformer and Translator of the Bible, who was probably born
at North Nibley (3), the village at the foot of the Knoll,
the Church of which can be seen to the right. Just over the
foot of the Knoll can be seen part of Kingswood (2), the site
of a once-famous monastery, now a small village under the
shadow of Wotton-under-Edge, a town similar in size and
position to Dursley, but as completely separated from its
sister-town as three miles and a half of hilly country can
make it. It lies out of sight to the left of Kingswood.

The horizon now begins to recede, bounded by the Cotswolds, on which the camps of Horton and Sodbury may be
distinguished by those who know the country. The line is
next broken by the Lansdowne Monument (5) above Bath,
'beyond which the Cotswolds reach their southern extremity.
Just above where they fail, on the slope of a far distant hill
may be seen in fine weather another monument (6) which
seems to be Alfred's Tower near Taunton. [At this point the
end of Drakestone Point (7) obstructs much of the view,
unless a move be made to the extreme edge.]

Bristol (8) is the next conspicuous object, of which little
but smoke and tall chimneys can usually be distinguished,
the high ground between Horfield and Stapleton hiding
most of the city. But in Clifton (10) can be seen Christ
Church and the Observatory, possibly even the piers of the
Suspension Bridge. Immediately above Clifton stands the
Tower of Dundry Church (9), a well-known beacon about

Q

four miles from Bristol, behind and above which appear the
Quantock Hills. The valley of the Avon may be traced
until Portishead (13) is seen over the ships in Kings-Road,
jutting out into the Bristol Channel, while off the point, ten
miles further distant, are the Steep and Flat Holmes, the
former distinguished by its high round outline, the latter by
a lighthouse. Much nearer, a little to the right, is Denny
Island. In ordinary weather all beyond these objects seems
open sea, but occasionally the line of the Somersetshire coast
by Weston, Clevedon, Watchet, and even parts of Exmoor
to the border of Devonshire bound the view, stretching completely across till they meet the Glamorganshire shore.
Below this last the bold outline of Aust Cliff (15), *Trajectus
Augusti*, strikes the eye, which with St. Tecla's Isle (16) at
the mouth of the Wye, marks the point where the Bristol
Channel ends and the Severn begins.

Turning attention to the nearer view, the eye rests upon
the line of the Midland Railway. Immediately below
Clifton is Tortworth Tower (11), in the churchyard of
which to the left of the Church is the old tree that has been
a landmark since the days of King John. To the right, just
above the trees, can be discerned the top of Tortworth Court,
Lord Ducie's seat. The large wood nearer the spectator to
the right is Michaelwood Chase (12), once part of the Forest
of Kingswood: above the northern extremity of it, about
four miles from Aust Cliff, is Thornbury (14), with its
richly-decorated tower.

Beyond the river and above the mouth of the Wye are
the Glamorganshire Hills, in the shadow of which is Cardiff,
hardly discernible. Tracing the course of the Wye we see
Chepstow (17) and, less easy to find, the Windcliff (18),
900 feet high and well wooded at the top. There is then
little to notice till we reach the Brecknock Beacons (20) and
the Sugar Loaf (21). The latter is unmistakable in fairly

clear weather from its shape; the former requires good sight at any time, to make out its three pinnacles rising above the nearer range. Abergavenny is out of sight at the foot of the Sugar Loaf, but the ridge of the Skirrid is visible a little to the right below the peak, and further still, just beneath a round tree-covered knoll, is Stanton Hill, above Monmouth. The long line above and behind these objects, terminating in a bold bluff, is the so-called Black Forest. Next comes the nearer tract of undulating woodland called the Forest of Dean (24), now unfortunately easily recognised by the smoke which overhangs it night and day from iron works.

Returning now to the Gloucestershire side of the Severn, Berkeley (19) though not easily found by the eye, may usually be traced by the blue smoke of the town and the walls of the Castle on the left "by yon tuft of trees" [*Shakespeare. Rich. II. 2, 3, 53*]. Where the river disappears behind Sharpness Point, may be seen the outlet of the Gloucester and Berkeley Canal (22), while glimpses of the Canal itself appear at intervals most of the way to Gloucester, and, sometimes ships' masts moving among the trees. The Church Spire (23) between us and the Point, just beneath our Hill belongs to the pretty village of Stinchcombe, where Isaac Williams lived, and from which the Hill takes its name. Following the course of the Severn we come to the Horse Shoe, a large bend of the river, beginning near Frampton Church (31) and winding round Barrow Hill (28) by Fretherne, and on the further side by Newnham (25) and Westbury-on-Severn (27). Above the last is May Hill (26) with its clump of trees, and, due north of us, the Malvern Hills (29), of which the highest peak is the Worcestershire Beacon, the next the North Hill, and the hill fortified with earthworks to the left the Hereford-shire Beacon. In the broad valley to the right there is nothing to notice except Highnam Church (32).

Gloucester Cathedral (34) next comes into sight, every detail of which can be made out with good glasses. Tewkesbury Abbey Tower is just above to the left, and on very exceptional days the Lickey Hills between Bromsgrove and Birmingham may be seen above all. At the Monument on Bredon Hill (35) beyond Cheltenham (which is itself hidden behind Robin Hood Hill to the right of Gloucester) the horizon begins to contract, the prospect being limited by the Cotswolds above Haresfield and Stonehouse (39) (where the line is broken by the Stroud Valley, affording a glimpse of the hills by Painswick), and nearer still by Frocester Hill (41).

Frocester Church (36) at some distance from the Hill is just visible, but to see Coaley (38), Lower Cam (37), and Upper Cam (40), a move must be made to the northern part of the Down.

To the right of Frocester Hill a small clump of trees marks the top of the beautiful Woodchester Valley which runs eastward towards Stroud, and a little further on is the celebrated chambered Tumulus near Uley (42), and the great Camp on Uley Bury (45). Beneath these last objects are the curious detached hills which characterize the Uley Valley (48). First is Cam Peak (44), a small conical hill hardly separated from the curved ridge of Long Down (43); next, more in the valley, Downham (46), with its trees and ruined fever-house on the summit. These with the spurs of Uley Bury form the northern wall of the valley, the narrow neck joining Stinchcombe Hill to the Cotswolds being the southern. Both ends of the valley are hidden from our view, for while at the village of Uley beneath the Bury small "combes" begin to ramify among the hills as far as to the source of the Cam, to Owlpen House (47) and to Nymphsfield, Dursley at the mouth of the valley is wholly concealed by its own down.

Little now remains to be noticed except the Ridge (49), and Stancombe House which lies in beautiful grounds at our feet, not far from the site of a Roman Villa, now covered up.[1] Above some trees to the right is the Hawkesbury Monument (50), near Badminton, close to which in appearance though not in reality is Tyndale's Monument, from which we began our description.

It may be worth while to remark that the Cotswolds from near Bristol to Bredon Hill—the whole of which line is visible from Stinchcombe Hill—were considered by the Romans so important a line of defence as to be protected by no less than twenty-five camps.

Having thus done our best to describe in humble prose the notable points of the prospect from Stinchcombe Hill, it may be interesting to the reader to see what a poet had to say on the subject a hundred and thirty years ago. The verses which we reprint, form a small folio pamphlet of twelve pages, and are entitled " Stinchcomb-Hill, a Poem: or, The Prospect. By the Reverend Mr. Edward Pickering Rich, of North-Cerney, Gloucestershire." But it would be unjust to the Author not to prefix his dedication, and so, we reproduce his work in its completeness.

" To the TRULY VIRTUOUS *Mrs. A. CHAMBERS.*

" MADAM,

" *THE following Rhymes were wrote under Your immediate Influence, for, if You remember, my Table was Your Knee ; we had no sooner viewed the delightful Prospect of* Stinchcomb-Hill, *in Gloucestershire, but You, with an agreeable Smile, commanded me to write something on it, which I immediately comply'd with, and wrote the following Piece ; in which, if there is any Thing that can please a Lady of Your nice distinguishing Taste, ascribe it all to Your all-inspiring Beauty ; and, when*

---

[1] An account of some Antiquities found on excavating this villa will be found in the Archæological Association's Journal.

I flag, kindly believe I was spent in Gazing on the too dazzling
Glory of Your bright Sun-like Beauty. The kind Appro-
bation it met with from You and a few other Ladies of the
highest Distinction and Fortune, makes it appear in public.
Therefore, I will make no Apology, since You are pleased to
like it; You, that I was always glad to please, smile on my well-
meant Essay, and accept the Poetical Endeavours of Your
    "Sincere *Inamorato*, and Most Obedient Servant,
                        " EDWARD PICKERING RICH.

" IF you, ye virtuous Fair, will fire my Breast,
And patronize my Muse, by Love distress'd ;
Henceforth I will commence a Priest of Fame,
And never tremble at a Critic's Name.

Fair *Amaryllis*, we'll a While retire,
From the low *Villa*, where the Hills aspire ;
Where the high Mountains emulate the Sky,
And Prospects wide and various charm the Eye.
Not *Alpine* Hills such glorious Scenes can show,
Tho' *Rome* and all its Splendor lay below :
Tho' boasted *Tyber* drew its wat'ry Store,
With mazy Error thro' that classic Shore :
Nor old *Olympus*, sung so oft in Lays,
Can justly merit so sincere a Praise,
As *Stinchcomb's* tow'ing Height, that soaring Hill,
That does with Wonder all Spectators fill.
Observe, bright Maid, and ope your glorious Eyes,
And see the Prospects regularly rise.
First ken yon Mountains eminently high,
Which scorn the lower World, and mount the Sky ;
Where the old *Britons*, as they proudly go,
Look down with Trembling at the Deep below.
There, with a dismal melancholy Roar,
The raging Waters lash the sounding Shore ;

Severn 'tis called by all Historic Fame,
From drowned *Sabrine* it deriv'd its Name :
Here *Berkley's* antiquated Dome ascends,
And worn with Age most venerably bends ;
There erst a King as Chronicles relate,
Met with his cruel melancholy Fate.

Look where the Sun his glorious Beams displays,
And scatters gloriously his glittering Rays,
O'er yonder Tow'rs and Pinnacles that rise,
Brightly refulgent to the neighb'ring Skies ;
In that fair Vale the lovely City stands,
At once our Wonder and our Praise commands,
Gloucester eclypt.
A College there magnificently grand,
Built by some wond'rous Artist's wond'rous Hand ;
Where if two Lovers lend an amorous ear,
Widely divided, whisper and yet hear.
Leave now the City, and then turn your Eyes,
Where Sylvan Scenes and Rural Prospects rise ;
Promiscuous Villa's scatter'd here and there,
In artless Beauty innocently fair ;
Their pleasant Meadows in a cheerful Green
Delight the Eyes and drive away the Spleen.
But that's not all, that we do much out-do
All other Countries, for a length'ning View ;
That we the World in Prospect will excel,
And high above the rest car' off the Bell :
But then our Bells are so exceeding bright,
That all around they cast a glorious Light ;
They're unaffected with their pretty Meins
Of Innocence and Beauty, Rural Queens.
Tho' now in general I have sung the Fair,
Yet one above the rest my choicest care ; .

So in a charming starry glittering Night,
When every Star then glitters in our Sight,
Yet all agree the Moon's the softer Light.
So *Amaryllis*, so, my brighter Maid,
When you appear, all other Beauties fade;
Fain would I strive your wond'rous Charms to paint,
But Words can't speak 'em and Description's faint:
A Goddess' Form let Gods alone express,
For who are fit to draw it, who are less—— ?
Oh! that I'd *Mylton's* Style, that Heav'nly Song,
To you bright Maid such Verses do belong!
Then would I give the World a glimmering View
Of wond'rous Virtues center'd all in you.
My Muse, sweet Maid, bids us the Hill descend,
And warns me for to hasten to the end:
Therefore, accept my careful Conduct down,
From the high Summit to your humbler Town:
So the first Pair were forc'd to leave behind
Their dear lost Eden, with reluctant Mind."

ULEY.

This pleasant and prettily situated village was once of considerable importance as a seat of the West of England cloth manufacture, and in the height of its prosperity must have rivalled in size the neighbouring town of Dursley. It is situated in a hollow of the Cotswolds, about two and a half miles north-east of Dursley, and is shut in by hills on all sides but the west. Many springs take their rise in these hills, and flowing down into the valley form the little stream called the Ewelme; which, running on to Dursley, is augmented by the waters of the Broadwell, and afterwards becomes the Cam.

But Uley became a clothing village not much earlier than the reign of Queen Elizabeth, and it had nestled down in its quiet valley for many ages before that time. When men first built their homes here and gave them a name is hard to say,[1] but it seems to have been in those early days when their language designated as " Wl ley" what we should now call a " wool valley," and as " Wl pen " what we should now call a " wool down or hill: " and thus the primitive inhabitants were no doubt as great in the growth of long wool as their descendants were in the manufacture of it into broad-cloth. Later on, perhaps, when Norman gentry came to live among the primitive shepherds of the place, people bethought them of another characteristic of the locality, and especially of the

---

[1] Canon Lysons considers that the name of Uley may be traced to the Hebrew " Olah " a " burnt offering " or " a high place, a place of whole burnt offerings, a place of lifting up of sacrifice, and the voice in prayer." [Lysons' *Our British Ancestors*, p. 146.]

village itself, and so they called it "Eau ley" because of the many springs, which are visible in the village street and under every hedge in the parish, in the shape of gushing fountains or of crystal wells.

But long before any peaceful village grew up in the valley, men of war had taken possession of the hill. There, once, were ancient Britons who dyed themselves with the woad which their descendants used for dyeing their broad-cloth coats;[1] and they have left their mark in the well-known Cairn with its interior cluster of walled graves. After them came the Romans, who maintained a considerable force in the district, and obliterating most of the marks of their pre-decessors, have left their own in the shape of the camp earth-works which are still conspicuous on Uley Bury. Probably those earth-works were not unfrequently occupied in the ages of war which followed the departure of the Romans, and it was in the midst of them, no doubt, that the three Godwins encamped their armies when they marched from their three counties to their Castle at Beverston, and thence to over awe the last of the old English Kings by displaying their force within sight of his court at Gloucester. [See page 100.]

And when the Godwins encamped at Uley they encamped on their own ground, for the parish was part of the great Manor of Berkeley in their time and in the time of Robert Fitzhardinge, the next subject who possessed it. Later on it went to the Berkeleys of Stoke Giffard, who lived at their Manor House of "White Court," with its two deer parks, a house which has long vanished, but the name of which still lingers in a little hamlet that has grown up near its site. But the parish was broken up into several freeholds even in the days of the Plantagenets, and beside White Court there

---

[1] Dyer's woad was grown in Uley fields within the memory of persons still living, but it is now superseded by Indigo, which in its turn is being superseded by Aniline, manufactured from gas tar.

were separate estates and houses named Basset's Court, Bencombe, Stout's Hill, Wresden, Angeston, and Rockstowes. Of these and of the families associated with them, however, there is not much known.

White Court was evidently the principal place of the parish, and is called the Manor of Uley in ancient records. The house was situated where the hamlet of the name now stands, and probably covered a good deal of land, for it was surrounded by two deer parks, or by one large park divided by the high road. It was made into an estate for a junior branch of the Fitz-hardinges, the Berkeleys of Stoke Giffard, and was broken up into small holdings and farms by Sir Richard Berkeley, in A.D. 1565.

Basset's Court was made over by Thomas Lord Berkeley, about A.D. 1216, to Margaret his daughter, who was the wife of Anselm Basset, and continued in that family until the eighteenth century, when it also was broken up by Elizabeth,—daughter of Sir William Basset, of Claverton, the last male heir,—who was married to William Westcombe.

Bencombe, in the thirteenth century, gave its name to a family of whom one member, Robert de Bencombe, is on record. In the sixteenth century it belonged to John Poyntz, and from him it descended to the Dorneys, of whom the last representative in the male line died in 1845 and lies in Uley Church, with the following inscription to commemorate her, and her arms, on a lozenge gules a chevron between three crescents or. "✠ Near this Spot Lieth the Body of Elizabeth Dorney of Bencomb, who died April 6th 1846, Aged 90 years, The last Descendant in the Male line of an Ancient Family. A faithful and pious Churchwoman. A gentle and liberal Neighbour. She forgot not to do good and to distribute And walk humbly with her God. ✠ This Monument is erected by her Grateful and Affectionate Kinsman the Revd. John Harding." This nephew was Rector of Coity

R 2

and Coychurch in Glamorganshire, and his son was Sir John Dorney Harding, a distinguished Ecclesiastical Judge.

Stout's Hill is the name of a house situated on high ground to the south of the village of Uley, built in the style which, in the last century, was intended for Gothic, but which may be more exactly defined as the Strawberry Hill style. In a house of earlier date lived the father of Samuel Rudder, the laborious compiler of the folio History of Gloucestershire. He lies in the churchyard of Uley on the south side of the Chancel, and his grave stone has a brass plate inserted in it which records a very remarkable fact in the following words:—" Underneath lie the remains of Roger Rutter *alias* Rudder, Eldest Son of John Rutter of Uley, who was buried August 30, 1771 aged 84 years, having never eaten Flesh, Fish, or Fowl, during the course of his long life." Tradition says that this strict vegetarian lived mainly on " Dump" in various toothsome forms. Usually he ate " plain Dump" made of flour and suet: when he grew tired of Plain dump he changed his diet to " Hard Dump: " and when he was in a special state of exhilaration he added the variety of " Apple Dump" to his very moderate fare. The writer is reminded of a hospitable squire of his acquaintance—Consule Planco—who took pride in the eels and pike which flourished in the stream that ran through his estate. On Monday he would help you, with much bonhommie, to a plate of eels, on Tuesday to a plate of pike, on Wednesday to a plate of eels and pike reposing side by side in genial companionship : and on Thursday you began again.

Samuel Rudder, the son of the above vegetarian, was the second great historian of the County of Gloucester ;—second to Sir Robert Atkyns in time but hardly second in industry, accuracy, and research. He was a printer and bookseller in Cirencester, where he published his large folio work, and where he died at the aged of 75 in the year 1801. In describing Stout's Hill he says, " This is also the place of the writer's nativity, where he collected his first ideas, and for which he still indulges a natural partiality."

The present house has an interesting association also with the family of Lloyd Baker; the present representative of the families of Lloyd and Baker, Thomas Barwick Lloyd Baker, Esqre, of Hardwicke Court near Gloucester, being the descendant, by a double line, of William Lloyd, Bishop of Norwich, who was one of the Seven Bishops committed to the Tower for Protestantism by the Popish James II., and deprived of their sees for Popery by the Presbyterian William III. The Bishop's great grand-daughter, Mary, who died in 1819, and was buried in Uley Church, was the wife of Mr. William Lloyd Baker who died in 1830, and whose mother, Mary, was grand-daughter of the Bishop.[1] The present Mr. Lloyd-Baker is a well-known writer on the Condition of the Labouring Classes, on the Poor Laws, and on Prison Management.

Early in this century the hospitality of Stout's Hill was offered to the poet Bloomfield, at a time when he was recovering from a severe illness. He spent a fortnight in the house in 1807, and during the course of his visit a pleasant driving party was made for an excursion through South Wales, which led to the composition of the poem entitled

---

1 LLOYD-BAKER of Stout's Hill and of Hardwicke Court.

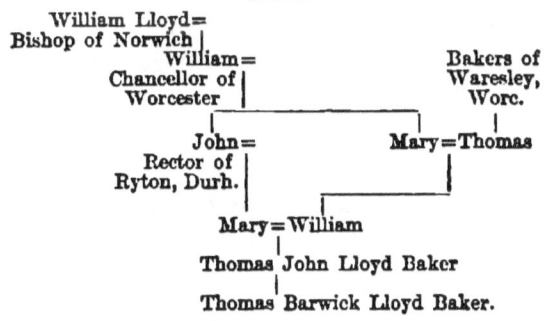

"The Banks of Wye." Bloomfield mentions the occasion of his writing the poem in his preface, and dedicates it to his hospitable entertainers in the following terms:—" To Thomas John Lloyd Baker, Esqre., of Stout's Hill, Uley, and his excellent lady: and Robert Bransby Cooper, Esqre., of Ferney Hill, Dursley, in the County of Gloucester, and all the members of his family: this journal is dedicated, with sentiments of high esteem and a lively recollection of past pleasures."

The poet celebrates his arrival at Stout's Hill with the pretty lines;—

" Soon the deep dell appeared and the clear brow
    Of Uley Bury smiled o'er all below
    O'er mansion, flock, and circling woods that hung
    Round the sweet pastures where the skylark sung,"

and after invoking the muse in the received style of pastoral poetry, he describes the start of the party on the " ten day's leisure " which " ten day's joy shall prove."

" One August morn, with spirits high,
    Sound health, bright hopes, and cloudless sky,
    A cheerful group their farewell bade
    To Dursley tower, to Uley's shade;
    And where bold Stinchcombe's greenwood side
    Heaves in the van of highland pride,
    Scour'd the broad vale of Severn; where
    The foes of verse shall never dare
    Genius to scorn, or hound its power,
    There blood-stained Berkeley's turrets low'r
    A name that cannot pass away,
    Till time forgets ' the Bard' of Gray."

The smooth but not very exciting verses flow on through about two thousand lines of such descriptions of scenery as our grandfathers delighted in, and then once more Uley and Dursley come to the front ;—

" The setting sun, on Dursley tower,
Welcomed us home, and forward bade,
To Uley valley's peaceful shade."

Bloomfield was a poet whose writings charmed a large circle of readers in the generation which preceded Wordsworth; and his poems are as conspicuous as those of his great successor for their single heartedness and purity.

Uley can also boast of an association even more direct with that saintly poet John Keble. His grandfather, John Keble of Fairford, died in 1780, leaving several daughters and an only son, also named John, who became Vicar of Coln St. Aldwyn's near Fairford, in 1782. There being at that time no suitable residence in his parish, Mr. Keble lived in his own house in Fairford, and there he took home, in 1785, the mother of his two sons, one of whom was the John Keble so dear to the hearts of the millions who have read the Christian Year; and whose memory has also been perpetuated by the noble College at Oxford which bears his name. Mrs. Keble, born Sarah Maule, was one of a family of that name which was well known among the principal residents of Uley.

Uley Broad-Cloth.

This parish was once specially famous for the manufacture of that blue "Kerseymere" cloth which our grandfathers used to wear in the form of long-tailed coats freely adorned behind and before with buttons of gilded brass.

Of "Cloathing" says Fuller " as good as any in England for fineness and colour is wrought in this county, where the Cloathiers have a double advantage, First, plenty of the best Wooll growing therein on Cotwold hills: so that whereas Cloathiers in some Counties fetch their wool far off, with great cost, it is here but the removing of it from the Backs of the Sheep into their Worke Houses. Secondly they have the benefit of an Water for colouring their Cloath, being the sweet Rivulet of Strowd, which arising about Branfield, runneth across this Shire into the Severn.

"Now no rational man will deny Occult qualities of perfection in some above other waters (whereby Spanish Steele *non natura sed tinctura* becomes more tough than ours in England) as the best Reds (a colour which always carried somewhat of Magistracy therein) are died in Stroud water. Hence it is that this Shire hath afforded many wealthy Cloathiers, whereof some may seem in their Loomes to have interwoven their own names into their Cloaths, (called Webscloath and Clutterbucks) after the names of the first makers of them, for many years after."

The blue cloth of Uley was as famous as the scarlet of Stroud. For this fame no doubt it was indebted to the "Occult qualities" of the "sweet Rivulet" of Ewelme, flowing through the fields of Woad, and brightening the texture of the fabrics which came from the looms, so that when they were drawn out of the dyeing vats they shone a resplendent true-blue, such as would gladden the heart of the Tory Squire for his Sunday duties, even as the scarlet of Stroudwater gladdened it on Monday for the duties of the field. The first to manufacture that particular kind of cloth, at least in Uley, was one John Eyles, of Wresden,[1] whose monument in the Church still bears testimony to the achieve-

---

[1] Wresden is an ancient homestead in the Parish which was sold by Sir Richard Berkeley, of Stoke Giffard, to Giles Browning, in 1566, and which belonged to the Eyles family not long afterwards. Mr. John Phillimore, of Cheshunt and New Broad Street, London, came into possession of it afterwards, and made a gift of it and of The Thing on Cam Green to his brother Robert ; from whom it has descended to the present owner W. Stiff Phillimore, Esqre., of Snenton, Nottingham. The house is an interesting specimen of a seventeenth century middle-class residence ; and in one of the bed-rooms is a fine old Jacobean bedstead which was once, no doubt, occupied by John Eyles himself.

ment by the following inscription with John Eyles' trade-mark in the place of arms:—

Behind this Wall lyes the Body of
John Eyles aged 91 years and $\overline{y}^{e}$
first that ever made Spanish Cloath
in $\overline{y}^{s}$ psh To whose gratefull memory
this Monument was erected by M.
Bayly Gent of Wresden.

1731

But famous as the blue broad-cloth of Uley once was, its fame could not save the manufacturing industry of the parish from the influence of an age in which so many landmarks have been changed. Within the memory of those still living the village was more than double its present size, many looms being at work in it, and also fulling mills and dyeing houses; but steam and Yorkshire energy began to underbid the Uley clothiers about half a century ago, and strikes for wages which would leave no profits to the manufacturers finished what Northern rivalry had begun. This destruction of the local clothing trade led to a time of terrible poverty among those who had been the working population of the place ; and Mr. Lloyd-Baker, who was at that time resident in the parish, states that in 1830 the Poor's rate stood as high as eighteen shillings in the pound on the real value of the land, although the poor received as little as it was thought possible for them to live on. From that time the manufacturing industry of Uley has passed away, and when the present writer recently made enquiries on the spot, he found two looms alone remaining at work in the hands of an ancient weaver and weaveress to testify to the former prosperous trade which was carried on here.

ECCLESIASTICAL ULEY.

The Parish Church of Uley is an entirely modern structure, erected on the site of the old one in the year 1858 at a cost of £3,000. It is a structure in the Early English style of a late period, and was designed by Mr. S. Teulon, Architect, of London. The stained glass windows are of some local interest, but not of high artistic character. The tower is lofty and handsome and contains a fine-toned tenor bell, which was taken from the ancient Church.

The old Church, dedicated like its successor to St. Giles, was an unpretending structure which had been much pulled to pieces for the addition of pews and galleries. On the south side alone there were three exterior stair-cases leading to the latter. The tower was supposed to be of great antiquity, but no records remain respecting it. The whole Church was in such a condition that restoration was found to be impossible, and it was entirely removed at the above date.

The parochial records of Uley are not of any great interest, although the Register begins as early as the year 1668.[1]

But there are some entries respecting excommunication which show that the discipline of the Church was exercised at a later date than is sometimes supposed.

---

[1] It may however be mentioned that the trade of "Rugger" or "Rug-weaver" seems to have been a common one before the intro - duction of Broad cloth weaving.

And the following names may be added to the list printed at page 179 :—

Dionisia	Unis	Temperance	Modesty
Baersheba	Germanicus	Lucina	Tryphena daug. of
Archilaus	Troilus	Paphroditus	Rich. and Lohurama

On February 5th, 1697 the following occurs:—
"By virtue of an Order directed to me by Richard Parsones
Doctr of the Laws I did denounce and declare the marriage
of William Manninge of Uley and Elizabeth Manninge
yᵉ late wife of John Manninge his deceased brother to be
void and null to all intents and purposes: witnesse my Hand
William Heart."

The next entry of the kind indicates the nature of the
spiritual offence for which these excommunications were probably issued.

"Eliz: yᵉ base born child of Eliz: Tilly buried February
yᵉ 8th Annoqu. Dom: 171$\frac{4}{5}$.   Yᵉ reputed father of this
childe was John Cook who afterward married her and after
marriage were both denounced excommunicated in our parish
church of Uley"

The next shows that it was not the poor alone who were
subjected to the censures of the Church.

"April 26th 1778. Mr. Edward Dorney of this Parish was
excommunicated   John Gregory Rector."

The sentence of excommunication not having been revoked
at the death of this gentleman in 1795 he was buried at
midnight without the usual Service.

"April 3rd 1785. Sarah Talboys of this Parish was excommunicated. John Gregory: Rector."   This entry is followed
by another, undated, "Sarah Talboys's sentence of excommunication was revoked by me Ralph Lockey Curate;" so
that it may be hoped that she at any rate was penitent for
her misdeeds, whatever they were.

It may be well to add that sentences of excommunication
were not issued by the parochial clergyman who had to read
them in Church (according to the rubric after the Nicene
Creed) at his own will, but by formal process in the Bishop's
or Archdeacon's Court, after "presentation" by the Clergyman or Churchwardens.

THE RECTORS OF ULEY.

THOMAS MAINWARING	
JAMES DALTON	1611
HERBERT CROFTS	
WILLIAM HEART	1667
JOHN JACKSON	
RICE WILLIAMS	
THOMAS GREGORY	1748
JOHN GREGORY	1778
THOMAS ESBURY PARTRIDGE	1793
MARLOW WATTS WILKINSON	1823
CHARLES CHAPMAN BROWNE	1867

CHURCHWARDENS SINCE 1807.

Rice Williams	1807	James Kathro	1842
Samuel Went	1807	William Hurcombe	1846
William Hill	1811	John Legge Clarke	1847
Reuben Howell	1812	Thomas Legge Clarke	1848
Joseph Jeens	1814	Edward Bloxsome, Jun.	1850
Thomas Went	1814	Robert Arthur Fitzhardinge Kingscote	1852
William Hinton	1818		
George Adey	1824	John George Rowley	1855
Samuel Price	1825	Charles Price	1860
John Feribee	1825	William Hurcombe	1860
George Blackwell	1827	John George Rowley	1868
James Haile	1830	Charles Norris	1868
John Norris	1832	Cornelius Harris Holloway	1869
David Bailey	1834	A. E. Burmester, C.B.	1870
John Norris	1837	William Hill	1870
Joseph Powell	1838	Thomas Clarke	1871
Henry Moreland Jeens	1840	John Hamlyn Borrer	1875
Thomas Stiff	1841		

ULEY CHARITIES.

On a Monument upon the Wall of the Church is the following record :—

" Near this place lyeth enterred the body of HENRY PEGLER of this Parish Gent. who dyed the 12th day of August

1695, aged 85. He gave a parcel of land and 10 Pounds in Money to the Use of the poor of this Parish for ever."

On the Tables of Benefactions in the Church Tower.

MR. PARSLOW gave ten shillings per annum, to be paid out of the Fancis in Uley, to be given away in Bread to the poor on St. John's Day.

CAPT. PEGLER gave ten shillings per annum, to be paid out of Broadstone field in Uley, five shillings to be given away in Bread to the poor, and five shillings to the Minister for a Sermon on the 17th day of February.

MR. HOLLINS gave five shillings per annum, to be paid by the Overseer of Uley, being interest of Five Pounds put in his hands, to be given away in Bread to the poor on the 17th day of February.

MRS. ANN WENT, by her Will dated 7th January, 1825, gave One Hundred Pounds to the Parish, to be placed out at interest on Government Security in the names of the Minister and Churchwardens for the time being, two fifth parts of such interest to be distributed amongst the poor by the said Minister and Churchwardens at Christmas Annually, and the remaining three fifth parts thereof, to be paid towards the support of the Church Sunday School established in this Parish.

MR. THOMAS GREGORY of Dursley, by his Will dated May, 1837, gave Eighty Pounds to the Parish, to be placed out at interest in Government Security in the names of the Minister and Churchwardens, the interest arising therefrom to be distributed amongst the poor in Bread on St. Stephen's Day.

MR. TETHERS gave forty shillings per annum, to be paid out of the Estate called Oldminster, in the Parish of Berkeley, thirty shillings to be given away in Bread to the poor, and ten to the Minister for a Sermon on St. John's Day.

MR. RICHARD HOPKINS gave twenty-five shillings per annum, to be paid out of the House formerly called, The Bell and Apple Tree Inn in Dursley, to be given away in Bread to the poor on Easter Tuesday.

MRS. CATHE. WORLOCK gave forty-three shillings and four-pence, the interest of Eighty Pounds in the funds, to be given away by the Minister and Churchwardens to the poor Widows that are Housekeepers on St. John's Day.

The Tumulus, or Grave-mound.

Just outside the village of Uley, about an hundred yards to the left of the road leading to Nymphsfield, there is an artificial hillock about ten feet high, the construction of which is thought by antiquaries to date from a period some hundreds of years before the Christian era, perhaps as far back as the reign of King David; though, to judge by its local name, " Hetty Pegler's Tump," a much more recent date has been assigned to it by those who live in its immediate neighbour-hood.[1] It is a great heart-shaped heap of stones, 120 feet long by 85 feet wide in its broadest part, which has been piled over an ancient sepulchre constructed of large "plank" stones, and over which a layer of earth and turf has accu-mulated. In former times it presented simply the appearance of a hillock on a rising ground which leads towards the Roman Camp and overlooks a most beautiful view of the Severn valley and of the hills of South and Mid Wales, but the approach to its interior being now left open its artificial character is at once apparent.

---

[1] This name appears to be associated with the wife of Henry Pegler, whose benefaction to the poor of Uley is recorded at page 225. After the inscription commemorating him there follows "Also the body of Hester his wife, who died the 26th day of Nov. 1694, aged 69." Perhaps Mrs. Pegler had some explorations made in the "tump" and so gave her name to it.

This Grave-mound is one of a class which antiquaries have
named the "Chambered Long Barrow" type, to distinguish
them from other forms, such as the round, disc-shaped, and
unchambered, barrows: and it is one of the finest of all that
are known.

The construction of such grave-mounds is not simply that
of a stone chamber over which stones and earth have been
piled up. The dry stone-wall on either side of the entrance

ENTRANCE OF TUMULUS.

is part of a heart-shaped wall which runs round the whole
of the mound as a kind of support by which its original form
is preserved. At the broad end, or entrance, which points
towards sunrise, a second wall of a similar kind occurs at
a distance of several feet behind the one which is visible, so
as to form a double breast-work in front of the stone-chambers
beyond: and at the smaller end one longitudinal, and two
transverse walls exist; all these walls being buried under the
superincumbent stones and earth, except where the entrance
has been laid open in modern times.

These structural walls end at the entrance to the chambered part of the barrow and their place is taken by plank stones set up on edge, the stones not having been tooled in any way but being put together just as they were lifted out of the bed, the interstices between the irregular edges being filled in with smaller stones of the same description. The plank stone walls which thus continue the rubble walls of the entrance run parallel to each other for a distance of 22 feet, being 4½ feet apart and 5 feet in height; and the passage thus formed is roofed over with similar stones. In the sides of this square tunnel there were four polygonal chambers made in exactly the same way, which were the sepulchral vaults of those for whom this burial mound was constructed: but only the two on the left hand remain in a perfect condition. It is probable that the chambers and the passage to them were first built up, that the heart-shaped walls were then erected to regulate the size and form of the mound, and that the whole was afterwards buried under the rubble and earth of which the substance of the hillock is composed.

The Uley barrow was accidentally broken into in 1820, and the chambers on the north side were destroyed by the labourers. In the following year it was carefully opened in the presence of antiquaries, and after being thoroughly examined it was closed again until 1854, when it was once more opened and explored under the direction of the late Dr. Thurnam, the greatest authority in England on the subject of grave-mounds. Since that time the tumulus has not again been closed except by a small wooden door.[1]

The entrance to the interior of this barrow is under the lower edge of a massive stone eight feet long which is set

---

[1] Some notes of the examination made in 1821 were taken by T. J. Lloyd Baker, Esq., F.S.A., of Stouts Hill, and these were incorporated by Dr. Thurnam with a paper on the examination of 1854 which he contributed to the Archæological Journal, vol. xi. 315.

upright and supported by two side stones at the height of
about two-and-a-half feet from the ground. Creeping through
this low doorway the explorer finds himself in the long
passage described above, and on his left hand are the two
sepulchral chambers which remain perfect. The passage is
partly divided into two by the projection into it of the great
stones which form the divisions between each pair of chambers,
and the easternmost half of it is again divided off in a
similar manner about a yard from the entrance. The end of
the passage is blocked by a large slab of the same kind as
those which form the sides and roof. The ground plan of
the whole thus takes the form of a cross, and this is so
frequently found in pre-Christian days, and among heathen
nations, that there can be little doubt it had some meaning,
though what meaning is not now evident.

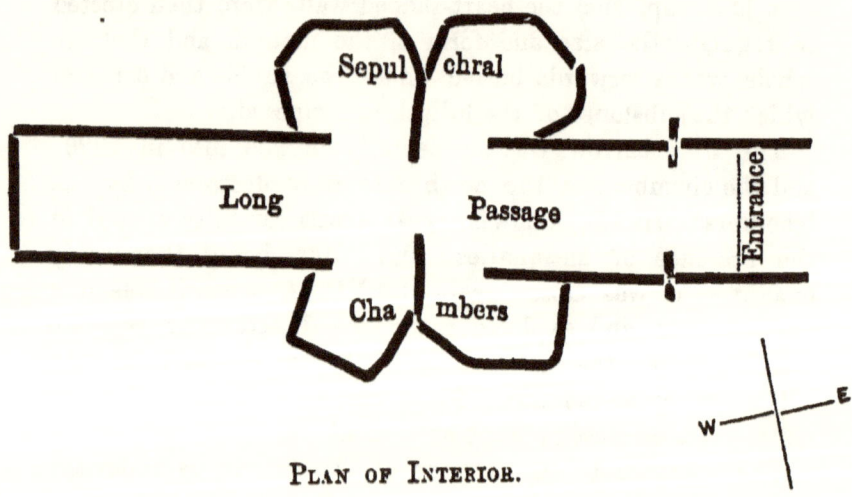

PLAN OF INTERIOR.

The sepulchral chambers are entered by narrow doorways,
but these were each closed up with a wall as the chambers
became the resting places of the bodies for which they were
constructed, and the one furthest from the entrance was so

found when the mound was explored in 1821. The roofs also were originally formed in rude domes by making courses of plank stones overlap each other in succession until the whole of the chamber was covered; but these are not now in their original condition.

When the mound was examined in 1821 the central passage and the side chambers were found to be filled with soil and rubble, part of which had no doubt accumulated by infiltration, and part from the rough and incomplete explorations of those who had searched there for treasures in some far distant day. · In the central passage there were uncovered the remains of as many as six skeletons, and two others lay between the rubble walls in front of the entrance. In the chamber nearest the entrance on the left hand were the remains of four other skeletons, the bones of which were so irregularly placed as to show that the chamber had been previously explored and the skeletons displaced from their original position. In the soil and rubble with which they were covered there were some fragments of pottery, and one small vessel which is described as being shaped like a lachrymatory. In the further chamber there were also a few human bones with some fragments of pottery and charcoal. There were also, besides these human remains, the lower jaws, teeth, and tusks, of several wild boars, as well as a few bones and the teeth of some ruminant animal.

Thirty-four years afterwards, as has been said, the sepulchre was again explored, and a heap of these bones were then found piled together at the furthest end of the passage. They included fragments of eight or nine skulls, but only two perfect ones, these being of the type called by the very learned name of "dolichocephalic" which means "long-headed." A singular peculiarity was discovered in the spines of some of the skeletons, the two upper dorsal vertebræ, that is, two of the joints of the spine between the "shoulder-

blades," being cemented into one or "anchylosed," so that
some at least of these long-headed Britons must have been
very stiff about the back. The bones are preserved in the
Museum of Guy's Hospital, where also are some fragments
of flint arrow-heads which were discovered near them.[1]

In the upper part of the mound, close to the surface and
therefore high above the roofs of the ancient sepulchral
chambers below, another skeleton was discovered, and the
date of this later grave was fixed by the fact that near the
remains of its occupant there were found three coins of the
sons of Constantine the Great, belonging to the middle of
the fourth century. Fifteen hundred years ago, therefore,
this grave-mound was an ancient structure; and those whose
bodies were laid in its chambers may have looked out from
Uley Bury on the Valley of the Severn in times when the
world was yet young, and when the name Roman had not
yet been heard. Perhaps the bones which have now been so
recklessly scattered were those of warriors belonging to a
race of Britons contemporary with the earlier days of the
Hebrew monarchy; and the "very great heap of stones"
which they laid over the body of Absalom in the wood of
Ephraim [2 *Sam.* xviii. 17] may have been a grave-mound of
the same period as that at Uley.

---

[1] Since the account of Beverston was printed the writer had occasion
to excavate a portion of a field in front of his house for the purpose of
making a new approach to the latter: when the labourers came across
many fragments of pottery bearing the mark of fire, much charcoal
of apple tree wood, some of it only partially burnt, many bones,
some human and some the bones of animals, a flint arrow-head, a flint
core, a very thin disc of yellow metal four inches in diameter made
of three pieces rivetted together, a single white stone, and a hair
bodkin of bone, four inches long. The fragments of pottery were
without ornament, and belonged to eight or ten urns. All these
relics lay within about eighteen inches of the turf, and the grave had
no doubt been often disturbed before by the plough.

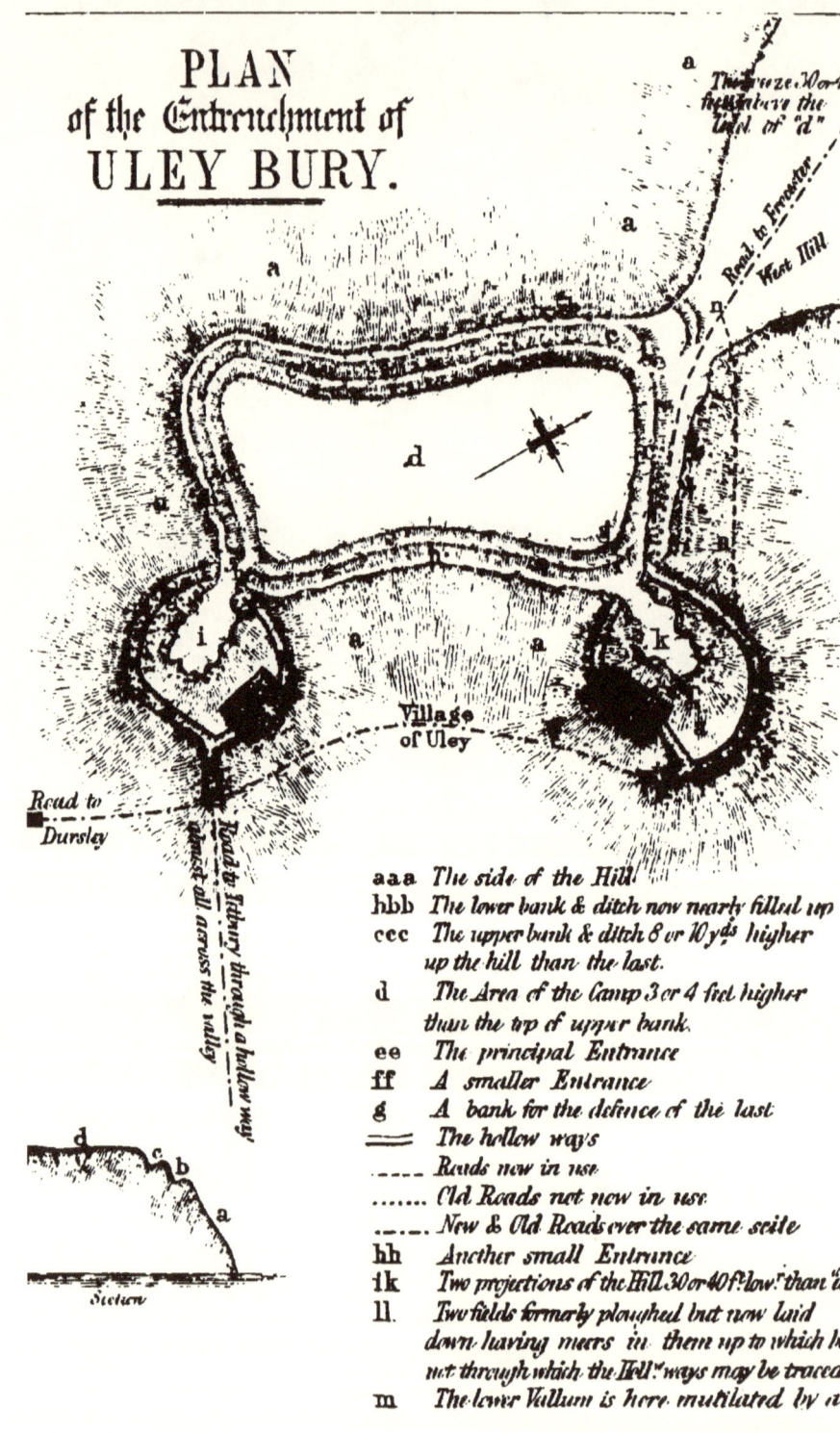

PLAN
of the Entrenchment of
ULEY BURY.

The Breeze Work feeble above the level of "d"

Road to Forester

West Hill

a

a

a

a

d

a

a

i

a

a

k

Village of Uley

Road to Dursley

Road to Tetbury through a hollow way almost all across the valley

Section
d
c
b
a

aaa   The side of the Hill

bbb   The lower bank & ditch now nearly filled up

ccc   The upper bank & ditch 8 or 10 y.ds higher up the hill than the last.

d   The Area of the Camp 3 or 4 feet higher than the top of upper bank.

ee   The principal Entrance

ff   A smaller Entrance

g   A bank for the defence of the last

══   The hollow ways

----   Roads now in use

······   Old Roads not now in use

-·-·-   New & Old Roads over the same scile

hh   Another small Entrance

ik   Two projections of the Hill 30 or 40 f.t low.r than it

ll   Two fields formerly ploughed but now laid down having meers in them up to which but not through which the Holl.w ways may be traced

m   The lower Vallum is here mutilated by a

The Roman Camp.

All along the Valley of the Severn for forty miles, that is from Clifton Down and Bath at one extremity to Bredon Hill at the other, the ridges which form its boundary on the south-western side and the hilly places in the valley itself are crowned with Roman encampments. That of Uley Bury is the fifteenth, reckoning from the one on Clifton Down, and that on Bredon Hill is the twenty-fifth.[1] But the Uley Bury Camp is the largest and finest of them all, and was probably considered to be the key to the position which was occupied by these extensive lines of earthworks.

The Roman armies never halted, even for a single night, without throwing up earthworks in the form of a regular entrenchment, which should be large enough in area to enclose the whole body of fighting men and their transport corps. So important was the construction of such protecting lines considered, that even, when a military force was actually

---

[1] These are enumerated and their positions indicated in a paper giving "An Account of a Chain of Ancient Fortresses extending through the South Western part of Gloucestershire ; By Thomas John Lloyd Baker Esqre F.S.A., with a map reduced from Taylor and a plan of the entrenchment at Uley Bury," in the Archæologia of the Royal Society of Antiquaries, vol xix. 161. They are as follows :—

Clifton Down	Dyrham	Churchdown
Kings Weston Hill	Old Sodbury	High Brotheridge
Blaize Castle	Horton	Whitcombe
Knoll	Westridge	Crickley Hill
Elberton	Drakestone	Leckhampton Hill
Oldbury	ULEY BURY	Cleeve Hill
The Abbey	Broadridge Green	Nottingham Hill
Bloody Acre	Painswick Beacon	Bredon Hill
Bury Hill		

These were all so placed that they could communicate with each other by signals ; and they doubtless had roads also in communication. It is said that this chain of permanent camps can be still further traced, through Warwickshire and Northamptonshire, as far as the Ely fens.

engaged with the enemy, parties of the soldiers were told off to lay out the camp for shelter and rest, and to pitch the tents on a regular and well-understood plan, so that every corps might be able to march at once to its own quarters.

But encampments of a more permanent kind were some-times necessary, where an army could be quartered, perhaps for years, in a position that would command a hostile country, and then the earthworks were made of a more solid and durable character, while the men were quartered not in tents but in huts of turf, wood, or even stone. Uley Bury Camp was one of this kind, and being placed in so favourable a position upon a spur of the Cotswolds, it overlooked an exten-sive range of country in the Vale of Severn, and was a very important part of the frontier fortifications by which the Romans compelled the Britons to keep within the hill country of Wales, to which they had retired before the conquering forces of the invaders.

The Uley Bury Camp was probably a fortified city of the Britons long before it was occupied by the Romans, and the grave-mound adjacent may be only one of many in which the more distinguished of its inhabitants were interred. The Romans are thought to have brought it into its present form in the time of Caractacus, about the middle of the first century of the Christian era. At this time Publius Ostorius Scapula held the chief command of the Roman forces in Britain, his command lasting from A.D. 47 to A.D. 51.[1] The Roman historian Tacitus records of Ostorius that he con-

---

[1] His predecessor was Aulus Plautius; whose wife Pomponia Græcina was accused of being a Christian on her return to Rome in A.D. 47. Doubtless some of those who were quartered within the entrenched lines on the Cotswold hills during the latter half of the first century had been among the number of those whom Paul "received" in "his own hired house" at Rome, and had heard him "preaching the kingdom of God" . . no man forbidding him." [Acts xxviii. 30, 31].

structed a series of camps along the lines of the Avon and the Severn [Tacitus' *Annals* xij. 31], having had very hard work to drive Caractacus and his army out of Gloucestershire, and endeavouring by means of these garrisoned posts to secure the country he had won from the British King.

The hill on which the Camp is situated is 823 feet in perpendicular altitude, and has a deep slope on all four of its sides, being entirely detached from the neighbouring heights, except at the northern corner where a narrow isthmus connects it with Crawley Hill, and with the road to the Severn on the west and to Gloucester on the north. The top of the hill is a level parallelogram from 560 to 600 yards long by about 250 yards wide, and at each of the two corners on the south-east side there are projecting buttresses of nature's own construction, the tops of which are about 30 feet lower than the area of the hill itself.

The camp occupied the whole of the level surface and was thus about thirty-two acres in extent. It was defended by two banks and ditches which ran all round, and large portions of which still remain. The highest of the defences was formed by digging a trench on the edge of the hill six or eight feet below the level of the area, and forming a bank of the earth which was thrown up on the outside of it, this bank been surmounted by a further defence of stakes. The lower trench and bank were made in the same manner about five and twenty feet further down the hill. When there was danger of attack these trenches were occupied by the garrison, and under cover of the walls the defenders could effectively hurl their missiles down on their assailants, while the latter would have little chance of doing them any damage except by achieving the very difficult task of storming the trenches in the midst of their opponents' fire.

The principal entrance to the camp was by a fortified gateway at the north corner, where the ridge which forms the isthmus is only about fifty yards across. This gateway was protected by three trenches and banks which ran across the ridge, and by mounds corresponding to the towers of a castle barbican, each of which would be provided with a rampart of earth or stone. On this side the camp is overlooked by higher ground, and there were probably outlying defences beyond the entrance which are not now to be traced.

Two smaller entrances to the camp were provided on the two buttresses of the hill, and these were protected by mounds on either side. The roads which led to them were hollow ways descending round the buttresses and communicating with the road which ran across the valley and up the opposite hill towards Beverston and Tetbury.

This general plan of the Uley Bury Camp will be understood by the annexed engraving, which is copied from the paper in the Archæologia referred to in a note on page 233. How it was laid out cannot now be traced from any remains, but may be inferred from the ordinary practice of the Romans.

Around the rampart were placed engines for throwing darts and arrows, and for slinging stones, engines which were originally invented by the Jews [2 Chron. xxvi. 15], but were adopted by the Assyrians, as their sculptures in the British Museum show, and by their successors in empire the Greeks and the Romans. Behind these engines there was a wide space of forty or fifty yards which was used as parade ground and for the safe keeping of cattle and other booty. Down the centre of the enclosure was a principal street an hundred feet wide, and on either side were as many others, fifty feet wide, as the space would contain. The huts of the soldiers and officers were built up on either side of these streets, the huts being so arranged that every company of an hundred soldiers was quartered together around its own centurion, and the companies of each division in close proximity to each other ready to fall in to their ranks immediately without confusion in the wide street of the camp, and to march out of it in the order in which they were to take their places on the field of battle. "In the midst of all," says Josephus the Jewish historian, who wrote about the time when Uley Bury was first occupied by the Romans, "is the general's own tent, built like a temple; and the whole camp looks like a city suddenly springing into existence, with its market place, and a quarter for handicraft trades, and places for the superior and subordinate officers where they can hear and determine causes if any differences arise." [Josephus' *Wars of the Jews*. III. v.] The morning parade, the daily drill and exercise, the posting of sentries, and the giving of orders and the watch-word, the historian describes in such a manner as to show that a modern Aldershott inherits the traditions of a Roman Uley Bury; and that, where modern artillery has not necessitated changes, military mankind of the first century were not very different in their habits from those of the nineteenth.

The Roman Camp on Uley Bury was probably used by later armies, taken and re-taken by Dane, Saxon, and Briton, and sometimes occupied even down to the time of the Conquest: but like many others it has been a place for the grazing of peaceful sheep now for many a generation. But some Roman Aldershotts became the centres of large populations and ultimately the sites of mediæval cities; and there is usually a trace of their origin in the regular arrangement of their principal streets, and in the name "castra" which still clings to them in the English form of "cester" or "chester."

Heights on the Cotswolds.

It may be convenient to the reader of the preceding pages to know the altitudes of the principal hills in the Cotswold district, and of some of the places that have been named. Those which follow are most of them taken from a paper by Mr. Hyett in the first volume of the papers of the Cotswold Naturalists' Club :—

	Feet above the Sea Level.
Ordnance Bench Mark /|\ on the north side of Dursley Church Tower	242
Beverston Castle	600
Stinchcombe Hill	725
Uley Bury	823
Symond's Hall Down	802
Finger Post on top of Frocester Hill	780
Robin's Wood Hill	652
Standish Hill	715
Oxenton Hill	733
Painswick Beacon	929
Birdlip Hill	969
Leckhampton Hill	978
Base of Bredon Hill Tower	979
Broadway Beacon	1000
Cleeve Hill	1081

INDEX.

WHITMORE, STEAM PRINTER, STAMP OFFICE, DURSLEY.

Also, price Five Shillings.

TEWKESBURY ABBEY

AND

ITS ASSOCIATIONS.

BY

JOHN HENRY BLUNT, M.A., F.S.A.,

RECTOR OF BEVERSTON, GLOUC.

With 17 Illustrations.

LONDON : SIMPKIN, MARSHALL, & CO.
TEWKESBURY : W. NORTH.
1875.

Published by Rivingtons, London, Oxford, and Cambridge.

The Compendious Edition of the Annotated Book

of Common Prayer, forming a concise Commentary on the Devotional System of the Church of England. Crown 8vo, 10*s.* 6*d.*; in half-morocco, 16*s.*; or in morocco limp, 17*s.* 6*d.*

The Annotated Book of Common Prayer; being

an Historical, Ritual, and Theological Commentary on the Devotional System of the Church of England. By various Writers. Sixth Edition. Imperial 8vo, 36*s.*; or in half-morocco, 48*s.*

[This large edition contains the Latin and Greek originals, together with technical Ritual Annotations, Marginal References, &c., which are necessarily omitted for want of room in the Compendious Edition.]

"Whether as, historically, showing how the Prayer Book came to be what it is, or, ritually, how it designs itself to be rendered from word into act, or, theologically, as exhibiting the relation between doctrine and worship on which it is framed, the book amasses a world of information, carefully digested, and errs commonly, if at all, on the side of excess."—GUARDIAN.

Dictionary of Sects, Heresies, Ecclesiastical Parties,

and Schools of Religious Thought. By various Writers. Imperial 8vo, 36*s.*; or in half-morocco, 48*s.*

"A very comprehensive and bold undertaking, and is certainly executed with a sufficient amount of ability and knowledge to entitle the book to rank very high in point of utility."—GUARDIAN.
"It will be useful to all who possess it, on account of the immense amount of information carefully collected and arranged; having in this respect no rival in England."—LONDON QUARTERLY REVIEW.

"That this is a work of some learning and research is a fact which soon becomes obvious to the reader."—SPECTATOR.
"The quantity of information it presents in a convenient and accessible form is enormous, and having once appeared, it becomes indispensable to the theological student."—CHURCH TIMES.
"A whole library is condensed into this admirable volume."—NOTES AND QUERIES.

Dictionary of Doctrinal and Historical Theology,

By various Writers. Second Edition. Imperial 8vo, 42*s.*; or in half-morocco, 52*s.* 6*d.*

"We know of no book of its size and bulk which supplies the information here given at all; far less which supplies it in an arrangement so accessible, with a completeness of information so thorough, and with an ability in the treatment of profound subjects so great."—GUARDIAN.
"Within the sphere it has marked out for itself, no equally useful book of reference exists in English for the elucidation of theological problems."—CHURCH TIMES.

"Infinitely the best book of the kind in the language; and, if not the best conceivable, it is perhaps the best we are ever likely to see within its compass as to size and scope. The book is sure to make its own way by sheer force of usefulness."—LITERARY CHURCHMAN.
"It will be found of admirable service to all students of theology, as advancing and maintaining the Church's views on all subjects as fall within the range of fair argument and inquiry."—STANDARD.

Published by Rivingtons, London, Oxford, and Cambridge.

The Book of Church Law; being an Exposition
of the legal rights and duties of the Parochial Clergy, and the Laity, of the Church of England. Revised by W. G. F. Phillimore, D.C.L., Barrister at Law, and Chancellor of the Diocese of Lincoln. Second Edition. Crown 8vo. 7s. 6d.

The Reformation of the Church of England: its
History, Principles, and Results. A.D. 1514-1547. New Edition. 8vo 16s.

The Sacraments and Sacramental Ordinances of
the Church: being a plain Exposition of their History, Meaning, and Effects. Small 8vo. 4s. 6d.

Household Theology; a Handbook of Religious
Information respecting the Holy Bible, the Prayer Book, the Church, the Ministry, Divine Worship, the Creeds, &c, &c. New Edition. Small 8vo. 3s. 6d.

Directorium Pastorale. The Principles and Prac-
tice of Pastoral Work in the Church of England. New Edition. Crown 8vo. 7s. 6d.

A Companion to the Old Testament; being a Plain
Commentary on Scripture History, down to the Birth of Our Lord. Small 8vo. 3s. 6d.

Also in 2 Parts :

Part I.—The Creation of the World to the Reign of Saul.
Part II.—The Reign of Saul to the Birth of Our Lord.
Small 8v. 2s. each

[Especially adapted for use in Training Colleges and Schools.]

A Key to the Knowledge and Use of the Holy
Bible. New Edition. Small 8vo. 2s. 6d.

A Key to the Knowledge and Use of the Book of
Common Prayer. New Edition. Small 8vo. 2s. 6d.

A Key to Christian Doctrine and Practice
(Founded on the Church Catechism). Small 8vo. 2s. 6d.

A Key to the Knowledge of Church History
(Ancient). Edited by John Henry Blunt, M.A. Small 8vo. 2s. 6d.

Published by Rivingtons, London, Oxford, and Cambridge.

A Key to the Knowledge of Church History
(Modern). Edited by John Henry Blunt, M.A. Small 8vo. 2*s*. 6*d*.

A Christian View of Christian History, from
Apostolic to Mediæval Times. Crown 8vo. 7*s*.

Published by Masters, London.

The Atonement and the At-one-Maker. A Volume
of Lectures on the Apostle's Creed. Small 8vo. 5*s*.

Published by Trübner & Co., London, for the Early English Text Society.

The Myroure of oure Ladye, containing a Devo-
tional Treatise on Divine Service, with a Translation of the Offices used by the Sisters of the Brigittine Monastery of Sion, at Isleworth, during the 15th and 16th centuries; with Introduction and Notes. 8vo. 24*s*. Large Paper. 42*s*.

Published by Simpkin, Marshall, & Co., London, and Whitmore, Dursley.

Dursley and its Neighbourhood, being Historical
Memorials of Dursley, Beverston, Cam, and Uley. Eleven Illustrations. Small 8vo. 5s.